Microsoft Office 365
for Beginners

M.L. HUMPHREY

CONTENTS

Word 365 for Beginners

WORD 365 ESSENTIALS - BOOK 1

M.L. HUMPHREY

CONTENTS

Introduction

Microsoft Word is a staple in the modern business world. I spent twenty years working with a variety of organizations as both a regulator and consultant in the financial services industry and every single entity I interacted with used Word for their word processing. It was also ubiquitous at every school I attended.

And while there may be industries that default to using other programs or people may have started using newer programs that do the same thing but are free, Microsoft Word is still the go-to program to learn for drafting documents.

I wrote the original *Word for Beginners* using Word 2013 to introduce users of any version of Microsoft Office to the core skills you need to use Word. That book is still a valid introduction to Word that any user could use today to get started.

But in the five years since that book was published, Microsoft has released newer versions of Word. And, of course, Word 365, which this book covers, is the constantly-evolving, most-recent, latest and greatest version of Word. Those new versions have changed the appearance of Word, which is why I wanted to publish this book with updated screenshots.

I am writing this book in January 2023 and for our purposes—a basic introduction to the core functions of Microsoft Word—you should be able to use this book for years to come and not have a problem. The basic functionality of Word does not change much. If anything, they add more bells and whistles to Word, they don't take them away.

Our focus in this book is going to be limited to just what you need to know to get started. The problem with the Microsoft Office programs is that they're so powerful that sometimes it can be overwhelming for a new user to learn what they need to know without getting bogged down in a lot of extraneous information they don't need. So we're going to focus in.

What are we going to cover?

I am going to start you off with the absolute basics of opening, saving, closing, deleting, and renaming a file. Then we'll cover how to add, delete, and move text in a Word document.

Next, we'll cover how to format that text at both the word and paragraph levels, including the use of basic bulleted and numbered lists.

We'll also cover find and replace, spelling and grammar check, and how to get a word count as well as how to add basic headers and footers, including page numbers, and also how to do some document-level formatting.

Finally, we'll cover how to print and customize your settings.

By the time we're done here you'll know about 90% of what you need to know to use Word on a daily basis, maybe more. I am not covering topics like track changes and tables, which you may also need, but which are also more complicated topics that I consider intermediate-level. They are covered in the next book in this series, *Intermediate Word 365*.

You don't have to continue to that book. I will give you in this book a strong foundation to build from when you're ready to add those other areas to your knowledge. Word has a great Help function you can use, and there are also numerous online resources out there.

Okay, then. Let's get started with a discussion of Office Themes so we can make sure that your screen looks like my screenshots.

Screenshots and Office Theme

Some of you who are brand new to Word may not be ready to change your Office Theme yet, because you don't know how to open a Word file and aren't familiar with the terminology I'm going to use, so will need to come back to this chapter later.

But for the rest of you, I wanted to cover this before you see your first set of screenshots so that we can all be on the same page.

As I mentioned above, one of the reasons I'm publishing this book rather than just letting everybody use *Word for Beginners,* which is still a perfectly adequate introduction to Word, is that the appearance of Microsoft Word changed with the release of Word 2021. And it changed enough to be noticeable.

I wanted to publish a book that had updated screenshots for users of Word 2021 or Word 365. But within Microsoft Office there are a number of "themes" that you can choose from that will impact the appearance of your document, so my screenshots still may not look the same as your version of Word.

Which is why, before we start I wanted to show you what I'm using for the rest of the book so that you can change those settings to match mine if that is important to you.

Okay, then. Here goes.

When I open Microsoft Word, I have the option to click on Account in the bottom left corner to go to the Account screen:

That screen has a dropdown that is labeled Office Theme. As you can see here, my theme is currently set to the Colorful theme. And that's the theme I will use for the rest of the book.

Here is an example of what the top left corner of a new document looks like using that theme:

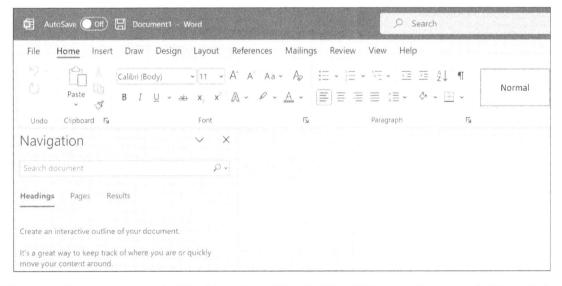

The top of the workspace in Word is colored blue. In Excel it's green. I assume in PowerPoint it's orange and in Access it's red. Most of the text is black and the background is a fairly light gray. The main document where you type is white.

Most of the screenshots I use in this book will not include that top bar, so if you're using the White theme, it will look much the same. Here that one is:

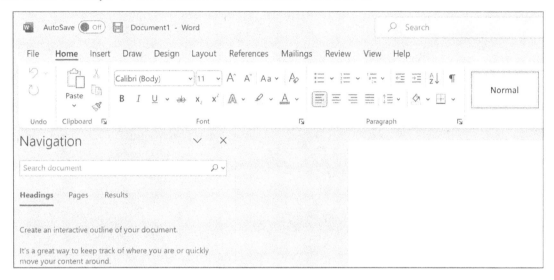

Note that the bar across the top is that light gray instead of blue, but for the most part the rest of it looks the same.

Where there can be bigger differences are with the Dark Gray and Black themes. Here is Dark Gray:

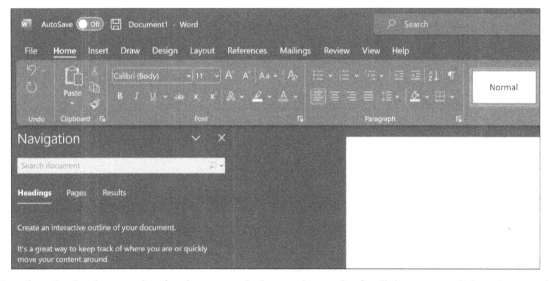

See that the background color is now a dark gray instead of a light gray and that the text is now white instead of black. But the main document is still white.

Here is the Black theme:

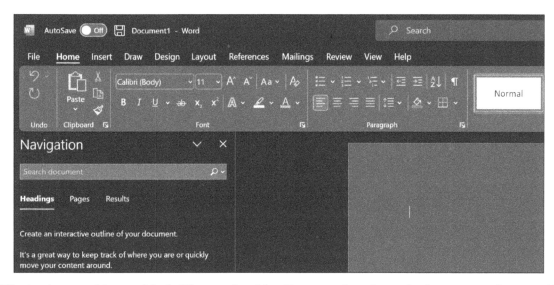

The background is now black. The text is white. But note that the main document where you'd type text is now a dark gray.

For most of what we do, those differences won't matter, but I wanted you to know about them because for me, for example, the difference between the Colorful or White themes and the Black theme are enough to be disconcerting. It throws me off to look at the Black theme.

So. If you want to have the same appearance as my screenshots and know that the colors I reference for dropdown items, etc. are the same, be sure to use the Colorful theme option. If you don't care, don't worry about it.

Also, another way to change this is to click on Options in that bottom left corner to open the Word Options dialogue box. You can change the Office Theme in the General section under Personalize Your Copy of Microsoft Office.

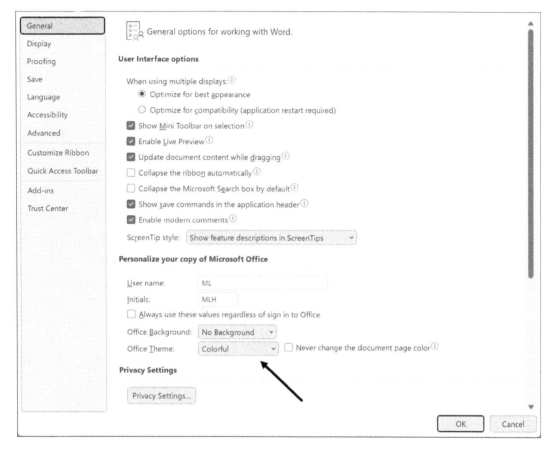

Note that any change you make to the theme applies to all Office programs, not just Word.

If your appearance still doesn't match mine it may be due to your computer's appearance settings which can also impact how Word appears on the screen.

Alright, now let's cover basic terminology so that we're all on the same page.

.

Basic Terminology

Most of these terms are used by everyone who uses Word, but a few may be my own quirk, so even if you're familiar with Word, please be sure to skim through.

Tab

When I refer to a tab in Microsoft Word, I will be referring to the menu options at the top of the screen. In older versions of Word when a menu option was selected it had the appearance of an old-time file tab, hence the name. But in the latest version of Word (Word 365 as of January 2023) they removed that. Now when a tab is selected, it's just underlined as you can see here with the Home tab.

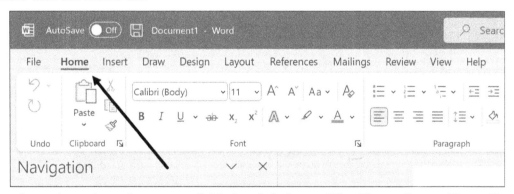

The other tab options that are available by default are File, Home, Insert, Draw, Design, Layout, References, Mailings, Review, View, and Help.

Each tab you select will show you different options or tasks. As you can see above, the Home tab allows you to Redo/Undo, Paste/Copy/Cut/Format Sweep, apply Font settings, apply Paragraph settings, and more. (We'll cover most of the Home tab in this book.)

Click

If I tell you to click on something, that means to move your cursor over to that location and then either right-click or left-click. If I don't say which to do, left-click.

Left-Click / Right-Click

If you look at a standard mouse, it's divided into two sides. Press down on the left side and that's a left-click. Press down on the right side and that's a right-click. You can also left- and right-click using your laptop's trackpad, but it won't always be obvious where to click. Usually it will be in the bottom of the trackpad. Pushing on the bottom left will left-click. Pushing on the bottom right will right-click.

A left-click is generally for selecting something. A right-click is generally for opening a dropdown menu.

Left-Click and Drag

If I ever tell you to left-click and drag, that means to left-click and then hold that left-click as you move your cursor. This is one way, for example, to select a range of text. You left-click at one end of the text and then hold that left-click as you move your mouse until all of the text you want is selected. It can also be a way to move an object.

Select or Highlight

There will be times when I tell you to select a range of text. Like here where I've selected the words "sample text":

This is sample text and I've selected the words that say that

When text is selected it will be highlighted or shaded a different color. In my Office theme, it is shaded a light gray.

As I noted above, one way to select text is to left-click and drag. You can left-click at either end of the range of text you want to select and then hold that left-click and drag your mouse until all of it is highlighted in gray.

Another option is to click at one end of the text, hold down the Shift key and use the arrow keys to select your text. The right and left arrows will move one character space at a time. The up and down arrows will move one row of text at a time.

If you need to select text that is not touching, you can do so using the Ctrl key. Select your first range of text, then hold down Ctrl while you left-click and drag to select your next range of text. (Using the arrow keys does not work. It will remove the first text selection.)

To select all of the text in a document you can use Ctrl + A.

Dropdown Menu

A dropdown menu is a list of choices. There are many dropdown menus in Word. One of the main ones is in the main workspace. Right-click on your document and you should see a dropdown menu that looks like this:

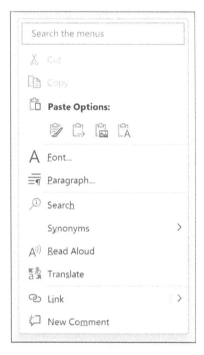

You can then select any of those choices from that dropdown to perform that task. Some dropdowns, like Synonyms, have a secondary dropdown menu. Hold your mouse over that arrow to the right of the option and you'll see another dropdown menu:

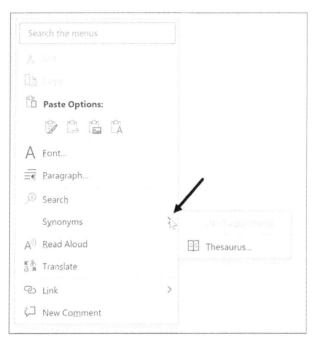

Many of the options in the tabs at the top of the workspace also have dropdown menus. They are indicated by an arrow either to the right of the option or below it. Here, for example, is the Font Color dropdown menu that you can see because I clicked on the arrow next to the red capital A.

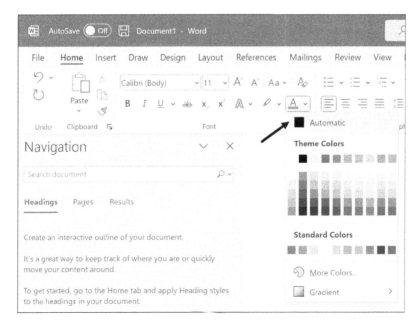

There is also a dropdown arrow under the Paste option on the left-hand side, as well as the underline, change case, text effects, bullets, numbering, and multi-level lists dropdowns that are visible in that screenshot.

(Don't worry if you don't know which is which, we'll cover most of them later.)

Expansion Arrow

The tasks under each tab are divided into different sections. So above you can see the Undo, Clipboard, Font, and Paragraph sections of the Home tab.

In the bottom right corner of most of those sections you will see an arrow. That's what I refer to as an expansion arrow. Click on that to see more options. Often it will open a dialogue box. (Which we'll define next.)

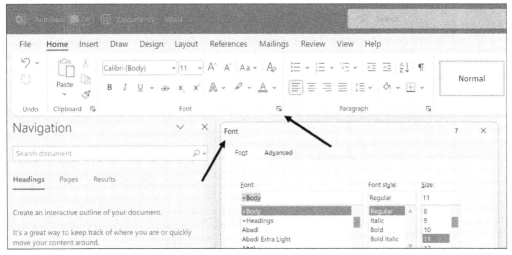

Here you can see that I clicked on the expansion arrow for the Font section and it opened the Font dialogue box.

Clicking on an expansion arrow is often the way to see the largest number of options, although I find I rarely need to do that.

Dialogue Box

Here is the full Font dialogue box that opened above:

A dialogue box is a pop-up box that will open on top of your workspace and will usually include the largest number of choices for that particular setting or task. For example, here you can see that for Effects there are choices for strikethrough and double strikethrough. In the Home tab we only had the choice for strikethrough.

So if there's ever anything you want to do that you think should be possible, try opening a dialogue box to see if that option is listed.

To close a dialogue box, click on OK after you've made your selection or click on the X in the top right corner.

If you have more than one Word document open, you may need to close any open dialogue box before you can move between documents.

Scroll Bar

Once you have more text in your document than will fit on the screen, you will see scroll bars appear. In Word they usually are on the right-hand side. If you have your workspace zoomed to a level that won't show all of the text across a line, then you'll also see a scroll bar along the bottom. Like you can see here where the arrows point to the scroll bars, one on the top right, one along the bottom:

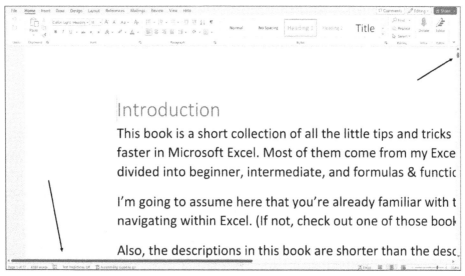

Note that the scroll bars are different sizes. The more text that isn't visible, the smaller the scroll bar will be.

Scroll bars may on occasion not be visible, but if you move your mouse over your document or over the edges where they should be located, they will reappear.

You can move through the document using the scrollbars in a number of ways. Left-click and drag the bar itself to flow through the document. Click in the lighter gray area at either end of the scroll bar to move one screen's worth of space. Left-click once on the arrows at the ends of the scroll bars to move about a line's worth of space. Or left-click and hold on those arrows to scroll through by about one line's worth of space at a time.

Scroll bars also appear for long lists of options where not all options fit on the screen. For example, the Font dropdown menu has a scroll bar on the right-hand side.

Task Pane

I believe by default you should have at least one task pane visible in your workspace for a new Word document. I do and I don't think I changed that setting. If so, it will be the Navigation task pane and be visible on the left-hand side of your workspace. Like so:

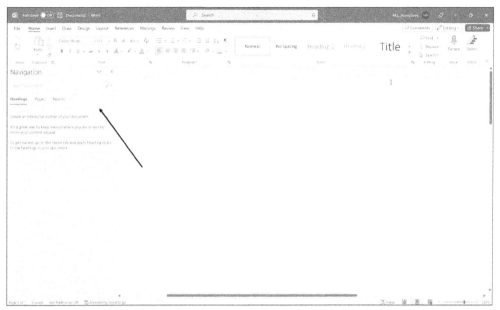

Task panes are a bit like dialogue boxes because they give you more options, but usually they will appear as part of your workspace, not on top of it like dialogue boxes do. Dialogue boxes are the old-school way of giving you more options. Task panes are the newer way of doing so. Which means for what we're doing in this book most of what you'll see are dialogue boxes.

You can open another task pane by going to the Help tab and clicking on Help, which will open the Help task pane on the right-hand side of your workspace.

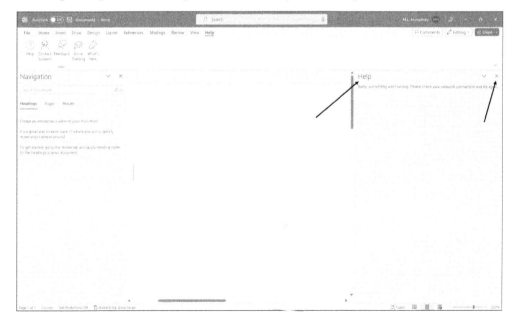

To close a task pane, click on the X in the top right corner of the pane. That arrow next to the X also allows you to move or resize the pane.

If you close a task pane and later need it, clicking on that task or using a Control shortcut for the related task will reopen it. To reopen the Navigation task pane, for example, you can use Ctrl + F, which is the control shortcut for Find.

Control Shortcuts

There are various shortcuts that you can use to perform common tasks in Word, such as Ctrl + C to copy. When I refer to those tasks, I will write them like I just did this one with the name of the keys that need to be used to execute the shortcut, separated by a plus sign. So Ctrl + C means hold down both the Ctrl key and the C key at the same time.

Even though I will write them using a capital letter, they do not require you to use a capital letter. Just hold down the letter indicated and you'll be fine. So Ctrl and the c key at the same time will copy your selection.

Absolute Basics

Now that we've established a common set of terms to use and you know how to make your screen look like mine, it's time to cover the absolute basics of opening, saving, closing, deleting, and renaming a Word file.

Open Word

If you're new to using Microsoft Word, then the first thing you need to learn is how to open it. The simplest way to open Word is to double-click on an existing Word file. That will not only open that file, but also open Word.

But if you don't have a file to open or don't want to open Word that way, then you have a few choices. The first is to go to your Start menu, which in Windows is usually located at the bottom of the screen. I always set mine so that it's in the left corner, but I believe the current Windows default puts it towards the center instead.

In Windows 11, left-click on the Windows icon and then find the Word icon in your pinned apps list or recently-used list. Here I've clicked on the Windows icon and then you can see that I have Word as one of my pinned programs:

If you can't see it there, then you can either type Word into the search bar at the top of the dropdown menu or you can click on All Apps and find it in the alphabetical listing of all of your applications.

I personally prefer to add the Word icon to my taskbar at the bottom of my screen so that I don't have to find it every time. Once it's there I can just left-click on the icon once to open Word.

You can see the Word icon in the taskbar in the screenshot above. It's the fourth one from the right at the very bottom of the screen, next to the ones for Excel, PowerPoint, and Access.

To put an icon in your taskbar, right-click on the application in the Start menu and choose Pin To Taskbar from the dropdown menu.

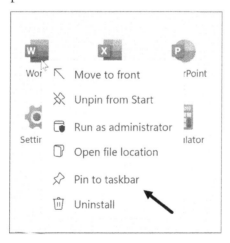

Once an icon has been added to your taskbar, you can left-click the icon and drag it to place it in the order you want. For example, I have my internet browsers grouped, then my Office programs, and then my audio/video programs.

New Word File

By default, Word is going to open to a Welcome screen.

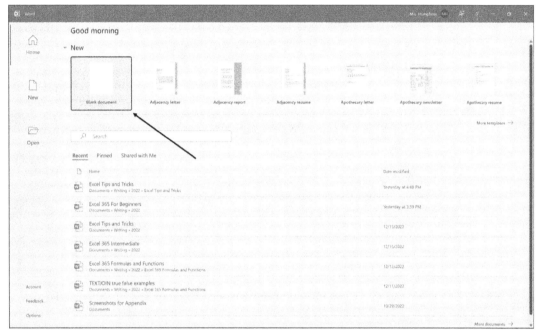

Click on Blank Document at the top to open a brand-new Word document. You can see in that same row that there are also a number of templates available to you. For this book, we're not going to use them. I think in the last ten years I've only used a Word template once.

For most basic writing tasks, you don't need them. But if you want to, feel free to explore them. You can see what each one will look like in the thumbnail and there is a More Templates option to click on at the end of that list.

You can also click on New on the left-hand side to start a new document but that will just take you to another screen that has Blank Document at the top and then a number of templates listed below that. So it's not necessary to do and doesn't give you any special options that you don't already have on the Welcome screen.

If you are already in a Word document and want to open an additional new Word document, you can use Ctrl + N to do so. Your other option is to go to the File menu up top which will take you back to the Welcome screen, and then click on Blank Document from there.

Open Existing Word File

To open an existing Word file, one option is to go to the file wherever you have it saved and double-click on it.

If it's a file I haven't used recently, this is generally the option I choose because I find it easier (or maybe more consistent) to navigate to my files outside of Word rather than through Word.

Your other option is to open Word first and then find the file you want to open through Word. This is the option I choose for files I've used recently.

On the Welcome screen there will be a listing of your Recent files as well as a tab you can click on to locate any files you've Pinned. (As you can see in the screenshot above.) If you see the file you want, just left-click on it.

The Open screen, which you can access by clicking on Open on the left-hand side or by using Ctrl + O has more options, so I want to walk through that one in detail. Here it is:

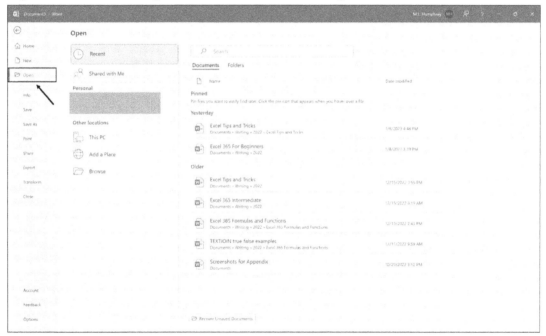

On the right-hand side is a listing of recently-used Word documents. You can see here that there are seven files listed for me right now in chronological order from most-recently-used to oldest. If you want to open one of those files, simply click on the name and the file will open.

If you have any files that you always want to have available to you, you can Pin those files and then they will be available in that Pinned section up top. (I'll show you how to do that in a moment.)

The default is a listing of your documents, but you can also click on Folders under the Search bar to see a list of folders that contain recently-opened documents:

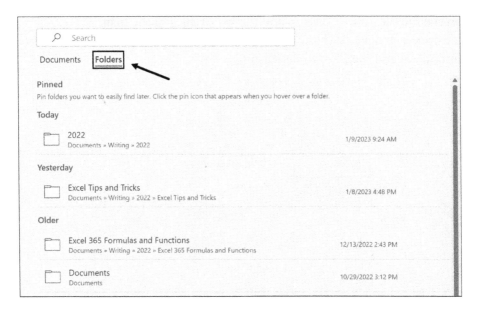

This is useful for when the file you want isn't listed, but it's located in a folder that you use often. For example, my 2022 folder has all folders and documents I worked on related to my writing in 2022.

Click on the folder name and that will show you any files in that folder as well as any sub-folders. You can keep navigating to the file you want by clicking through those sub-folders.

So, for example, here I clicked on 2022 in that original listing, and then the AML Compliance folder, and now I have four files I can choose from even though they weren't files I'd used recently:

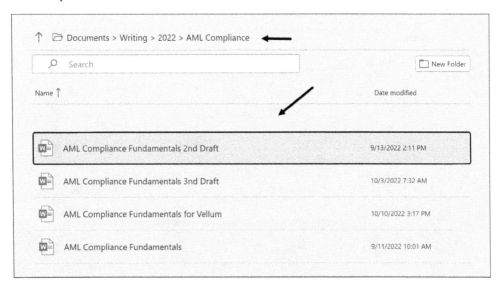

You can see the file path at the top and the list of files in the main space.

Another option if neither of those work is to navigate using the locations listed between the left-hand menu and the files/folders listing.

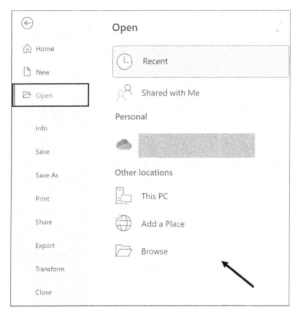

Right now I have the option to click on This PC, Browse, or OneDrive. (I personally don't use OneDrive because I'm a weird paranoid person and don't like storing my data "out there" somewhere, but it all works the same.)

If I click on Browse, that will open the Open dialogue box, which will then let me navigate to any file location on my computer and open my file from there:

Double-click on each of the folders in the main space (like Access DB for Writing) to open them or click once on the options on the left-hand side (like Desktop) to move to a location.

Once you find your Word document, click on it and then click on Open, or double-click on it to open it.

Pin a File

To pin a file, open it so that it's in your Recent files listing and then hold your mouse over that listing in the Welcome or Open screen.

On the right-hand side of the listing, under Date Modified you should see a little thumbtack image:

When you hold your mouse over it, it will say "Pin This Item to the List". Click on the thumbtack and the file will move to the Pinned section.

In the Welcome screen, that's a separate section where you have to click on Pinned to see it:

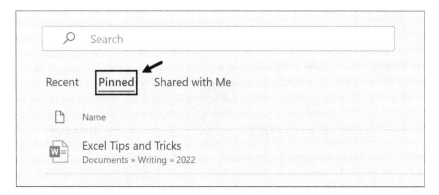

In the Open screen where we were before, it's just listed in a special area at the top of the list.

To unpin a file, just click on the thumbtack image again.

Close a File

To close a file, you have a few options there as well. I usually click on the X in the top right corner:

You can also go to the File tab and then choose Close from the left-hand menu. Or you can use Ctrl + W to close the current workbook.

The X in the top corner will also close out Word if you only had one file open or no files open.

Another option, if you have Word pinned to your taskbar, is to right-click on the Word icon and choose to Close Window (if you have one Word file open) or Close All Windows (if you have multiple Word files open) from there.

If you haven't made changes to your file(s) then Word will just close the file(s). But if you have, then Word will ask about saving the file.

Save a File

There are two types of saving in Word.

You can use Save to save an existing file as-is with the same name and location and file type. That will take the prior version of the file and overwrite it with the file as it exists right now.

Or you can use Save As which is for new files that don't already have a location or name as well as for existing files where you want to change the name, location, or file type or where you want to keep the old version as it was and also create a new version.

Let's walk through all of those scenarios now.

If you try to close a new file without saving first, Word will bring up a dialogue box asking if you want to save your changes to that file:

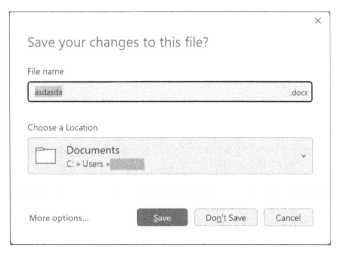

If you want to close the file without saving it, click on Don't Save. If you want to keep the file open for the time being and not save yet, click on Cancel.

If you do want to save the file, then give it a name in the File Name field, which should be highlighted by default.

Word will also display a default save location below that. In my case, it's my local Documents folder because I changed my options. Yours may default to OneDrive.

You can change the location by clicking on the dropdown arrow. That will show a list of options to choose from. For me, that list is recent locations I've saved to.

If none of those options work for you, click on More Locations at the bottom of the dropdown menu or More Options in the dialogue box. Both will open the Save As dialogue box:

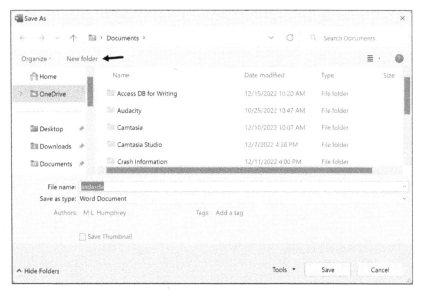

From there you can navigate to wherever you want to save your document. Note that at the top there is also an option for New Folder in case you want to save the file into a folder that doesn't already exist. Just navigate to where you want that folder to be, create it, name it, hit enter, and then select it to save to it.

Click on Save when you're ready.

Going back to the first dialogue box that appeared, you can see that Word 365 as of January 2023 defaults to using the .docx file type.

As of now, I'd say that's probably a fine format to use. Files that were created in any version of Word prior to Word 2007 were .doc files and for anyone working in one of those older versions of Word, they can't open a .docx file.

But I think at this point we're far enough away from that changeover that most people are able to open the newer file version and you're fine to always work in it.

(Five years ago, that was not my advice.)

If, however, you ever run into a situation where that isn't the case, then note that in the Save As dialogue box you can change the file type using that Save As Type dropdown:

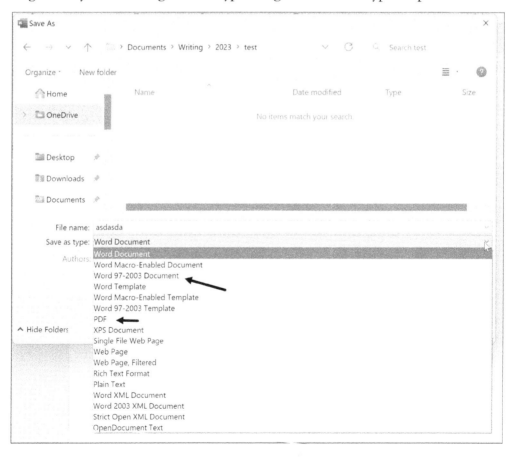

The option to use for older versions of Word is Word 97-2003 document. Also, this is where you can have Word save a document for you as a PDF file, which I've needed a few times.

(If you save as a PDF, however, be careful if the document you're using has images and image quality is important because the default image quality in Word is not a high enough standard for commercial printing. You may need to convert to a PDF using the Adobe website instead to get the quality of image you need.)

Okay. So that's one way to get to Save As. Just let Word do it for you with a new document. But if you want more control than that or if you're working with an existing document where you want to save it under a new name, new location, or new file type, then the better option is to go to File and then choose Save As on the left-hand side menu.

That will bring you to the Save As screen:

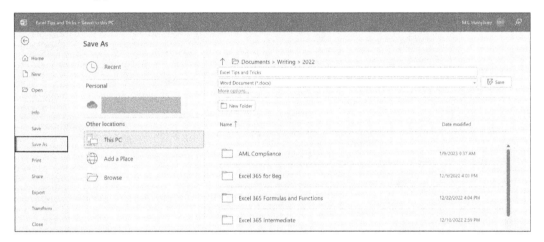

The document name and location will already be populated by default for an existing document, but you can click into the field for name to change that or you can navigate to a new location using the listed folders.

There is also a dropdown to change file format.

Once all those changes have been made, simply click on Save to save the file under its new name, location, and file type.

Clicking on More Options or Browse from this screen will open the Save As dialogue box, which we already discussed above.

I will note here that if you are just trying to move a file to a new location or trying to rename a file, this is not the way to do it, because the old version of the file will still exist. If you want to move a file or rename a file and not have that old version exist, then you need to move or rename the file outside of Word. We'll cover that in a minute.

So that was Save As. Usually, though, you'll just want to save your file before you close it.

Your first option is to just try to close the file. Word will display a dialogue box that asks if you want to save your changes. Click on Save to keep those changes, click on Don't Save to close the file without keeping the changes, or click on Cancel to keep the document open for now.

Your second option is to use Ctrl + S to save the document. You can do this at any point in time. You don't have to wait until you're ready to close the file to save your changes up to that point. I recently had a laptop that was crashing on me repeatedly, so I would use Ctrl + S after every significant change I made so that if my computer crashed I wouldn't lose that work.

(Word does have an AutoSave back-up feature. I believe the default right now is to save every 10 minutes. So you should never lose more than ten minutes of work, but when you do lose work that ten minutes can be a lot. I changed my settings to five minutes to help with that, but also saving frequently made a difference, too.)

Your third option, and again this is one you can do at any time, is to use the little disc icon at the top left corner of the screen.

It's meant to look like a little computer disc. Nobody uses those anymore, but that's what we

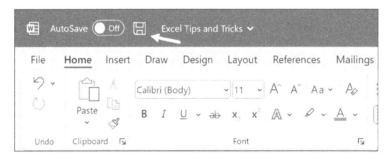

used to save information on rather than using a thumbdrive back in the day. Just click on the icon to save.

Finally, you could go to File and then choose Save, but given all the other options, that's the least efficient one to use. I just mention it because it's the most visible one.

Rename a File

As I mentioned above, if all you want to do is rename a file, doing so through Word is not the way to do it. The reason is because you end up with two files. The one with the old name and the one with the new name.

To rename a file and just have that one version of the file, you need to close the file and then go to where the file is saved. Click on the file once to select it. Click on it again to make the name editable. (The name will be highlighted when that happens.) And then make your changes and hit enter.

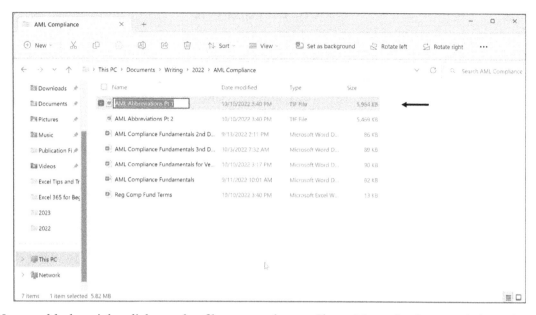

(You could also right-click on the file name, choose Show More Options, and then choose Rename from the dropdown menu, but the click and then click again option is faster and more consistent.)

When you rename a file, you cannot then open the file from your recent files listing. It may still display there under the old name, but you will get an error message that Word can't find the file. So the next time you open it you need to do so either from its current location or by navigating to the file through Word.

Move a File

As with renaming a file, the best way to relocate a file is to do so outside of Word so you don't end up with multiple copies.

Find the file where it's currently located, click on it, use Ctrl + X to cut it from its current location, go to where you want to move the file, and use Ctrl + V to paste it.

(And again, you could do this with right-click and finding the menu options for Cut and Paste, but the control shortcuts are faster.)

As with renaming a file, when you move a file you will then need to open that file directly the next time you use it in Word because the recent file listing won't work.

I often run into this issue because I have a habit of tidying up when I finish a project. I move my files into a Published sub-folder. Since that relocates the files, the next time I want to open them in Word, they're no longer where they were, so Word can't find them.

Delete a Word File

Finally, we need to discuss how to delete a Word file. Once more, this cannot be done in Word itself. You need to navigate to where the file is saved.

Click on the file name so that it's selected and then click on the trash can icon at the top of the dialogue box. Or, click on the file name and use the Delete key.

Or, you can right-click on the file name and click on the trash can icon there. Or, you can right-click on the file name, choose Show More Options, and then choose Delete from the dropdown menu.

Many available choices. The key is that it must be done where the file is saved and can't be done through Word.

Inputting Information

Now it's time to talk about how to actually input information in Word.

At its most basic, inputting information in Word is very easy to do if you're not working with a template. Simply open a new Word document and start typing.

But there are a few things in Word 365 that you may not like and so want to turn off. And there are some general tips and tricks I want to share with you to make using Word easier.

First up, Text Predictions.

Text Predictions

One of the unpleasant surprises I had when I first started using Word 365 in late 2022 was that it defaults to having Text Predictions turned On. What this does is as you type, it tries to figure out what the next words you want are and it suggests them for you. It was highly distracting for me and I immediately wanted it gone.

Of course, this morning as I was trying to demonstrate this so I could take a screenshot and show you, it let me write entire paragraphs without making any suggestions. The only example I could get to work was this one:

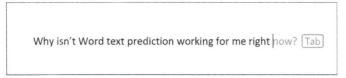

I typed the words "Why isn't Word text prediction working for me right" and then typed a space.

Word suggested "now?" to complete the sentence.

You can see that in the screenshot above. The suggested text is a light gray instead of black and it shows Tab next to that text. If I wanted to use the suggestion, I could use the Tab key or the right arrow key and Word would insert the suggested text for me and then I could keep going with the next text I want to type.

For me, as someone who did not grow up with predictive text, that interferes with my writing ability. It makes me slow down and assess whether the suggestion is an accurate one or not and then I have to think to use a Tab or right arrow key to accept that change.

But if you're new to Word then it might really help speed up your writing. Especially if you're writing something where it wants to make suggestions for you.

The first time I used Word 365 if felt like it was suggesting every other word to me. Now I'm writing entire paragraphs and it isn't.

My preference is to just turn it off. If you also want to do that, then go to the bottom left side of the screen and click on Text Predictions.

That will bring up the Word Options dialogue box to the Advanced tab.

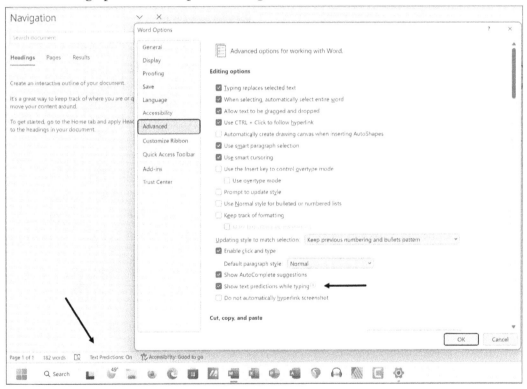

Click on the box for "Show Text Predictions While Typing" to turn that off. Once you've done that, you can just type what you want to type and Word will not have an opinion on it. Well, at least not about what the next word should be. It will still, by default, have opinions about your spelling and grammar.

So let's talk about that next.

Spelling and Grammar Flags As You Type

Here are a few of those paragraphs I typed trying to get it to make a prediction:

> I want to write something that is very basic and simple so that Word will predict what I am going to write next. It would help if Word would suggest a word for me now and again so that I can see how text prediction actually works in Word and tell others about it. But right now I'm doing a lot of typing and not seeing anything happen.
>
> What do I have to type to have Word predict my next words. There was a door in between me and my destination. Nope, that didn't work. What other phrases can I type that Word will understand in time to make a suggestion for me?
>
> I was able to get it to work on why isn't Word working for me right now? But now it won't do it again and I don't understand.

If you look closely at the text (because they've made this less obvious in the latest version of Word), you will see that some of my text has a dotted blue line under it and some of my text has a double blue underline.

You can right-click on the flagged text to see what Word's identified issue is:

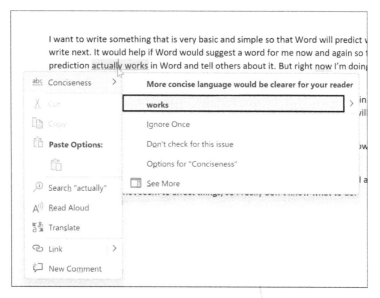

So, here, for the dotted blue line it is telling me that I could use more concise language. It would prefer that I use "prediction works in Word" instead of "prediction actually works in Word."

If I agree, I can click on that suggested text and it will change it for me.

I can also tell it to ignore that one suggestion or to stop checking for that particular issue by clicking on those options in the dropdown.

Here is one of the double-underlined examples:

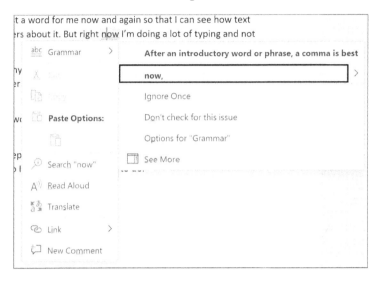

In this case, it thinks I'm violating a grammar rule. According to Word, a comma is best after an introductory word or phrase. It wants me to have used "But right now, I'm…" instead of "But right now I'm…"

Fair enough.

Personally, I don't want to stop while I'm writing and consider grammar issues, so I often will have this turned off in my version of Word.

But before I show you how to do that, let's misspell a few things. Here I've gone back to the first paragraph and deliberately misspelled "write" and "basic". For spelling errors, Word uses a red squiggly line under the text.

I want to writte something that is very basiic and simple so that Word will predict what I am going to write next. It would help if Word would suggest a word for me now and again so that I can see how text prediction actually works in Word and tell others about it. But right now I'm doing a lot of typing and not seeing anything happen.

Once more, you can right-click on the word that was flagged and Word will provide suggestions:

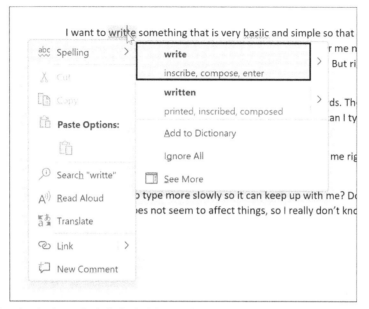

In this case, it also includes a brief definition of each suggested word so that you can choose between, for example, discrete and discreet, correctly.

If the word that it flagged is one that you use often that was not recognized by Word, you can click on the Add to Dictionary option to add that word into the dictionary that Word uses for your documents so it's not flagged anymore.

I usually do not do this, just in case I'm wrong. What I instead do is use the Ignore All option which will ignore all uses of that word in that document. But you need to know that it's very specific. It will only do that form of that word and will not include plurals or possessives.

Let me show you:

Here I have two sentences that use two made-up words, "Gramdy's favorite past time was to play with gregorns. Gramdy really like a good gregorn."

(I'm leaving that typo in there so we can discuss that in a minute.)

In that second sentence, I told Word to ignore both "Gramdy" and "gregorn". But note that "Gramdy's" and "gregorns" are still flagged as spelling errors in the first sentence.

That's because when you choose the Ignore All option, Word will only ignore that very specific combination of letters. It doesn't extrapolate to possessives or plurals.

Which is fine. You just need to know that's the case, because likely you will also end up needing to tell it to ignore a possessive or a plural as well.

Now, let's go back to that second sentence. "Gramdy really like a good gregorn." That should be liked not like. Or maybe likes if we didn't have the first sentence to give the past tense use. But like is not correct.

And yet, it was not flagged.

You can't rely 100% on the grammar and spelling check in Word. It misses things sometimes.

It's also wrong sometimes. And it has a very specific approach to grammar that is not necessarily the appropriate choice for writing fiction or less-formal prose. Also, be very careful when it flags its vs it's because about 20% of the time it gets it wrong.

I personally prefer to run the spelling and grammar check at the end rather than try to deal with that as I'm typing. So let's cover two things, real quick. One, how to turn off grammar check as you're typing as well as how to turn off specific rules. And, two, how to run a spelling and grammar check on your entire document.

Turn Off Grammar or Spell Check as You Type

To disable the grammar or spelling check as you type, go to File and then choose Options at the bottom-left corner of the screen to open the Word Options dialogue box. Go to the Proofing tab.

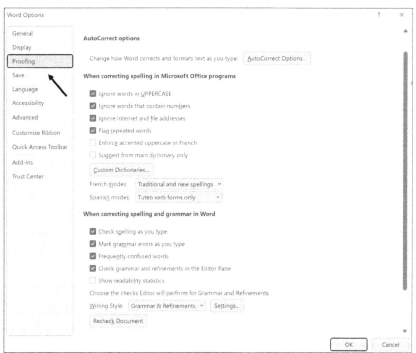

You can see that there are a number of options here. The ones that are blue and checked are the ones that are currently active.

To turn off grammar and/or spelling checks as you type, go to the section titled When Correcting Spelling and Grammar in Word and then check the box for "Check Spelling As You Type" and/or "Mark Grammar Errors As You Type" to turn them off.

My preference is to usually turn off grammar check but leave on spellcheck. That's because I'm usually catching and correcting a misspelled word as soon as I type it so I don't find that distracting in the same way I do the grammar error flags.

Run a Spelling and Grammar Check On Your Document

Where I do the bulk of my spelling and grammar check is at the end when the document is finished. I go to the Proofing section of the Review tab and click on the Spelling and Grammar option:

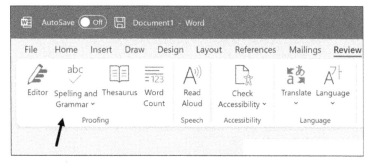

(The dropdown menu there will let you choose to just review Spelling instead if you want.)

When you click on Spelling and Grammar, an Editor task pane will open on the right-hand side of the workspace and you'll see the first identified issue:

In this case it was a grammar issue. It shows the sentence that contains the error, flags the text that was identified as an issue, and then below that lists a suggestion for how to fix it.

You can either click on the suggestion to apply it, click on Ignore Once, click on the option to not check for this issue, or use the arrows at the top of the task pane to move to the next identified issue.

Here it is for a spelling error:

If you click on a solution, like I just clicked on basic for that spelling error, it will immediately move to the next flagged issue, so be careful on that one that you don't make a mistake.

Another option you have is to go directly into the document and make your change there. So, for example, maybe it flagged "Gramdy" and that is wrong, but none of the suggestions are right because it's supposed to be Gramby. In that case, you can click into the document, make your change, and then click on Resume Checking Corrections when you're done.

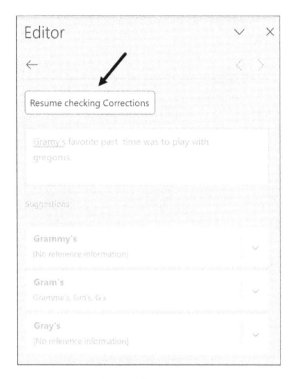

AutoCorrect

Another thing that Word likes to do to help, and sometimes it is a help, is to autocorrect common errors. One of my personal issues is that I will often type "teh" instead of "the". Word knows this happens a lot so it changes that immediately as soon as I move on to the next word.

Which is great when you want that to happen. But it's something to watch out for. For example, I had to undo that change when it did it to me above. (Ctrl + Z will do that if you notice it right away.)

It also has certain tricks that you can use to type common symbols or characters. Often those are great to have around, like the double hyphen that gets turned into a dash, but sometimes they get in the way. My background is in securities regulation. So I am far more likely to write about Rule 3070(c) than I am to need the copyright symbol. But by default in Word using (c) creates the copyright symbol.

You can turn off any AutoCorrect option you want in the Word Options dialogue box. In this case I opened the dialogue box by clicking on Text Prediction at the bottom of the workspace and then went to the Proofing page. At the top is an AutoCorrect options button that will open the AutoCorrect dialogue box when you click on it:

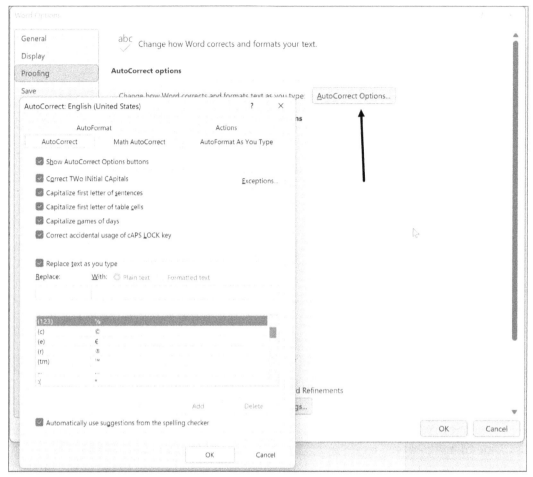

You can see both dialogue boxes in the image above.

Uncheck any option you don't want Word to use. You can also click on one of those AutoCorrect choices that's listed down below, like turning (123) into one-eighth and then click on Delete to remove it. And you can add your own custom autocorrect options if you want using the Add option.

For some options, like replacing straight quotes with smart quotes, you may need to turn it off on more than one tab. Both the AutoFormat tab and the AutoFormat As You Type tab sometimes overlap.

Undo

I just mentioned this above, but if you ever do anything in Word that you want to undo, the best way to do so is to use Ctrl + Z. That will undo the last thing you did. So if AutoCorrect changes something you didn't want it to change, Ctrl + Z will reverse that.

It can also undo formatting or typing or anything else. With text it often undoes a word or phrase at a time so may undo more than you want.

There is also an Undo menu option on the far left-hand side of the Home tab. It has a dropdown menu that lets you undo multiple steps at once.

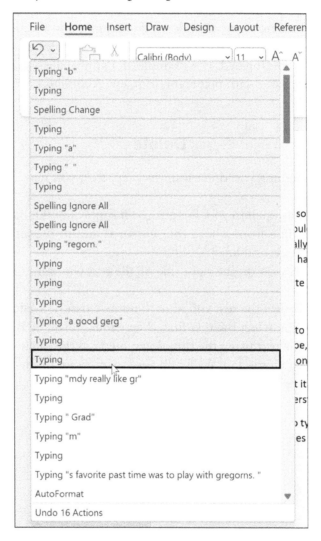

The further down that list you click, the more steps you will undo. As you move your mouse down that list you will see all of the steps above highlighted in gray to indicate that those steps will all be undone when you make that selection. In the screenshot above I'd be undoing 16 actions at once if I made that selection.

Redo

If you ever undo something and change your mind, you can Redo. Ctrl + Y will redo the last action.

There is also a Redo option on the left-hand side of the Home tab, but in Word you can only redo one action at a time so the dropdown doesn't give any additional choices.

If you have no action that you undid, Ctrl + Y or the Redo option in the Home tab will perform the last task you performed. For example, if I apply italics to text, Ctrl + Y will then let me apply italics again. Same with text color, font, etc. Although I found it to be glitchy with text highlight color.

Delete

Finally, if you type something you don't want to keep, then you need to remove that text by deleting it.

There are a few options open to you. First, you can simply use the Backspace key to remove any text one letter at a time from where your cursor is and to the left. (When you're in the document the cursor is a vertical line.)

If you are for some reason on the right side of the text you want to delete, use the Delete key instead.

Another option is to select the text you want to remove first (left-click and drag or use Shift and the arrow keys.) If you select the text first, then either Delete or Backspace will work.

You could also Cut the text using the dropdown menu in the main workspace or from the Clipboard section of the Home tab. We'll talk about Cut more in the next chapter when we talk about moving your text around.

Moving Information

Once you have information in your document, there may come a time when you need to move that information around. Maybe you want to reorder the document or maybe you wrote part of a report and someone else wrote another part in another Word document and now you want to combine those two.

Let's talk now about how to do that.

Select All

First up, if you want to select everything in a document, including text, images, and headers/footers, you can do so using Select All. The easiest way is to use Ctrl + A.

You can also go to the Editing section of the Home tab and click on Select to open the dropdown menu there which will then let you choose to Select All, Select Objects, Select All Text with Similar Formatting, or to open the Selection Pane which will list any objects (like shapes or charts) in your document.

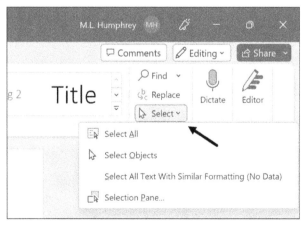

For our purposes in this book, that first option, Select All, is the one to remember.

You may also at some point want to use Select Text With Similar Formatting to easily change the formatting of different selections from your document at once. For example, when I write these books I use bolded text for the section headers within each chapter. If I decide that I want to quickly apply a different font size, font, font color, etc. to all of those headings at once, I can use this option and then apply my formatting (which we will cover soon) and all similarly-formatted entries will update.

Okay. Now let's go back to that example where you have two documents and you want to take the text from one and put it in the other. Step one was to select all of that text. For me, that's Ctrl + A. Done.

Copy or Cut Text

The next step would then be to copy or to cut that text. When you Copy, you keep the text where it was originally and take a copy of it. When you Cut, you remove the text from its original location and have a copy of it that you can paste elsewhere.

So the choice of which one to use comes down to whether you want to leave a version in the original location. In our example here where we're taking text from one document and putting it in another, it really doesn't matter. Because even if I Cut that text from the first document as long as I close that document without saving changes, that document remains as it was.

When moving sections of text around within a document, use Cut. When reusing text from one location in another, use Copy.

How to do this.

The simplest way, and definitely memorize these, is to use the Control shortcuts. Ctrl + C will copy. Ctrl + X will cut. Select your text first and then use the shortcut you want.

If you don't remember the shortcuts or don't want to use them, then you can right-click after selecting your text and choose Copy or Cut from the dropdown menu:

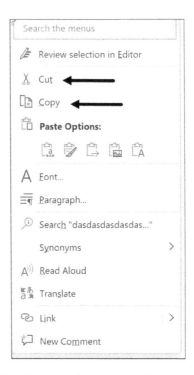

Your final option is to go to the Clipboard section of the Home tab and choose the cut or copy option from there. Cut is represented by a pair of scissors. Copy is represented by two pages stacked on top of each other. (We'll see that in a moment when we discuss how to paste text.)

Paste Text

Once you have selected your text and copied or cut that text, then it's time to paste the text. Go to the point in the document where you want to place the text and, if you have no special changes that need to be made to that text, simply use Ctrl + V to paste it.

Your other options are to right-click and choose one of the Paste options from the dropdown menu. (See above.) Or to go to the Clipboard section of the Home tab and click on the Paste option there.

If you want to paste the text but with changes, then you need to use one of the Paste Special options available either through the dropdown menu in the main workspace or by clicking on the dropdown arrow under Paste in the Clipboard section of the Home tab:

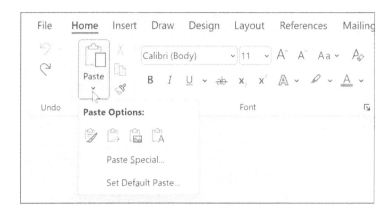

Clicking on Paste Special in that dropdown will bring up the Paste Special dialogue box, but we're just going to cover the four options you can see there which are, from left to right, Keep Source Formatting, Merge Formatting, Picture, and Keep Text Only.

For basic text that doesn't have a lot of formatting and where the source and destination formatting is similar, you won't see much difference between those options. But often I find I need this when someone, for example, wrote their portion of a document in the default Word font (Calibri) and now I'm pasting that into a document using a different font like Times New Roman. Or when I'm taking text from Excel and need to paste it into a formatted Word document.

Let's look at a very basic example:

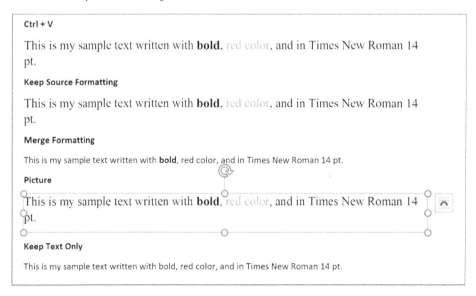

I took a sentence and I changed the font to Times New Roman, 14 point (so larger), changed the text "red color" to red, and applied bold formatting to the word "bold". I then selected that text and pasted it into a new Word document which by default is using Calibri 11 point font.

That first example is using Ctrl + V and the text pasted in exactly like it was formatted in the first document. Same for the next option where I used Keep Source Formatting.

Where things get interesting is starting with the Merge Formatting option. It kept the bolded text, but changed the font, font size, and font color.

Picture looks like it's the same as the first two options, but you can see that I clicked on that one to show you that it's in fact a picture now. You cannot edit or format that text, it's like taking a snapshot of the text and dropping it into the document.

Finally, Keep Text Only pasted the text in but removed the bolding and red text and also changed the font and font size to the default for the document the text was pasted into.

Usually, when I need one of these options, it is the Keep Text Only option I need so that whatever I'm pasting into the document matches what's already there.

One final thing to note. It is possible to have multiple snippets of text copied or cut at one time and to then be able to paste all or one of them into your document. To see which text snippets are available to you to paste, you need to open the Clipboard task pane.

To do that, click on the expansion arrow in the Clipboard section of the Home tab. You should see something like this on the left-hand side of your workspace:

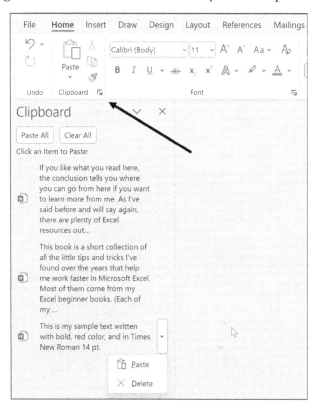

You can click on an individual entry to paste it. Or you can click on the arrow next to the snippet like I have above and choose Paste that way. Or you can use that Paste All option at the top to paste all of the snippets at once.

If you don't want one of those snippets there, click on the arrow next to it and choose Delete. (The arrow only shows when you hold your mouse over each snippet.)

I will admit I've never used this in real-life. But it's there if you need it. And could be very useful if you have multiple phrases or sections of text that you will need to paste into a document multiple times. You could copy each of them and then just quickly go through and click on the one you need to paste it into the document as it's needed.

* * *

Okay, so that was the easy part of working in Word. Open a new document and type away and then copy or cut and paste your text around as needed. Now we get into the "fun" of formatting, starting with text formatting, some of which you've seen me do already.

Text Formatting

Text and paragraph formatting is key to working in Word. I have yet to work for an employer who wanted their staff to use Calibri as the font on documents. And I don't think I've ever written a book that didn't use italics or bold. So this chapter is a very important one to master if you're going to use Word.

The text formatting options can be accessed in a number of ways.

First, there are control shortcuts for some of the most basic formatting like Bold (Ctrl + B), Italics (Ctrl + I), and Underline (Ctrl + U).

Second, in the Font section of the Home tab you can find the most common formatting choices:

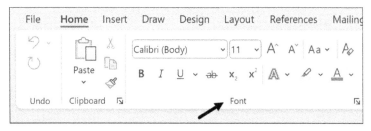

Third, the expansion arrow there as well as right-clicking and choosing Font from the dropdown menu in your document will both open the Font dialogue box. This can also be opened by using Ctrl + D.

Finally, there is a mini formatting menu that you can see if you right-click in your document:

For each of the above options, first select the text you want to format, and then apply the formatting option using the method you prefer.

Let's now walk through what your formatting options are. I'm going to do this alphabetically so you can easily return to this chapter when needed, although you can also use the index in the back of the print version of this book or search in the ebook.

Bold

To bold text I usually just use Ctrl + B.

The Font dialogue box allows you to choose either Bold or Bold Italic.

You can also click on the capital B on the left-hand side of the Font section of the Home tab or the mini formatting menu.

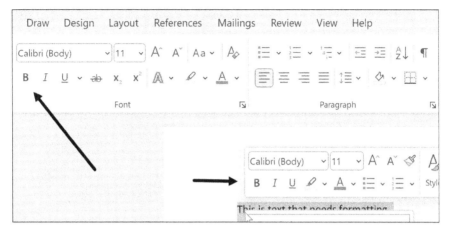

To remove bolding from text, you can either use Ctrl + B again, click on the capital B once more, or in the Font dialogue box change the Font Style to Regular or Italic.

For the first three options, if the text you selected was partially bolded and partially not, the first time you select the option it will bold all of the text, so you will need to do it twice to remove the bolding. (That usually happens to me if I select a range of text and there's a space at the end that wasn't formatted as bold that I can't tell isn't formatted the same way.)

Change Case

It is possible to change your selected text so that all of the letters are in uppercase, lowercase, sentence case (where the first letter of each sentence is upper case but the rest is lower case), toggle case (where the first letter of each word is lower case and the rest are in upper case), or where each word is capitalized but the rest of the letters are lower case.

I do this through the Font section of the Home tab using the Change Case option in the top row on the right-hand side. It's represented by an Aa where there is a capital letter A next to a lower-case one.

Here you can see the dropdown choices as well as examples of each one in the document:

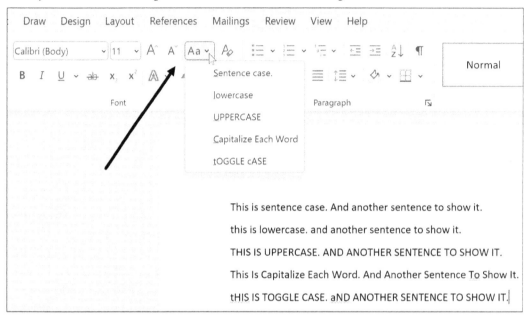

Change case is also an option in the mini formatting menu.

The Font dialogue box also has checkboxes for Small Caps and All Caps.

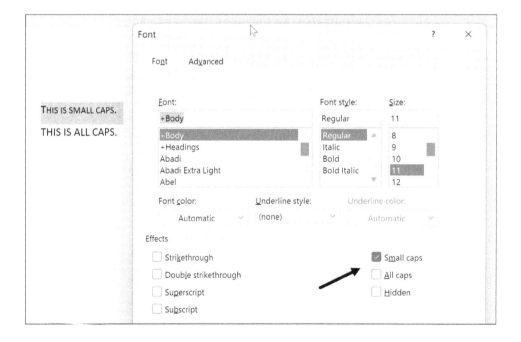

Font Color

Font color is another one that I usually apply using the Font section of the Home tab. It's the A with a red line under it, at least by default. (Once you change the color that new color will be the color under the A.) It is also available in the mini formatting menu as well as in the Font Color dropdown menu of the Font dialogue box.

In the Home tab, if you just want the color shown under the A (which is red by default), click on the A. Otherwise, click on the dropdown arrow to see seventy different font colors you can choose from:

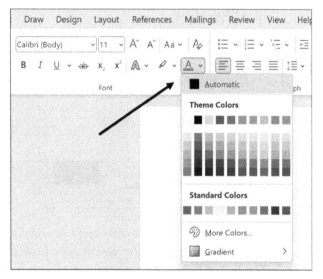

If one of those seventy colors isn't what you want or you have a specific color that you're required to use, click on More Colors to bring up the Colors dialogue box.

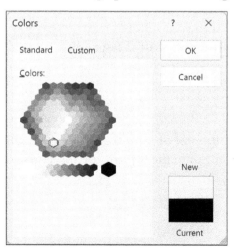

The first tab of that dialogue box is labeled Standard and shows a honeycomb of colors. Click on any of those colors in the honeycomb or in the white-to-gray-to-black line below that to choose a color. The new color will show at the top of the square in the bottom right corner of the dialogue box. The old color will show on the bottom of that square.

Click OK to apply the new color or use the X in the top right corner to close the dialogue box without applying a new color.

If you need to use a custom color, click over to the Custom tab.

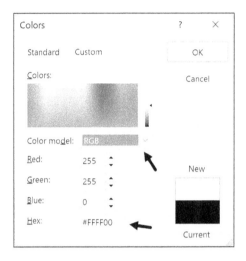

It has a rainbow color grid that you can click into and then use the slider on the side to adjust the degree of black included in the color. But the real power in this tab is below that. The dropdown lets you choose between RGB or HSL colors and there is also a Hex Code box at the very bottom.

If you have a custom color you must use, which many corporations do, you can get the exact color you need by providing the RGB, HSL, or Hex Code value on this tab. Once you've done so, click OK to apply it to your selected text.

The mini formatting menu and Font dialogue box work the exact same way. They both have a dropdown menu of colors to choose from.

Font Size

If you ever need to change the size of your text, there are a number of options available. The one I use is the dropdown menu in the top row of the Font section of the Home tab:

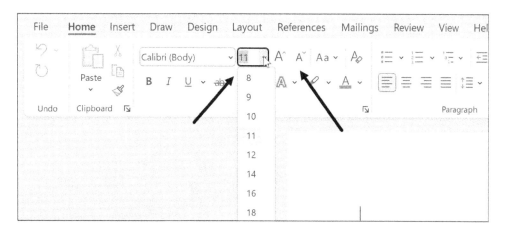

Click on the dropdown arrow and choose the font size you want from there. The default in Word is 11 pt, so a number less than that will be smaller text and a number greater than that will be larger. If you're not sure what size you want, you can hold your mouse over the different values and the text will change size within your document. To keep that change, click on the value.

You can also click into that box and type a value if you want. As you can see in the dropdown, it only includes the most popular sizes, so if you want something like 13 pt text you need to manually enter that value.

Another option is located to the right of that dropdown. There are two A's there, one with an up arrow, one with a down arrow. Clicking on those options will move the font size up or down one size. The font sizes used for that are the same as the ones in the dropdown. So you would move from 12 pt to 14 pt to 16 pt, for example.

The mini formatting menu also has those same options available. And the Font dialogue box has a list of popular font sizes to choose from as well as a box where you can type in a value.

Font Type

To the left of the font size dropdown is the Font dropdown. This is available in the Font section of the Home tab, in the mini formatting menu, and also in the Font dialogue box.

Here is the font dropdown from the Home tab:

The default font in Word is Calibri. If you use a different Theme in Word you may have a different default. Those Theme Fonts will be listed first. Next you will see Recently Used Fonts listed. And then finally you will see an alphabetical listing of all available fonts.

Which fonts are listed will depend on your computer. Word comes with a number of default fonts, but it is possible to buy additional fonts as well. I have a number of those so my font listing may be different from yours.

If you know the font you want, you can click into the box with the current font name in it and start typing the font name like I've done here:

I typed "Gara" and Word took me to that portion of my fonts list and also suggested the

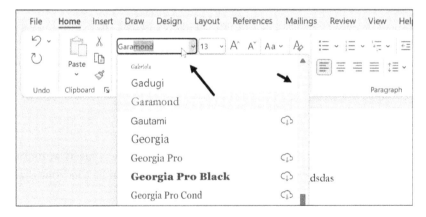

Garamond font which is the only one that starts with those letters.

There are also scroll bars available on the right-hand side of the font listing that you can use to scroll through your listed fonts.

Each font is written using that font so you can see what it looks like. That's why, for example, Georgia Pro Black is so dark compared to the rest, because a black-weight font is a very bold weight. You can also see there the difference between Gautami, which is a non-serif font, and Georgia, which is a serifed font.

Usually, in a corporate or school environment you will be told which font or fonts to use. For example, with writing, Times New Roman is a common one to use. In the past Courier was a common one. One employer I worked for preferred Palatino for everything.

If no one gives you guidance on which font to use, keep in mind your goal or purpose. In general, that is going to be legibility. You want people to be able to read the words you write.

For a standard audience reading a book like this one, that means using a serifed font, like Times New Roman or Palatino. Serifed fonts have little feet at the bottom of the letters which are supposed to make it easier to read words.

For those who have difficulty with sight, so large-print readers for example, often a non-serifed font is a better choice. For my large print fiction titles, for example, I use Verdana.

Save the display fonts (like Algerian) and script fonts (like Cochocib) for signage or book covers or report covers. And even then, be careful to make sure that people can actually read the text.

Now, there is a new quirk in Word 365 that we should also discuss and that's those little cloud download options in that font listing. Those are fonts that are available to you to use through Word, but that are not installed on your computer. To use one of those fonts, you'd need to click on that cloud to download the font.

It is possible to disable this if they annoy you and you don't want them. To do so, go to File and then click on Account at the bottom left corner of the screen. From the Account page click on Manage Settings under Account Privacy. That will open a Privacy Settings dialogue box. You can then uncheck the box for Experiences That Download Online Content.

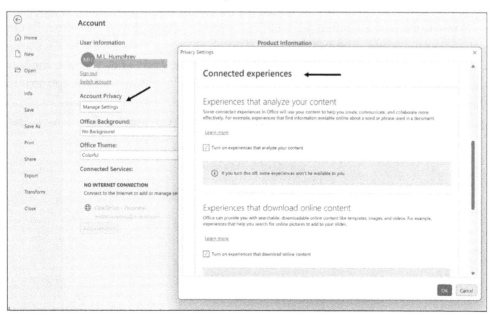

When you restart Word, you should no longer have those downloadable fonts listed. Much cleaner:

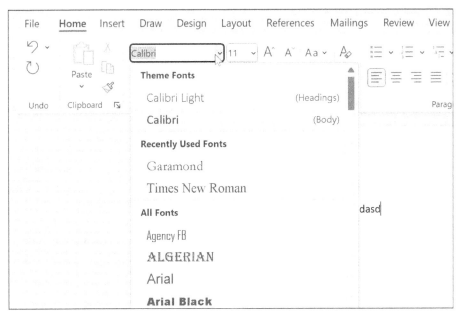

(And I should note here that I actually scrolled a little below that and unchecked the box for everything. But now I have to go and check it again so I can keep writing this book for you. There are quirks in Word 365 that are driven by those settings or by being online. For example, I learned that the Read Aloud voice in Word 365 is the old mechanical male-sounding horrible one if you're offline but a woman who almost sounds decent if you're online. Technology. Always changing.)

One more thing to mention here is that different fonts, even ones that are the same font size, will appear different sizes on the page. So choose your font before you do any final formatting or arrangement of elements.

Here are a few examples of good, solid, reliable fonts you can use that also demonstrates that:

Serif-Font Examples

Times New Roman

Palatino Linotype

Garamond

Each of the fonts in the list above are the same font pt size.

Highlight Text

If you ever want to highlight text, like you would physically with a highlighter, you can do that using the Text Highlight Color option. By default it's going to have a bright yellow line under what looks like a marker. It's located in the bottom row of the Font section of the Home tab next to font color.

Select your text and then if all you want is yellow highlight, click on that image.

If you want to choose a different color, like I did here with a bright green, use the dropdown arrow:

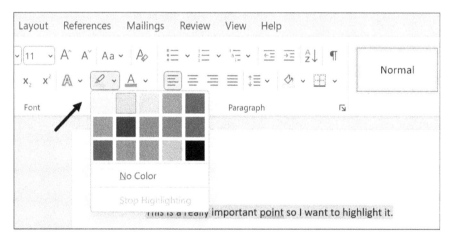

To remove a highlight, use the No Color option.

The highlight color option is also available in the mini formatting menu.

Do not confuse this with adding fill color to a cell in a table. Also, it's better to use track changes and comments to flag any issues in a document rather than use the highlighter for that purpose. Track changes, comments, and tables are intermediate-level topics covered in the next book in this series, but I just wanted to mention it here in case.

Italicize

To italicize text, the easiest way is to use Ctrl + I. But the Font section of the Home tab and the mini formatting menu also have a slanted I that you can click on in the bottom row under the font dropdown. And the Font dialogue box has options for both Italic and Bold Italic under font style.

To remove italics, select your text and then once more use Ctrl + I or click on the slanted I in the Font section of the Home tab or in the mini formatting menu. You can also change the font style back to Regular or to Bold in the Font dialogue box. As with bolding, if you select text that is partially italicized you will need to use Ctrl + I or click on the slanted I twice because the first time will apply it to all of the text and the second will remove it.

Strikethrough

To add a basic strikethrough to text, you can use the ab with a strikethrough in the Font section of the Home tab or the mini formatting menu. In the mini formatting menu it's off to the right side:

Above you can see an example of what that looks like when applied to the word "strikethrough" in the first line of text.

If you want a double strikethrough, like in the second line of text, then you need to use the Font dialogue box. There is a checkbox there for double strikethrough.

Subscript or Superscript

To apply subscript or superscript to text, use the options in the Font section of the Home tab.

Subscript looks like an X with a 2 in the subscript position. Superscript looks like an X with a 2 in the superscript position.

You can see examples of text using them in the screenshot on the next page.

Simply select the text that needs that formatting and then click on the option. So in the examples shown below, I selected the 2 in each line of text and then applied the appropriate formatting to it.

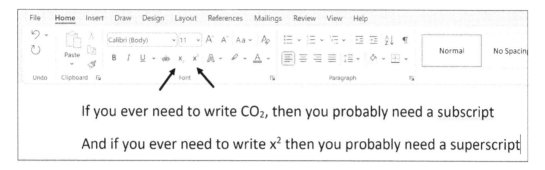

Subscript and superscript are also available as checkboxes in the Font dialogue box.

Text Effects

I'm only mentioning text effects here because they're included in the Font section of the Home tab. For new users to Word you are very unlikely to need these. But what they do is let you add an outline, shadow, reflection, glow, or other effect to your text. If you click on the dropdown arrow for Text Effects you'll see a number of pre-formatted options as well.

All I'll say here about these is that you should keep in mind your audience and effectively using text to convey your message. It is far too easy to add outlines and shadows and glow and reflections to text and end up overwhelming the text itself. So proceed with caution.

Underline

The easiest way to underline text is to use Ctrl + U. That will add a single-line underline below your selected text. You can also click on the underlined U in the Font section of the Home tab or in the mini formatting menu.

Unlike bold and italics, there is more than one underline option you can apply. To see a short list of choices, click on the dropdown arrow next to the underlined U in the Font section of the Home tab to see a list of your available choices:

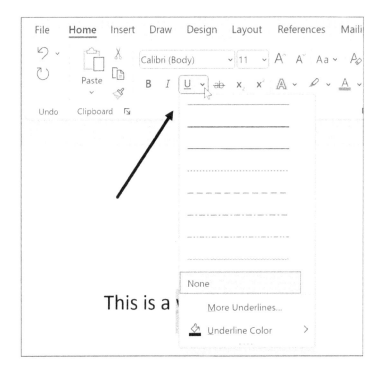

There is a single line, double line, thick line, dotted line, dashed line, two lines that have both dots and dashes, as well as a wavy line.

As you hold your mouse over each option, Word will apply it to your text so you can see what it will look like. Click on the one you want.

You can also choose a color for your underline at the bottom of that dropdown.

Clicking on More Underlines will open the Font dialogue box which has an Underline Style dropdown menu with even more choices available. Select the underline style you want there and then click OK to apply it.

The Words Only option will place a single underline under each of the selected words, but not carry through that underline between the words. Like so:

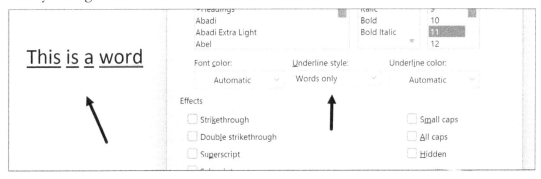

To remove an underline, use Ctrl + U or click on the underlined U once more. If you used an underline other than the default single-line option, you will have to do so twice because the first time will convert the existing underline to a single-line underline.

Another option for removing an underline is to use the dropdown for underline in the Font section of the Home tab and click on the None option towards the bottom.

The Font dialogue box also has a (none) option you can select.

$* * *$

Clear All Formatting

We just covered all of the formatting options in the Font section of the Home tab, but there's one more option in the top right corner there:

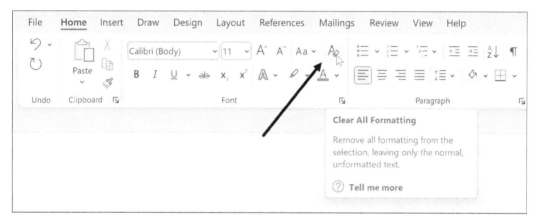

This is the Clear All Formatting option. Click on that to remove all formatting from your selected text. Below you can see text in the first row that has a change in font and font size as well as bold, italics, underline, strikethrough, text effects, highlight, and a red color applied.

This is a sentence that I want to test

This is a sentence that I want to test

In the second row is that same text after I used Clear All Formatting. It changed the font and font size back to the default of Calibri 11 pt and removed all other formatting except for the highlight.

Format Painter

The Format Painter is possibly my favorite tool in Microsoft Word. I cannot tell you how many projects I have worked on where there has been some weird slight difference between paragraphs written by different team members. No one ever knows how the change got in there and no one can figure out how to fix it.

The answer is to use the Format Painter tool. It is located in the Clipboard section of the Home tab and also available in the mini formatting menu:

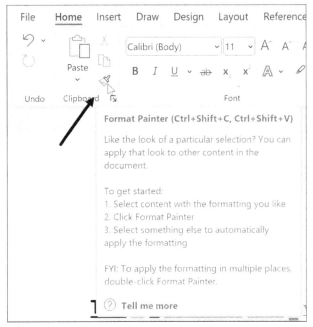

I always think of it as the format sweeper because it looks like a broom to me, but it's official name is the Format Painter.

What it does is takes the formatting of your selected text and places that formatting on other text that you select.

So step one is to select the text that has the formatting you want.

Step two is to click on the Format Painter. Double-click if you have more than one location where you want to transfer the formatting.

Step three is to select the text where you want to apply your formatting. Use the mouse or the trackpad to select the text. (Using the Shift and arrow keys doesn't work.)

If you have text that you select that has a wide variety of formatting, like in our example above for clear formatting, Word will generally go with the formatting that is at the beginning of the selection. So in that case it would transfer the bold and underline from "this" but not all the rest of the formatting.

Where Format Painter really shines in my opinion is when it's used to transfer paragraph formatting which can include the space before and after the paragraph, the space between lines in the paragraph, any indent that paragraph may have, etc. It will capture all of that.

And I don't know if this is still the case, but it's something to be aware of. Sometimes in the past it would matter whether I selected a paragraph from the first word to the last instead of from the last word to the first. So if I transferred formatting using the Format Painter and it didn't seem to fix the issue the first time, I'd go back and select the paragraph starting at the opposite end and try it again.

This can be especially true with numbered or bulleted lists.

Another trick to try is to select more than one paragraph if spacing between paragraphs matters.

Also, formatting can be transferred from one document to another. It doesn't have to be done within the same document.

When you transfer formatting this way, all of the existing formatting in the paragraph you're transferring to will be removed. It's all or nothing. (That includes italics, for example, so if you have italics in text in your document and you use the Format Painter you will lose that word-level formatting.)

If you double-click on the Format Painter so you can use it in more than one location, use Esc or click on it once more in the menu bar to turn it off when you're done.

* * *

Okay, now on to paragraph-level formatting.

Paragraph Formatting

In the last chapter the focus was on how to format individual words. Sure, you can apply that kind of formatting to every word in a document, but the formatting itself happens at the word level. Now it's time to move up to the paragraph level.

Most paragraph formatting options are located in the Paragraph section of the Home tab. Some of the options are also available in the mini formatting menu.

There is also a Paragraph dialogue box that includes the most options which can either be opened by clicking on the expansion arrow in the Paragraph section of the Home tab or by right-clicking in the main workspace and choosing Paragraph from the dropdown menu.

We are not going to cover every single option in the Paragraph section of the Home tab in this book. Multilevel lists, shading, and borders are covered in the next book in the series. As is Sort.

So, without further ado:

Paragraph Alignment

In the bottom row of the Paragraph section of the Home tab there are a series of images that show four lines. If you look closely at those lines you'll see that they represent different alignments. The left-hand one has all lines aligned along the left side, the next one has all lines centered, etc.

These are your alignment choices.

They each also have a control shortcut, which you'll see listed if you hold your mouse over each option. Align Left is Ctrl + L, Center is Ctrl + E, Align Right is Ctrl + R, and Justify is Ctrl + J.

Here are examples of all four:

> This is a sample paragraph to show you paragraph alignment. The text in this paragraph is **left-aligned**. I am going to write another sentence here just so we can get to three lines of text. Okay. Done.

> This is a sample paragraph to show you paragraph alignment. The text in this paragraph is **centered**. I am going to write another sentence here just so we can get to three lines of text. Okay. Done.

> This is a sample paragraph to show you paragraph alignment. The text in this paragraph is **right-aligned**. I am going to write another sentence here just so we can get to three lines of text. Okay. Done.

> This is a sample paragraph to show you paragraph alignment. The text in this paragraph is **justified**. I am going to write another sentence here just so we can get to three lines of text. Okay. Done.

Notice that with left- and right-aligned every row lines up along that side but that the opposite side is "ragged" so ends at different points. With centered each row is ragged at both ends and by an equal amount so that the line is centered within that space. With justified the spacing between the words is stretched out so that each row except the last one is lined up on both the left-hand and right-hand side.

Most documents will use either left-aligned or justified paragraphs but centered is often used for things like section headers. Right-aligned I would say is rarely used, at least in languages that read left-to-right, but it can be useful for a side note in a formatted report.

The mini formatting bar is dynamic in Word 365, meaning the choices you see will change on you. By default, I believe your paragraph options will look like this:

You can see that there is an option for Center, but not the other alignment options.

However, after I was working on this section for a bit, mine looked like this:

Now I can also see options for Justify and Align Left but the Line and Paragraph Spacing option is gone. At other points I've seen it with options for Center and Justify but not Align Left.

Which to me makes it an option that would not be my first choice. It's there. You can try using it. But the options in the Paragraph section of the Home tab are more consistently available.

Your final paragraph alignment formatting option is the Paragraph dialogue box which you can open by clicking on the expansion arrow in the corner of the Paragraph section of the Home tab. Alignment is available in the top section in a dropdown under General in the Indents and Spacing tab:

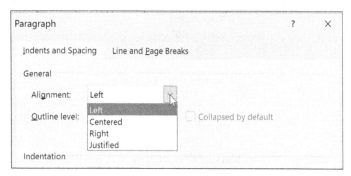

Line Spacing

Throughout school and also with submitting short stories I've always been asked to turn in double-spaced papers. But in the work world double-spaced looks horrible for a final report or memo. So chances are at some point in your life you will need to create a document that uses a different spacing than Word's default, which currently appears to be 1.08.

Here are examples of two paragraphs. The first has the default line spacing of 1.08. The second is double-spaced:

> This is a random paragraph written in Word to show you different paragraph spacing. This is the default spacing which is 1.08.
>
> This is a random paragraph written in Word to show you different paragraph spacing. This is double-spaced.

The way I usually adjust paragraph spacing is to use the Paragraph section of the Home tab. Just to the right of the alignment options in the bottom row is a dropdown menu of choices described as Line and Paragraph Spacing:

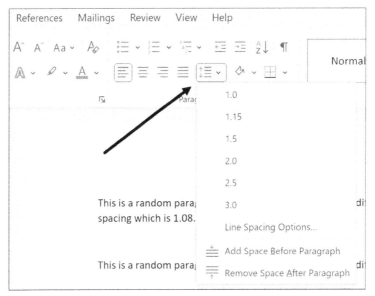

You can hold your mouse over each choice in the list to see what it will look like. Click on a choice to apply it.

If you click on Line Spacing Options in that dropdown it will open the Paragraph dialogue box. Line Spacing is located in the Spacing section on the right-hand side. There is a dropdown menu for Line Spacing there:

Sometimes I need to use that Exactly option which will then display a font size in the At box that you can adjust.

The mini formatting menu will usually also have the Line and Paragraph Spacing option which uses that same dropdown as in the Paragraph section of the Home tab, but as we saw above, not always.

There are also control shortcuts for paragraph spacing. I personally have never used them because I generally am only using one paragraph format in a document so can just use Ctrl + A to select all and then choose my format from that dropdown menu.

But if you want to use control shortcuts, Ctrl + 1 will give you single-spacing and Ctrl + 2 will give you double-spacing.

Space Between Paragraphs

I mentioned above that sometimes when formatting reports that combined portions written by different team members we'd run across a situation where the sections just didn't quite look the same. Tracking down that difference was a challenge so I'd use the Format Painter to sweep formatting from one paragraph to another. Often what was driving this was a difference in the spacing that was used between paragraphs in those different sections.

Also, this is a very useful setting to use for section headers or chapter headers. The inclination most people have is to use Enter to create space between a header and the text of that section, but the problem is that it doesn't work well when text breaks across a page. You suddenly end up with two blank lines at the top of a page, for example. Using spacing between paragraphs instead is a way to get that distance but not end up with those weird awkward blank lines in your document.

Space between paragraphs is also basically a necessity in the default way that Word formats paragraphs since there are no indents and having that space between your paragraphs is the only way to see that break in your text from paragraph to paragraph.

While the dropdown we just looked at for Line and Paragraph Spacing does have options for adding a space before a paragraph or removing a space after a paragraph, my default is to go straight to the Paragraph dialogue box for this one.

The settings are in the Spacing section on the left-hand side:

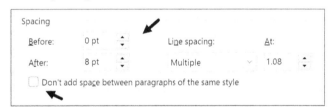

For a chapter header I put a space after. For a section header, though, I will often have values for both before and after. Same for any sort of separator. For me this is a visual setting where you basically play around with the values to see what works well for you.

You can also choose to not include those spaces when dealing with paragraphs of the same style by checking that box there.

Also, if you ever have different spacing at the bottom of one paragraph and at the top of the next, Word will use the larger of the two values, not combine them.

Keep Together

Since we're here and I'm thinking about it, I also want to mention that if you click over to the Line and Page Breaks tab in the Paragraph dialogue box that there are two useful checkboxes there.

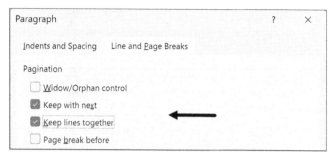

Keep With Next is good for any headers you have in your document because it will make sure that the header stays with the first paragraph of that section. Otherwise you can have a situation where your header is at the bottom of the page and then the text it's actually related to is on the next page, which doesn't look great.

Keep Lines Together is useful for if you have any headers that go across more than one line or if you ever want to make sure that all of the lines in a paragraph are displayed on the same page.

Just know that in order to make these both happen, Word is going to take all of the lines to the next page, which can result in excess white space at the bottom of the previous page. (If you're reading this book in print, you have very likely seen a few examples of that by now. I haven't formatted this book yet, but it happens in every one of these books that there is white space at the bottom of the page either to fit an image or to keep a header and its text together.)

Use these settings, though, to get that effect rather than trying to manually format your report. Because all it takes is someone adding a paragraph earlier in the document to ruin all of that manual formatting and cause you a lot of extra work.

Indents

There are two types of indents to consider. The first is the first-line indent that you see in many books that distinguishes the start of each paragraph. The second is when an entire section or paragraph is indented from the rest of the text.

The indent available in the Paragraph section of the Home tab is the full-section indent. You can click on a paragraph or select a series of paragraphs or bulleted or numbered entries (which we'll discuss in a moment) and then click on the increase indent option and it will move that text in one tab space.

Here I've taken three paragraphs and indented the second one once and the third one twice to show you what that looks like:

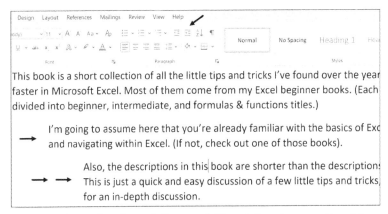

(Ignore the text, I was using a book on Microsoft Excel for the text for this one.)

To reverse an indent, use the indent option with the left-pointing arrow in the Paragraph section of the Home tab.

Once I indented those paragraphs the increase and decrease indent options were then also available on the mini formatting menu.

You can also adjust the indent using the Indentation section of the Paragraph dialogue box. See on the left-hand side in the screenshot below where the Left indent is 1". This is also where you need to go to apply a first-line indent to a paragraph.

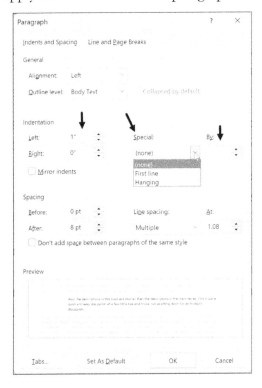

For the first-line indent, go to the Special option in the Indentation section and click on the dropdown. Select First Line and then type a value into the By field. It's going to default to a .5" indent, but that's generally going to be too much of an indent. Here is a .2" indent where I've also removed the spacing between those two paragraphs:

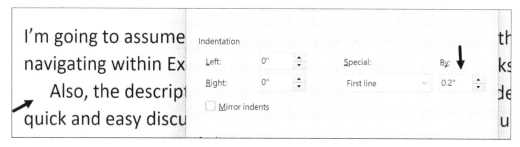

In general, you should either have spacing between your paragraphs and no first-line indent or no spacing between paragraphs but use a first-line indent. Don't do both.

Finally, another indenting option is the Tab key (and then Shift + Tab to reverse that), which will indent a single line and will create that first-line indent for you if used on a paragraph. But don't use it. There's more control and consistency in using the Paragraph dialogue box and choosing exactly the type and size of indent you want.

Bulleted Lists

Chances are that if you write enough corporate reports, at some point in time you will be asked to either create a bulleted list or a numbered list, so we're going to cover those now.

A bulleted list takes a series of text entries on different rows and puts bullet points in front of them. Like this:

- This is my first point
- This is my second one
- This is my third one and it's a real doozy.
- This is my fourth point.

Note that it indents those entries by default.

To apply bullets to a list, select your text and then go to the top row of the Paragraph section of the Home tab and click on the Bullets image. That will apply a standard bulleted list like you see above.

If you instead click on the dropdown arrow there, you can choose the type of bullet to use:

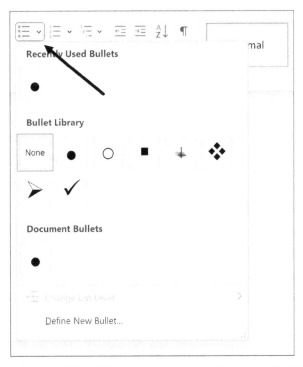

Because I just applied a bulleted list, I have a section at the top called Recently Used Bullets that shows the type of bullet I just used. Below that is the full list of bullets that you can choose from by default under the heading Bullet Library. And below that is a listing of any bullet types used in this particular document.

You can also click on that Define New Bullet option at the bottom to create a brand-new bullet type, but we're not going to do that here.

It's pretty basic to create a bulleted list.

Once a line of text is bulleted, when you hit enter from that line, the next line will also be bulleted.

You can remove that bullet by using the Backspace key, but you will still be indented to align with the text entry in the line above. If you Backspace two more times that should take you to the left-hand side of the page.

Another option is to hit Enter twice from a bulleted line. That will also remove the bullet point and take you back to the left-hand side of the page.

With bulleted lists the continuity of the list isn't an issue the way it is with numbered lists. But if you start adjusting the indent of various lines and are using bullets in multiple locations in your document you can end up with a situation where the appearance of a bulleted list on one page does not match that on another. So be careful if you go down that road.

Also, if you start a bulleted list and then have indented bullets, those indented bullets will be different by default. Like so:

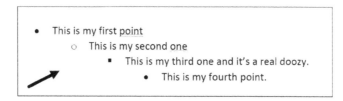

Word does this automatically as you indent each level and will automatically apply that bullet consistently for that indent level. Note that it cycled back to the first bullet type when I reached the fourth level.

You can customize this, too, using the Bullets dropdown, but exercise caution when doing so.

I indented each line there using the Tab key after clicking in front of the first letter of each row, but you can also go back to the Bullets dropdown and use the Change List Level secondary menu to choose an indent level for each line.

Shift + Tab will reverse the text one indent level.

You can also use the Decrease and Increase Indent options in the Paragraph section of the Home tab. The advantage of using those is that you can click anywhere on that line of text, you don't have to click at the start of the line like you do when using Tab or Shift + Tab.

To remove bullets from a bulleted list, select your list and then click on the bulleted list option again.

The mini formatting menu also includes the Bullets dropdown menu.

Numbered Lists

At their most basic, numbered lists work much the same way as bulleted lists. Select your rows of text and then click on the Numbering option in the top row of the Paragraph section of the Home tab. Word will turn your entries into a numbered list that looks like this:

1. This is my first point
2. This is my second one
3. This is my third one and it's a real doozy.
4. This is my fourth point.

Note that the numbered list is indented by default.

You can also start a numbered list by simply typing the first entry (1., A., etc.) and Word will convert that into a numbered list for you. (If you don't want that, just use Undo, Ctrl + X, right away.)

If you hit enter from a line that's a numbered entry it will either continue the numbering (if at the bottom of the list) or insert a new numbered entry and then renumber all other entries in the list (if in the midst of a numbered list).

You can remove a numbered entry using the Backspace key. When you do that, like I have below with what would have been number 2 in this list, Word will renumber any subsequent numbered entries to maintain a numbered list that goes from 1 to 2 to 3, etc.

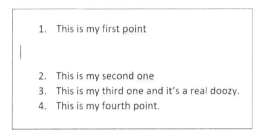

There is a Numbering dropdown menu that lets you choose other numbering styles:

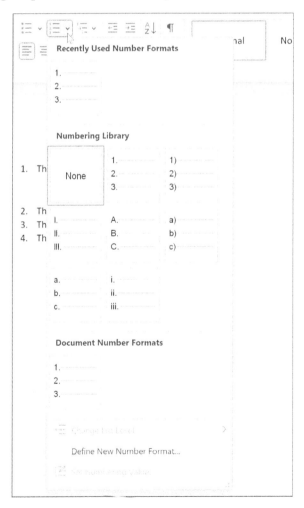

If you click on one of your numbered entries and then choose a different format from that dropdown it will change all of your entries to the new format.

Select the Set Numbering Value option at the bottom of that dropdown menu to open the Set Numbering dialogue box:

This dialogue box allows you to start a new numbered list instead of continuing the prior one or to continue a numbered list from earlier in the document. You can also choose the value for that entry.

To create a multi-level list using the Numbering option, use Tab or the Indent option to move the text to that next level. Word will automatically assign a numbering option for that next level.

Here you can see it went 1, a, i, and then back to 1 again.

1. This is my first item.
    a. And here's my subpoint
    b. And another one
            i.   And then a sub-subpoint
            ii. And another one
                1. And then another

When I changed the first level to an A. instead, it still went with a, i, and then 1 for the next three levels. So it doesn't follow the standard format for an outline that I was taught in school.

If you really need to go down that route, the Multilevel List option will give you far more control, but we're not covering it here because it can be very finicky in my experience.

Also, be very, very careful using either multiple numbered lists in a large document or using numbered lists where there are large gaps between the entries.

It's possible to do and I have certainly done so more than once. But this is one of those areas where I have wasted more time and energy than I can count going back and forth between different sections of a document to make sure that a change on page 10 didn't renumber my entries on page 65 or vice versa.

This may be more of an issue with Multilevel Lists, but it's definitely something to watch for. At the very end, when you are done making all other edits, if you are using numbered lists, make sure that you walk through your document from start to finish to confirm that all of the lists are working as expected.

To remove numbering, select your entries and then click on the numbering option once more.

The mini formatting menu also includes a Numbering dropdown menu.

Page and Document Formatting

Okay, that was the paragraph level. Now on to the page and document level. I'm not going to cover everything here, just the basics you need to get started.

Headers and Footers

You can insert text into the header or footer of your document. This is text that is kept separate from the main body of your document. The header is the text at the top of the document, the footer is the text at the bottom.

Often, for example, on a multi-page report you will want to have a header that states the title of the report and maybe the author of the report. Or maybe you want to include a corporate logo on the top of every page.

And usually you'll want a page number in the footer of the document. (Page numbers are covered specifically in the next section.)

To insert a header or footer go to the Header & Footer section of the Insert tab and then click on the dropdown arrow for the one you want. Word will give you a series of choices, some of which are very fancy:

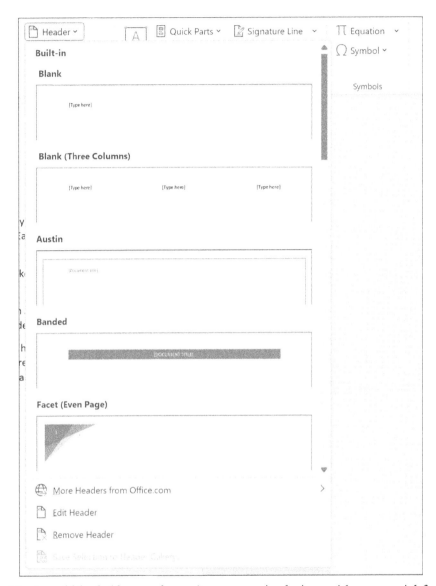

The top two, blank and blank (three columns), are generic choices with no special formatting that allow you to provide your own text in the spots that say [Text here].

The ones below that are fancier. You can also go to the web for even more choices using the Office.com option below the list of built-in choices. The ones that use [Author Name] or [Document Title] are going to pull in properties of the document to populate those particular fields, so be wary of using those.

If you choose one of the blank options it will insert text fields that say [Type here] that you then can click on and delete or replace with text. Here I've entered text for the first of the three-part footer option:

Footer		
Really Important Report	[Type here]	[Type here]

The Insert section of the Header & Footer tab includes options to insert Date & Time information, document information such as Author, File Name, File Path, and Document Title, or pictures. I had one employer where we would regularly insert the corporate logo in the header, for example.

The Options section of the Header & Footer tab also includes checkboxes for if you want a different header or footer for the first page or different header or footer for odd and even pages. I use these often because I usually need to have a different header for the first page of the document since a first-page header usually doesn't include text.

To return to your document from your header or footer, double-click back onto the text of your document or use the Esc key. You can also click on the Close Header and Footer option in the Header & Footer tab.

To return to the header or footer, just double-click on the header or footer text. You can also right-click on that text and choose Edit Header or Edit Footer, whichever option appears. This second option works even when there is no text in that header or footer.

Now let's talk about page numbering.

Page Numbering

First, if you already have a text-based header or footer that you've inserted, you can click into the header or footer and then go to the Page Number dropdown in the Header & Footer section of the Header & Footer tab and choose Current Position to insert a page number there. The top option in the secondary dropdown menu will insert a basic page number, but there are other options shown below that.

If you don't already have a header or footer in your document and you want to insert a page number, go to the Header & Footer section of the Insert tab and click on the Page Number dropdown arrow to see a list of options that include Top of Page, Bottom of Page, Page Margins, and Current Position.

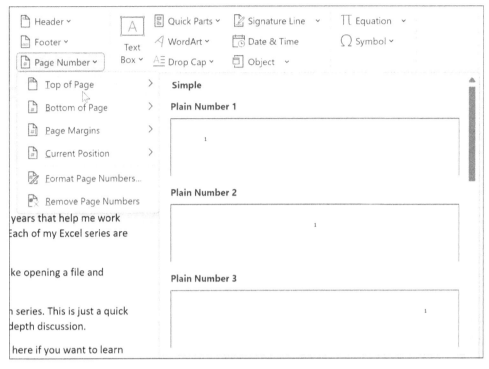

These are all locations where you can place that page number. Top of page, bottom of page, etc. And each has a secondary dropdown menu that will provide a number of options to choose from as you can see above for Top of Page.

Be sure to use the scroll bars to see the full range of choices. You can't preview the choices in your actual document, but when you click on a choice it will be inserted and formatted based on your choice. You'll also see that the header, footer, etc. section is now the section of the document that you're working in:

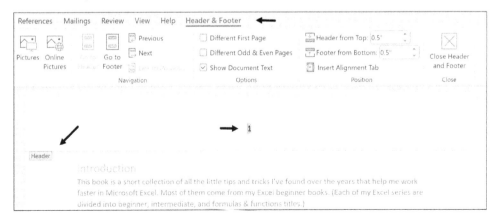

In the Header & Footer section in the far left-hand side of the Header & Footer tab is a Page Number dropdown. You can click on that and select Format Page Numbers to bring up the Page Number Format dialogue box:

This will allow you to choose a number format (1, 2, 3 vs. i, ii, iii) for your pages as well as, if needed, restart the page numbering of your document.

For example, if you have a ten-page document but the first four pages are a cover page and introductory information you may want to have page numbering start on page five but with the number 1. You can do that using this dialogue box.

For the purposes of this book, that's as deep as we're going to go with this one, but know that you can use section breaks to have different headers and footers in different sections of your document if needed. So you could have those first five pages numbered i, ii, iii and then the main body of your document numbered 1, 2, 3, etc. But that requires section breaks which are covered in the next book in this series.

To exit where you inserted your page number, double-click back onto the text of your document or use the Esc key. You can also click on the Close Header and Footer option in the Header & Footer tab.

To return to editing your page number, right-click on where the page number is and choose Edit Header or Edit Footer, whichever option appears. If you put a page number into the margins, you will likely need to right-click where the header or footer would go to get back to editing that page number.

Another option is to double-click on the page number to re-open the header or footer, but for page numbers I find that unreliable.

Page Orientation

By default documents in Word are in Portrait orientation, meaning that the longer edge of the page is on the side and the shorter edge is along the top of the page. If you ever need to change that so that the longer edge is along the top, then the way to do that is to set the document orientation to Landscape.

One way to do this is using the Orientation dropdown in the Page Setup section of the Layout tab:

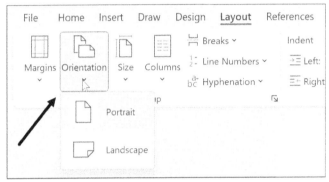

You can also do this when you go to print your document, but if I'm going to do this I usually prefer to set it that way before I start entering text and formatting.

Margins

The same goes for margins. Usually if I'm going to change those from their default I want to do so at the start not the end.

The Margins dropdown is also located in the Page Setup section of the Layout tab. Click on the dropdown arrow to see your available default choices:

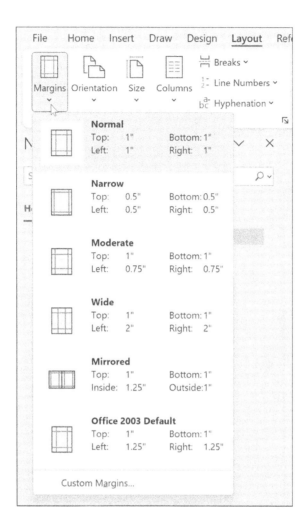

The Normal margin layout as of January 2023 is 1" on all sides, but there are options for Narrow, Moderate, Wide, Mirrored, and Office 2003 Default in that list. You can also completely customize your margins using the Custom Margins option at the bottom.

Paper Size

Another one you may want to change before you get started is the setting for the paper size you're going to use. This too is in the Page Setup section of the Layout tab under Size. Click on the dropdown arrow to see your available choices and then choose the one you want.

When you do so the page displayed in the main workspace will change to reflect your chosen paper size.

Other Basic Word Functionality

Real quick before we cover printing, I want to cover some other basic Word functionality like find and replace and zoom.

Zoom

By default I believe Word documents display at a 100% zoom level. That means that what you see on the screen is the same size as the text will be when it prints. But sometimes you may want what you see on the screen to be bigger or to be smaller.

You can make that happen by using Zoom. Now, to be clear, zoom only impacts your document. All of your menu options will stay the same size. To zoom your menu options you need to change your Windows settings.

So this is only for zooming in or out on the document you're working on.

The easiest way to do this is to use the slider in the bottom right corner:

You can left-click and drag that bar that is positioned along the line that shows a minus sign at one end and a plus sign at the other. The amount to which you are currently zoomed will show on the right-hand side. As you move to the right the text in your document will become larger. As you move to the left it will become smaller and you'll be able to see more of the document than you could before.

You can also just click on the line to either side of that bar. I find clicking and dragging allows me a little bit more control over the level to which I zoom.

There are also Zoom options in the Zoom section of the View tab.

I use the 100% option there to return my view to 100% because it's easier to get that exact value that way than to click around on the slider.

Click on Zoom to open the Zoom dialogue box which will give you pre-populated choices of 75%, 100%, or 200%. You can also enter a custom percentage.

The dialogue box also has options for zoom to page width, text width, whole page, and many pages.

The One Page option zooms out so you can see one single page on the screen. The Multiple Pages option shows two pages on the screen. The Page Width option zooms in so that the document covers the entire width of the workspace.

If you need this, play around with it to find the setting that works for you.

Views

It's generally best in my opinion to leave Word on its default view setting which is Print Layout. That's where you can see gray space on the sides and the document looks the way it will when it prints. But in the View tab there is a Views section that includes other options.

Read Mode hides your ribbon up top and shows two pages side by side with no gray space around them:

Use Esc to get out of it and go back to the Print Layout view.

Web Layout shows how your document would look as a webpage. It basically makes the document as wide as the entire workspace.

Outline shows your document in a bulleted outline format where each paragraph is displayed like an item in a bulleted list.

Draft shows just the text in the document not any objects.

I only bring Views up here because sometimes a document will get into one of these modes and you need to know how to get it back to the view you're used to. So if that happens to you, try Esc, Close [X View] option in the top menu, or change your view in the Views section of the View tab to Print Layout.

Find

Find and Replace are incredibly useful tools, but you have to be careful with Replace, so I'm going to cover Find first.

By default you should have a Navigation task pane open on the left-hand side of your workspace. If you do, click on Results below the search bar.

If you don't, use Ctrl + F to open it. It should look like this and if you used Ctrl + F your cursor should appear in the search bar already:

If you want to find text, just type the text you're looking for into that search bar, and hit Enter.

You should see a listing of results appear below that with snippets of the text surrounding each result, like here where I searched for shortcut and there were three results, one a chapter header and two that were part of paragraphs:

In the document itself each result will be highlighted in yellow.

In the Navigation task pane, you can either click on a specific result to go to that point in your document or you can use the up and down arrows on the right-hand side that are located just below the search bar to move between search results.

Using the search field works just fine for a basic text search.

But if you need something more advanced than that, X out your search term, and then click on the magnifying glass at the end of the search bar to choose a search type:

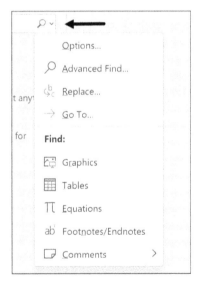

The Advanced Find option will open the Find and Replace dialogue box to the Find tab.

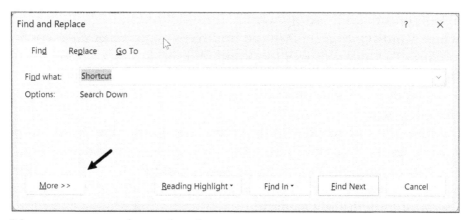

Click on More to see your advanced options:

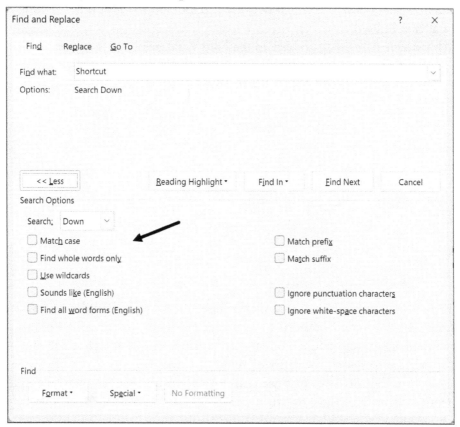

The two advanced options I use the most (and more so for Replace than Find, but we'll get there in a minute) are Match Case and Find Whole Words Only.

Match Case will only look for words that have the exact same capitalization as your search term. So if I want to look for "Word" as in Microsoft Word I would check that box so that the search doesn't return every use of "word", "foreword", etc.

Find Whole Words Only is another one that's very useful when there can be a lot of extraneous results. If I were to search for "excel" checking that box would keep Word from returning results for "excellent", "excellence", etc.

As you can see, there are other options there, too, so that you can find variations on a word with just that one search.

Down at the bottom are dropdowns for Format and Special. The Special dropdown lets you search for things like Paragraph Marks and Tab Characters. This can make fixing a poorly-formatted document much easier. If someone used paragraph marks to force the start of a new chapter in a document, for example, you can search and replace those paragraph marks with nothing. We'll cover that in a moment.

The Format dropdown has options for Font, Paragraph, Tabs, Language, Frame, Style, and Highlight. But usually I don't need that because I'm looking for simple formatting like all text in italics or all text in bold.

To search for all text in italics, go back to the Find What field, delete any text in that field, and then use Ctrl + I in that field. You should see a listing for Format appear that says Font: Italic.

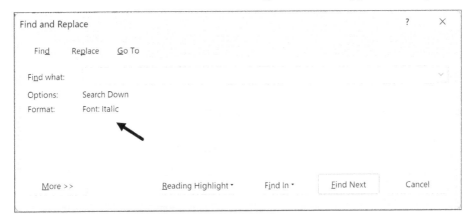

From there just click on Find Next to walk through and find all examples of italicized text.

Now. One warning here. You need to turn that off when you're done because Word will store that in the background and if you later try to do a simple search it will still be hanging on to that restriction to search for italicized text.

The way to turn that off is to just use Ctrl + I two more times in that Find What field to change it from Italic to Not Italic to off.

Replace

Now let's talk about Replace. Use Ctrl + H to open the Find and Replace dialogue box to the Replace tab.

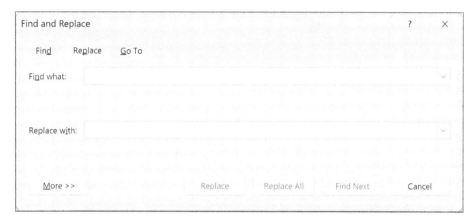

At its most basic what replace does is looks for the text you provide it in the Find What field and then replaces that text with the text you provide in the Replace With field.

Easy enough, right? Except…

It's very easy to mess up. Think of my example above where I want to find Excel. Let's say I just type that into the Find What field and say to replace with Word. Word will walk through the document and faithfully replace every instance of excel or Excel with Word. So I will end up with Wordlence instead of excellence and "the power to Word" instead of "the power to excel". Etc.

If you don't constrain the search portion properly you can have some truly horrible results. That's why using Match Case and Find Whole Words only on the Replace side of things is crucial most times.

Also, unless you're very confident that you won't have any issues like that it can be a best practice to walk through and use Find Next and then the Replace button instead of using the Replace All button so that you replace your entries one at a time and can verify that you won't replace something you shouldn't.

If you ever have something you need to delete, like extra enters in a document, just leave the Replace With field empty when you find and replace and that will have the effect of deleting what you searched for.

Word Count

In the Proofing section of the Review tab there is a Word Count option that will give you the number of pages, words, characters (no spaces), characters (with spaces), paragraphs, and lines in your document.

If you just need the number of words in the document, it's displayed in the bottom left corner. If you select a subset of your text, it will also display the number of words in your selected text as well.

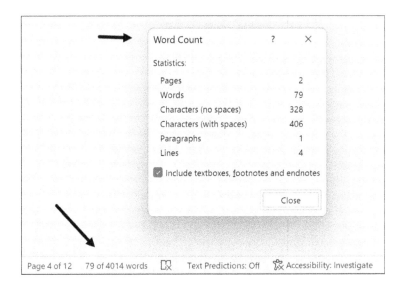

Show Paragraph Formatting

Sometimes I need to be able to see all of the little formatting marks in my text, like the paragraph marks and whether someone used spaces, the Tab key, or formatting to indent a paragraph. To see all of that, click on the little paragraph mark in the Paragraph section of the Home tab. It's on the top row on the far end. You can also use Ctrl + Shift + 8 to turn it on or off.

This is also useful for showing any page or section breaks in a document so we'll revisit it again in the intermediate book but just wanted to mention it quickly here.

Return to Last Place in Document

When you open a document you've been working on in Word, you should see on the right-hand side of the workspace towards the bottom, a pop-up box that asks if you want to return to where you were when you last closed the document.

This can be incredibly useful when you're working on a longer document because it saves you having to scroll through 50+ pages to get back to where you were.

Just click on that image to go to your last location in the document.

This also, of course, means that you should give some thought to where your cursor is when you close out a document. For example, if I need to format the chapter headers in my document before I close it, I can do that, but then it's helpful to click back to the place I want to be when the document reopens so this can work for me.

If you don't catch the message right away, it will turn into a little flag off to the side. You

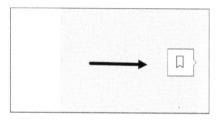

can still click on that to go to the last point in your document.

(If you hold your mouse over it, you'll see that welcome message again.)

Printing

Printing a document in Word is usually pretty straight-forward. (Nothing like printing in Excel.) The reason for that is because you can usually see exactly what the document is going to look like when printed as you're typing. If you're working in the Print Layout view, the document you're working on has your headers and footers and is the size and orientation it will be when printed.

Still. There are a number of printing options available that we should cover.

To print use Ctrl + P or go to File and then click on Print in the left-hand set of options. Both will take you to the Print screen:

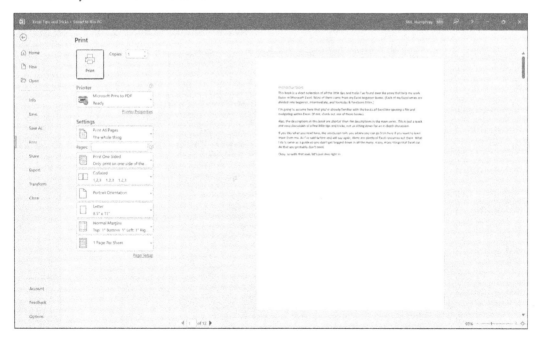

On the right-hand side is a preview of your document. You can see at the bottom of that space on the left-hand side the total number of pages and also which page of that total that you're currently viewing. There is a scroll bar on the right-hand side that you can use to move through the document or you can use those arrows down there by the number of pages.

On the left of that space is the print icon as well as all of your print choices. Let's look closer at those now:

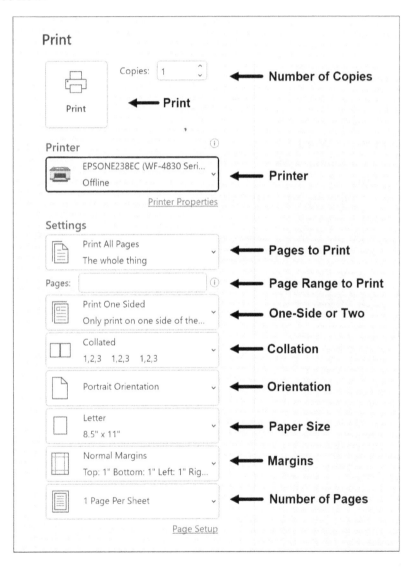

Print

At the very top on the left you can see a picture of a printer with the word Print underneath. That's what you click on when you're ready to print.

Copies

To the right of that is a white field labeled Copies. You can either click into that field and type a number or use the up and down arrows on the right-hand side to specify how many copies of the document to print.

Printer

Below that is where you tell Word what printer to use. Click on the dropdown arrow to see the list of available printers. You will also likely see a Microsoft Print to PDF option that will let you create a PDF version of the document. (I usually Save As a PDF instead.) Microsoft XPS Document Writer does something similar, but may not be as accessible to all other users as PDF.

At the bottom of the list you can add a printer if the one you want is not listed.

I will note here that a year or two ago I noticed that my Word and Excel programs were getting hung up. I want to say that they wouldn't close without a significant delay. I did some research and it turned out it was something to do with having my printer listed as the default printer. The issue went away when I changed the default printer to Microsoft Print to PDF. So if you ever experience that issue, maybe try that as a solution. You can always choose your printer from the list when you're ready to print.

Print All Pages / Print Selection / Print Current Page / Custom Print

Leave this on Print All Pages if you want to print the entire document. Print Selection will only be available if you selected text or objects within the document before choosing to print. Print Current Page will print whatever page you currently have visible in the print preview section. Custom Print uses the page range typed below that dropdown.

This dropdown also lets you print your document information, a list of tracked changes in the document, a list of styles used in the document, a list of items in the AutoText gallery, or a list of your custom shortcut keys.

You can also choose here whether to print the document with markup or not if you were using track changes.

And at the bottom of the dropdown you can choose to print only odd pages or only even pages.

Pages

If there are specific page numbers that you want to print instead of the whole document, you can enter those values in the white field next to where it says Pages. To print a page range write the first page number of the range and then a hyphen and then the last number of the range. You can also list multiple page numbers or ranges using a comma to separate each number or number range.

Hold your mouse over the small i next to that field for examples.

Print One Sided / Print on Both Sides (Long Edge) / Print on Both Sides (Short Edge) / Manually Print on Both Sides

If your printer can do so, you can choose to print on both sides of the page. If you do so, flipping on the long edge works best (in my opinion) for when you're using Portrait orientation and flipping on the short edge works best for when you're using Landscape.

Collated / Uncollated

This setting only matters when you're printing more than one copy of a document that is more than one page long. Your choices are to print all of page 1 first then all of page 2 then all of page 3, etc. Or to print one full copy of the document and then another full copy of the document and then another until all copies are done.

Collated is when you print one full copy at a time. Uncollated is when you print all of page 1 then all of page 2, etc.

Portrait Orientation / Landscape Orientation

We discussed the difference between these previously. Usually you should make this decision before you're ready to print your document so that you can see what the document will actually look like as you're writing it. But as a reminder, portrait is what a standard school report generally looks like with the long edge of the page on the side. Landscape is more what a PowerPoint presentation looks like with the long edge along the top.

Letter / A4 / Japan LPhoto / Etc.

This is the dropdown where you can choose which paper size to print to. Again, you should probably set this before you start to write, but I have had situations where I was in the UK and needed to switch to A4 at the last moment, so it does happen that you make this choice at the very end.

Normal Margins / Narrow Margins / Moderate Margins / Wide Margins / Mirrored Margins / Office 2003 Default

This is where you can set the margins for your document, but again, one that should probably be set at the start not the end.

1 Page Per Sheet / 2 Pages Per Sheet / 4 Pages Per Sheet / 6 Pages Per Sheet / 8 Pages Per Sheet / 16 Pages Per Sheet

This allows you to print more than one page of your document on a single sheet of paper. If you ever had a final exam where the professor told you that you could bring one page of notes, you may have tried this option. You know, write 16 pages of notes and then cram them all onto one page by printing it really small.

It's also sometimes useful for saving paper if you're doing a quick review of a report or document and don't need to see the text at full size.

Page Setup

Opens the Page Setup dialogue box, but it doesn't really give you any options that you haven't already addressed elsewhere.

Customize Settings

We touched on this briefly with the Theme setting and with AutoCorrect and a few other places, but before we wrap up I wanted to revisit how to customize your settings. Because as time goes on Office seems to add more and more, for lack of a better word, crap that's the default. Some of it raises privacy concerns, some of it is just not the way I prefer to work.

Now, I will say that the more you customize your version of Word the more you may get tripped up while working with someone else's version. But at this point I think it's kind of essential to know some of these settings.

So. First, go to File and then click on Options at the very bottom of the screen on the left-hand side. This will open the Word Options dialogue box to the General tab.

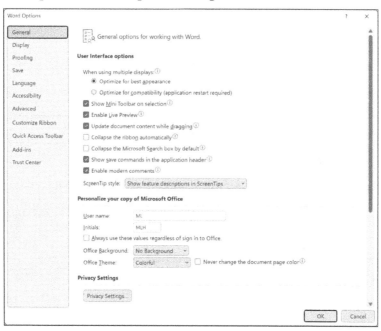

I suggest you scroll through all of these sections to see if there's anything there that you don't want. Or that you do. But I'm going to point out a few here.

General

- Enable or disable the Mini Toolbar
- Enable or disable Live Preview of a potential change
- Change your user name and initials for track changes
- Change your Office Theme
- Enable or disable LinkedIn features in your Office applications
- Enable or disable showing the Start screen when Word opens
- Use Privacy Settings to turn on or off connected experiences
- Enable or disable new style of track changes (this one looks like it's only temporary)

Display

- Enable or disable showing white space between pages in Print Layout view (if you don't do this all the pages run together like they're one long page.)
- Choose formatting marks that are always visible on the screen

Proofing

- Customize AutoCorrect Options
- Enable or disable various spelling and grammar check settings
- Enable or disable showing readability statistics when you ask for word count

Save

- Set timing for AutoRecover save
- Set where documents save by default (can save to computer instead of OneDrive)

Advanced

- Enable or disable default of select to select an entire word
- Set a default paragraph style
- Enable or disable text predictions while typing

- Set default settings for pasting text

- Set how images are or are not compressed when added to a document and the default resolution

- Set the number of Recent Documents and Recent Folders to list

- Enable or disable scroll bars

Customize Ribbon

Allows you to add or delete the items that are in each tab at the top of the screen. Be VERY CAREFUL in customizing this because it will make it more difficult to use other versions of Word either on someone else's computer or at a new employer or school.

Quick Access Toolbar

Allows you to add tasks that you perform frequently that you want to always have available regardless of the tab you're working in. For me, I usually have the options for Insert Page Break and Read Aloud up there because I use them often enough and they are not located in the Home tab and I don't want to go find them.

Click on the option you want and then use Add to move it to the Quick Access Toolbar and then be sure to click on Show Quick Access Toolbar at the bottom of the screen so it actually appears for you.

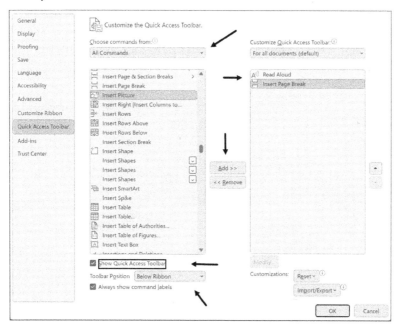

When you do that you'll have an option to show the Quick Access Toolbar either above the ribbon or below it. I actually prefer above so that it's next to that save icon. Here is what that looks like with Read Aloud and Insert Page Break added:

Trust Center

Opens the Trust Center dialogue box which contains a number of settings related to privacy and trust. The Privacy Options screen includes a Document Inspector that will review your document for any information that may not be visible but that you may want to remove before sharing.

Just be careful if you're using track changes that you don't remove user information unless it's really the final version of the document. If you remove user information and then continue to work on a document with a team, all edits from that point forward will simply be listed as edits by Author and you won't be able to see who did what.

That page also has a check box where you can enable warning before saving or sending a file that has track changes or comments in it. (Something that you may want to do if you use track changes since I have on occasion been on the receiving end of a "final" document that still had comments and track changes in it which made for a very interesting read.)

Conclusion

Okay, so that's the end of our introduction to Microsoft Word. There's a lot more that you can do in Word like use Text Styles to apply formatting, build tables, track changes, and use sections to apply different page formatting to different parts of a document. But for basic day-to-day use this should've been a solid introduction that will let you write a report or letter and format it properly.

From here, there are a few directions you can go. You can continue learning with me and move on to *Intermediate Word 365* which will cover the next level of information.

I don't have some exclusive super-secret insight, but what I do provide is a path forward so that you don't get lost trying to learn everything. Also, I sometimes provide opinions on certain things based on my corporate and educational experiences that a straight read of the help text won't give.

But you can learn as needed using Microsoft's Help function and website or by finding various blogs and tutorials online.

For Word's help, go to the Help tab and then click on Help.

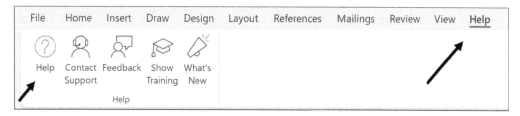

A task pane will appear on the right-hand side where you can then search for what you need. It does require internet access.

With a number of tasks in the top menu tabs you can also hold your mouse over the task and there will be a description of what it does. Some tasks have a Tell Me More option that you can click on to open the Help screen for that specific task, like here for Format Painter:

I'd say don't be afraid to try different things and see how they work. Ctrl + Z, Undo, is your friend if you do something that doesn't look right. Also, click around to the different tabs and see the options you have.

And if something I discussed was confusing or you can't find an answer, reach out to me. I'm happy to help and point you in the right direction.

Okay then. I hope this gave you a strong foundation to build from. Good luck with it. You can do this.

Control Shortcuts

Letter	Task
1	Single-Space
2	Double-Space
A	Select All
B	Bold
C	Copy
E	Center
F	Find
H	Replace
I	Italicize
J	Justify
L	Align Left
N	New File
P	Print Screen
R	Align Right
S	Save
U	Underline
V	Paste
X	Cut
Y	Redo
Z	Undo

Excel 365 for Beginners

EXCEL 365 ESSENTIALS - BOOK 1

M.L. HUMPHREY

CONTENTS

Why Learn Excel

Excel is great. I use it both in my professional life and my personal life. It allows me to organize and track key information in a quick and easy manner and to automate a lot of the calculations I need.

I have a budget worksheet that I look at at least every few days to track whether my bills have been paid and how much I need to keep in my bank account and just where I am overall financially.

(Which I shared in *Excel for Budgeting* and which you can also purchase a blank version of via my Payhip store if you're interested. Links available at https://mlhumphrey.com/business-and-personal-finance/)

In my professional career I've used Excel in a number of ways, from analyzing a series of financial transactions to see if a customer was overcharged to performing a comparison of regulatory requirements across multiple jurisdictions.

It's also the quickest and easiest way I've ever found to take rows of raw data and create summaries of that data.

While Excel works best for storing numbers and performing calculations, it is also often a good choice for text-based analysis, especially if you want to be able to sort your text results or filter out and isolate certain entries.

Excel also has very widespread usage. Every single corporate environment I ever worked in used Microsoft Office. I was in banking, finance, and consulting and all of those fields tend to default to Microsoft Office products.

More creative fields tend more towards Apple products, but your bread and butter corporations are very much still users of Office. So learning Excel (and Word and PowerPoint) is an essential skill if you want to be employed in those types of companies.

At least for the foreseeable future. Big companies do not like change.

And honestly, the skills you learn using Microsoft Excel can be applied to similar programs. I use Numbers on my Mac when I need to open a spreadsheet and other than remembering to do Command instead of Control for my shortcuts they work much the same way.

So Excel is definitely worth learning. It will help you with your own life and your career.

Now, real quick, I want to discuss the three main versions of Microsoft Office so you understand where this book fits.

Discussion of Different Office Versions

At this present moment (December 2022), Microsoft Office offers essentially three products that all share the same core functionality.

There is a free version of Microsoft Office that is available online. You can get access to Word, Excel, PowerPoint, and a number of other Microsoft tools by signing up for a free Microsoft account.

We'll call this one Office on the Web.

It has basic functionality that will work for most users, I suspect. But it's also all online. If you have a file on your computer and want to work with it in the free version you have to upload it and store it in a OneDrive account. It also has limited functionality, so it's not going to give you the full range of options as the paid products that Microsoft offers.

Second, are the old-school versions. That's what I have spent the last thirty years or so using. These are static versions of Office that are locked into place at a point in time.

As I write this, the latest static, or as Microsoft likes to call them, "on premise", version of Microsoft Office is Office 2021. The original Office Essentials books I wrote used Office 2013 and I also published a series of titles on Office 2019, but there have been many other versions of Office over the years.

Each of the static versions of Office are released with Office functionality as it exists at that time. They're not supposed to update if there are improvements made later.

(Although I've noticed that they have language about making updates and that sometimes they do seem to make updates, perhaps for security reasons, because I will sometimes notice that my old familiar program isn't working the way it used to.)

But the appearance and tasks do seem to stay fixed.

For example, they changed the appearance of Office with the release of Office 2021, but neither of my laptops, one running Office 2013 and one running Office 2019, were impacted. Also, with Office 2021 it looks like they released the function XLOOKUP to replace VLOOKUP and HLOOKUP, but I didn't get access to it.

One of the disadvantages of working with one of the static or "on premise" versions of Office is that you don't get future improvements like that.

You also, because Microsoft really wants to push people towards their subscription model, are generally limited to having that static version on only one computer. If that computer dies, oh well, you have to buy it again for the next computer. You can't transfer it.

(Again, that's what they say, but when I logged onto my new laptop with my Microsoft account they were ready to let me use Office 2019 on it even though I'd bought it for my old computer. So maybe it's more one computer at a time even though that is not what the license says.)

The advantage to the static versions, though, and the reason I like them, is that they are stable. I buy Office 2019, I figure out how it works, and I'm done until my computer dies.

I don't have to worry that I log in and they've changed things on me overnight. I am not a user who is on the cutting edge who needs the latest and greatest. And I don't collaborate which is where a lot of their more recent improvements seem to be focused so the changes they are making are generally ones that I don't need.

I just want things to stay the same so I don't have to think about anything when I'm ready to work.

Also, I like the static versions because I pay my $300 (or whatever the cost is at the time) once and never have to pay again or worry about losing the ability to edit my files.

But there are good reasons to use the third product option, Office 365, which is the subscription version of Office and the subject of this book.

One is that you can have access to Office across multiple devices. I have a few laptops and having Office 365, if I buy the right option, lets me have Office on my Mac as well as all of my laptops for one monthly fee.

If you're part of a family who all need access that can be a much cheaper option than paying to put Office on each computer.

Also, if everyone is using Office 365 then you know that everyone will be on the same page in terms of compatibility. One of the issues that I ran into professionally a number of years ago was that I was using a newer version of Office than one of my clients. I designed an entire workbook for them that did very complex calculations only to find out that they couldn't use the workbook because the Excel functions I relied on weren't available in the version of Office they were using. I had to redo the whole thing because they couldn't upgrade.

(Of course, that means that if you are going to use Office 365 or even Office 2021, and you're working with someone outside of your organization, you need to be very careful that you don't use something available to you (like XLOOKUP or TEXTJOIN) that that person can't use because they're using an older version of Office.)

Office 365 can also be far more portable if you're willing to put files on OneDrive. (I am not, because I'm a Luddite at heart.) But with Office 365 you can save your files to the cloud and then access them from your other devices.

Also, it can maybe be a much cheaper option for certain programs. I use Microsoft Access and to add that on to a Microsoft 2021 purchase was going to be a couple hundred dollars. But with Office 365 I can have Access along with everything else I need for, at the moment, $8.25 a month. (Go to the business licenses if you need this.)

It also spaces out the cost of the product. You don't have to plunk down all that money on Day 1. But overall Office 365 is probably more expensive for a single user on a single computer than just buying the product with a one-time fee. My laptop that's running Office 2013 is now five years old. If I were paying $8.25 a month I'd have spent $495 which I think is more than I paid up front. And (knock wood) that computer is still going strong.

So it's all about what trade offs you want to make.

To summarize.

There are technically three current versions of Office: (a) the free online one, (b) the static version, the most recent of which is currently Office 2021, and (c) the constantly updating version which is called Office 365.

At the beginner level the differences between the various version should not be significant.

What This Book Covers

Let's talk now about what you will learn in this book, because Excel is an incredibly complex and powerful tool, but it can also get a little overwhelming if you try to cover everything in one go.

So what I've done with the various Excel Essentials series is break that information on Excel down into digestible chunks. And I think I've succeeded at that. (At this point the original *Excel for Beginners* book, which was written for Excel 2013, has over a thousand ratings on Amazon and a rating average of 4.2, so people are generally happy with the level of information covered.)

This book is a version of that book but written for Excel 365. It focuses on the basics of using Excel. We'll cover how to navigate Excel, input data, format it, manipulate it through basic math formulas, filter it, sort it, and print your results.

That should be 95% of what you need to do in Excel day-to-day if you're an average user. I'll also cover at the end how to fill in that last 5% on your own.

(But if you want to keep going with me from there, then there's *Intermediate Excel 365* and *102 Useful Excel 365 Functions* which I'll discuss in a little more detail at the end.)

The other nice thing about Excel is that there are a number of ways to perform the same task. While I do strongly encourage you to learn the control shortcuts (like Ctrl + C to copy) that I mention throughout this book, there will usually be two or three or even more ways to perform a task that we'll cover. So if you have a preference for working in a certain way, it's likely that Excel can accommodate that.

My default is going to be those older ways of doing things because that lets you work across all versions of Excel you may encounter. But when I see that something new works better, I will definitely show that you that method as well.

Okay. So I hope at this point you know that Excel is worth learning.

And I want you to know before we begin that it doesn't have to be hard to learn. Trust me and stick with me through this book and you will have the solid foundation you need.

This book is written to be read start to finish. I want you to read the whole thing. But it's also hopefully organized in such a way that you can come back to it later and use it as a reference for years to come. In the print version there is an index at the end that lists everything we covered and where to find it. (In the ebook version, search will be your friend.)

Now, because this book is about Excel 365, I do need to warn you before we start that Office 365 is a moving target. It is always going to be the latest and greatest. Which means that this book is taking a snapshot of Office 365 as it exists in December 2022, but Office 365 changes monthly.

By the time you read this book, whenever that is, there may be *more* functionality available than I cover here.

Usually, though, that more is not going to impact beginner-level material. For example, the August 2022 update to Excel 365, added a new function (XLOOKUP) and the ability to have "sketched" shapes to make your diagrams and models look hand-drawn, thereby distinguishing ones that were "in progress." Not exactly things that will impact someone new to Excel.

So there will be some changes, but don't worry about them. If I ever think this book isn't a good beginner resource anymore, I will unpublish it or update it. So if you are buying this book new then that means I still think it works for new users and it will still teach you what you need to know to use Excel on a day-to-day basis.

I'm going to be working with the desktop version of Office 365. If you are working online your functionality may be more limited. (That is probably an especially good time to know the control shortcuts.)

Also, your save/open options may be slightly different due to that need to "upload" files or save them to OneDrive.

Okay, one more thing before we get started, which is how to change your appearance, and then we'll dive right in with terminology and absolute basics.

Appearance Settings

Depending on how you have your appearance set, your version of Microsoft Excel may look very different from the screenshots I'm going to use in this book. So before we start I wanted to show you how to change that appearance to match mine in case you want to do that.

If you are absolutely brand new to Excel you may have to come back to this chapter since it relies on having opened an Excel file and knowing some terminology, but I wanted to cover it here before I show you that first screenshot.

To change the appearance of your Office programs, open Excel. That should show you a welcome screen:

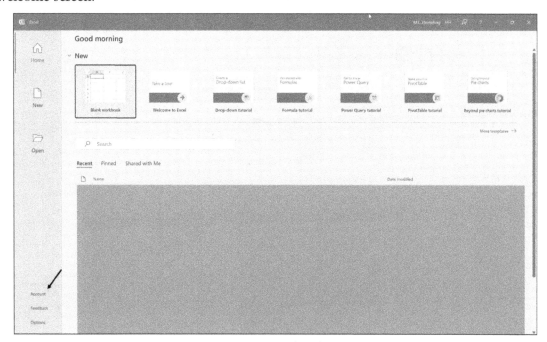

If you don't get that screen, open an Excel file and click on the File option in the top left corner. From there you have two choices. You can either click on Account or Options in the bottom left corner of the screen. Here I've clicked on Account. You can see in the main workspace that there is a dropdown menu for Office Theme. Note that I have mine currently set to Colorful.

If you click on Options instead, then you can find this same setting under Personalize Your Copy of Microsoft Office in the General section:

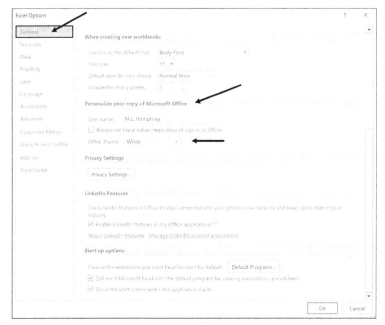

There will be a dropdown menu for Office Theme there as well. Let's look at the different options now.

This is the Dark Gray theme:

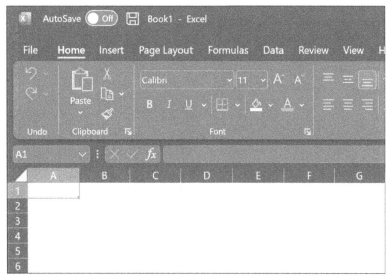

This is the Black theme (which is especially drastic in Word):

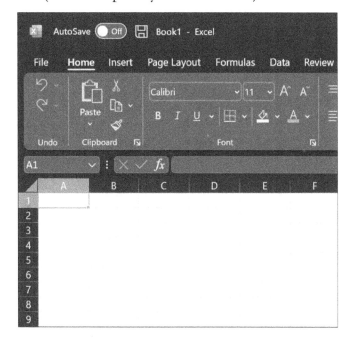

This is the Colorful theme:

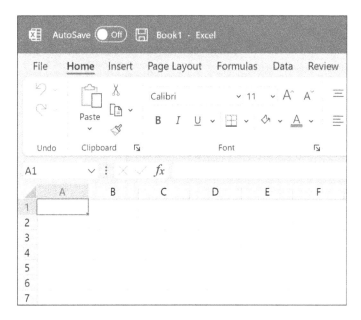

This is the White theme:

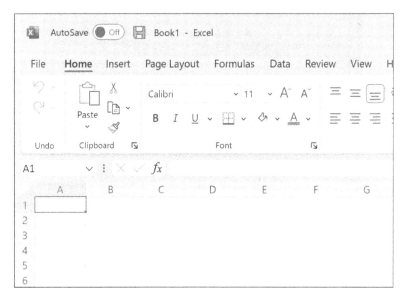

You can't see this in the black and white print version, but the Colorful theme uses blue for the top bar in Word, green for the top bar in Excel, and I would presume orange and red for PowerPoint and Access respectively.

There is also a system settings choice which I presume will be different for everyone based upon the Windows theme they're using. If you have any sort of sight impairment, there are some pretty funky choices you can make in the Windows settings that you may want to explore, but I'm not going to here. One of them for example uses black and bright yellow.

For the rest of this book I'll be using the Colorful theme but it will look just like the White theme most of the time because I won't include the very top of the screen in most of my screenshots.

Whichever choice you make will apply across all of your Office programs, so be careful there. Or be prepared to change it when you move between programs if you have different preferences in different programs.

Okay, now we can cover terminology.

Basic Terminology

Before we can dive in on how to do things, we need to cover some basic terms.

I'm going to assume here you really don't know any of the basics, so you can skim if you think you do, but be sure to at least glance at the headers because I may have my own idiosyncratic way of describing things that you won't have encountered elsewhere.

Workbook

A workbook is what Excel likes to call an Excel file. They define it as a file that contains one or more worksheets. In current versions of Excel a workbook will by default start with one worksheet in it, but you can add more as needed.

Worksheet

Excel defines a worksheet as the primary document you use in Excel to store and work with your data. It can also sometimes be referred to as a spreadsheet, but I will try to avoid using the term spreadsheet here because when I use the term spreadsheet I sometimes actually mean the whole workbook. So better to stick to workbook and worksheet whenever possible.

A worksheet is organized into Columns and Rows that form Cells.

Columns

Excel uses columns and rows to display information. Columns run across the top of the worksheet and, unless you've done something funky with your settings, are identified using letters of the alphabet.

As you can see below, each worksheet will start with A on the far left side for the first column and march right on through the alphabet (A, B, C, D, E, etc.) from there.

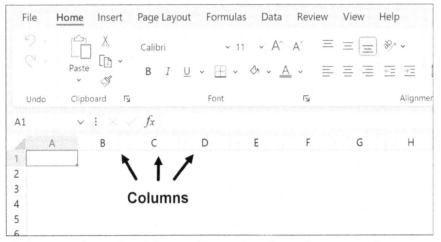

If you scroll far enough to the right, you'll see that the columns continue on to a double alphabet (AA, AB, AC, etc.) and then on to a triple alphabet (AAA, AAB, etc.).

As of right now the very last column in a worksheet is XFD.

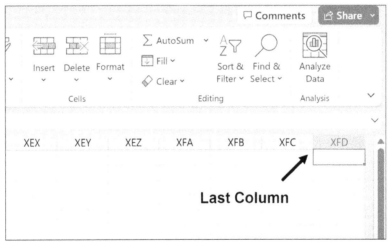

You can reach the very last column in a blank worksheet by holding down the Ctrl key and pressing the End key which is usually also the right arrow key.

If there is already data in that worksheet using Ctrl + End will take you to the last column that has data in it, so you'll need to use Ctrl + End again to go to the last column in the worksheet.

We'll touch on this again, but column letters are basically a way of numbering the columns, not an attribute that is specific to a column. So Column A is always the first column. Column B is always the second column. Etc. And there are always going to be the same number of columns in your worksheet regardless of whether you delete or insert columns.

When you delete or move information in a column you're just moving the data. The grid system doesn't move. So if I take Column A and I delete that column there will still be a Column A because there is still always a first column. And if I were to take all of the data in Column A and move that data three columns over it would now be in Column D.

So think of columns as location information that is actually separate from the data in the worksheet. (We'll work through this more, don't worry.)

Also, columns are one of those areas where you need to be careful if you're working with someone with an older version of Excel because they may not have as many columns in their worksheets in their version of Excel as you do.

For example, I have Excel 2013 on one of my laptops and my last column in that version is IV which means I have far far fewer columns in my version of Excel than anyone using Excel 365 does. This could mean that I would lose data if I open a file from an Excel 365 user in Excel 2013 if that file uses more columns than I have access to.

So always keep in the back of your mind that if you're working with others that aren't set up the same way you are in Office that you can have compatibility issues and one of the main ones you can have is number of rows and columns.

But let's get back to basic terms.

Rows

Rows run down the side of each worksheet and are numbered starting at 1 and up to a very high number. As of now that number is 1048576. That means a single Excel worksheet currently has over a million rows. You can hold down the Ctrl key in a blank worksheet while hitting the down arrow to see just how many rows your version of Excel has.

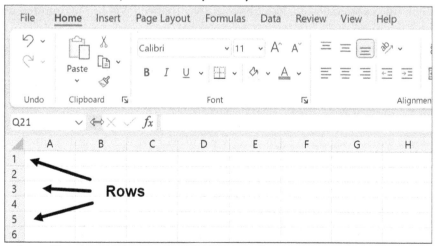

As a comparison, Excel 2013 had only 65,536 rows in a worksheet. Keep this in mind for compatibility issues when working with other users.

And, once more, those row numbers are locational information. The first row will always be numbered 1. The second row will always be numbered 2. And so on and so forth. And at least as of this moment there will always be 1,048,576 rows in every Excel worksheet at all times. So even if you delete or insert rows that will not change that fact.

You are deleting data not the number of rows in the worksheet.

Cells

Cells are where the row and column data all comes together. Think of it as map coordinates. Cell A1 is the first column and first row of the worksheet.

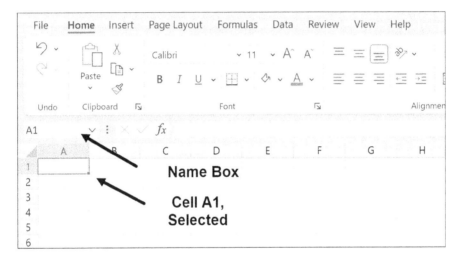

When you click onto a specific cell, like I have above, that cell will be surrounded with a darker border around the perimeter.

You can also look in the Name Box, noted above, to see the cell reference for that cell. These cell references are used when writing Excel formulas or using functions.

And remember, that these are coordinates, they are not fixed to your data. So if you have an entry in the first column of the first row of your worksheet and move that entry to the third column and third row of your worksheet that entry will now be in Cell C3 not Cell A1.

(Again, don't worry too much right now, we will work in Excel and you will see how this happens.)

Click

If I tell you to click on something, that means to use your mouse (or trackpad) to move the cursor on the screen over to a specific location and left-click or right-click on the option. (See the next definition for the difference between left-click and right-click).

If you left-click, this selects the item. If you right-click, this generally displays a dropdown list of options to choose from. If I don't tell you which to do, left- or right-click, then left-click.

Left-click/Right-click

If you look at your mouse you generally have two flat buttons to press. One is on the left side, one is on the right.

If I say left-click that means to press down on the button on the left. If I say right-click that means press down on the button on the right. (If you're used to using Word you may already do this without even thinking about it. So, if that's the case then think of left-click as what you usually use to select text and right-click as what you use to see a menu of choices.)

If you're using a track pad, not all track pads have the left- and right-hand areas visible. In that case, you'll basically want to press on either the bottom left-hand side of the track pad or the bottom right-hand side of the trackpad as needed.

Select

If I tell you to "select" cells, that means to highlight them. If the cells are next to each other, you can just left-click on the first one and drag the cursor (move your mouse or finger on the trackpad) as you hold that left-click until all of the cells are highlighted.

(I will refer to this action as left-click and drag.)

When you do this, all the selected cells will be shaded gray and surrounded by a dark box like below except for the first cell you clicked on which will be within the perimeter of the box but will be white.

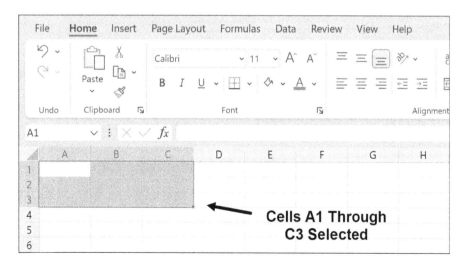

Cells A1 Through C3 Selected

You can also select cells that are not next to each other by holding down the Ctrl key as you left-click on each cell.

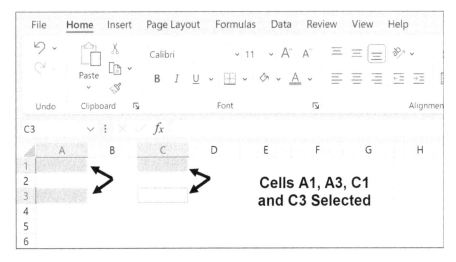

When you do that, each selected cell will be shaded gray except for the last selected cell which will be surrounded by a border but will be white. Above I selected Cells A1, A3, C1, and C3. C3 was selected last.

To select an entire column, click on the letter. To select an entire row, click on the number.

For any row or column where a cell is selected in that row or column, the number or letter for that row or column will be shaded differently. In my version right now with my settings it's shaded a darker gray and the number/letter turns green.

For any row or column where the whole row or column is selected that letter or number will change to a different shading. For my version with my settings it turns light green with a dark green number/letter.

Data

Data is the information you enter into your worksheet. It's the values and text that you input or calculate. I will also sometimes refer to this as information, values, or text.

Data Table

I may also sometimes refer to a data table or table of data. This is just a combination of cells that contain data in them.

One thing to keep in mind with Excel versus Word if you're coming from using Word is that in Word when you create a data table you are adding a specific number of rows and columns into Word to do that. But in Excel the number of rows and columns never changes.

What does change is how many of those rows or columns have your data in them.

Excel is smart enough to only print or focus on the rows or columns with data in them, but if you want something to print out and look like a table you could create in Word you'll want to put borders around your data in Excel. (We'll discuss how to do that, don't worry.)

(This is a question that came up a few times after I released *Excel for Beginners*, so I wanted to mention it here specifically. Data tables as you create them in Word are not the same as data tables as you use them in Excel.)

Arrow

I will sometimes tell you to arrow to somewhere. Or to arrow right, left, up, or down. This just means to use the arrow keys. Using arrows is one way to move between cells within an Excel worksheet.

The other ways are to left-click on a cell. Or you can use Tab and Shift + Tab to move right and left, respectively. And Enter to move to the next row.

Cursor Functions

The cursor is what moves around when you move your mouse or use the trackpad. In Excel the cursor changes its appearance depending on what functions you can perform. You can see this by opening an Excel file and moving your cursor over the cells and then along the edges of a row or column and then up to the menu options up top.

Tab

I am going to talk a lot about Tabs, which are the options you have to choose from at the top of the workspace.

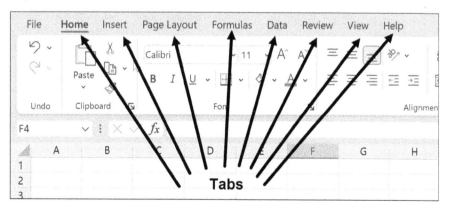

It used to be, in older versions of Excel that when you clicked on one of these options it took on the appearance of a tab like a file folder has. But in the latest versions of Excel that's no longer the case. The selected tab is just underlined. For example, in the image above, I have the Home tab selected which you can tell from the solid line under the word Home.

Each tab has a number of options available. Here is the left-hand set of options available under the Home tab, for example:

I can Undo, Copy/Paste/Format Sweep, choose my font attributes, choose my text alignment, etc.

The Home tab is the tab that will be selected by default. But you can click on the other tabs to see their available options.

Throughout this book I will often tell you to go to Y section of X tab and choose the task that we're trying to complete. For example, if I wanted you to change the font from Calibri to something else, I would say you could go to the Font section of the Home tab and click on the dropdown menu for font. (I will include screenshots most of the time so you can also see what I'm talking about.)

Dropdown Menus

A dropdown menu is a listing of available choices that you can see when you click on the arrow for that option or right-click in certain places such as the main workspace.

For example, here is the font dropdown menu:

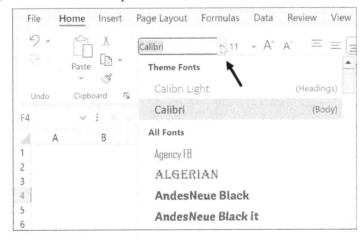

I clicked on the small arrow next to the current font name and that brought up a listing of choices. There are a large number of dropdown menus in Excel as you can see here where we have dropdown menus for Undo, Paste, Copy, Font, Font Size, Underline, Borders, Fill Color, Font Color, and Text Orientation:

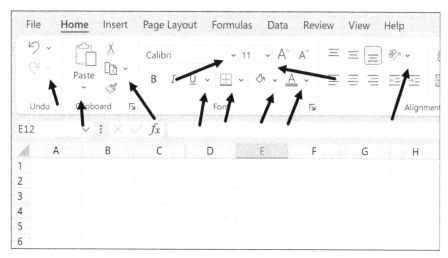

There are many more available in Excel. So any time I tell you to use a dropdown menu or anytime you're trying to find additional options, look for that little arrow to the right of or below the task you're trying to complete or try right-clicking on a worksheet name or in the main workspace.

Help Text

This isn't really a term and we'll discuss it again later, but I just wanted to mention that if you are ever unsure what task an image in the top menu is related to, you can usually hold your mouse over the image and Excel will tell you what it is. Here, for example, I held my cursor over the image of a bucket with a bright yellow line under it and Excel showed me a pop-up box that tells me that's for adding Fill Color and what that does. I can then click on Tell Me More to open Help and learn more about how it works.

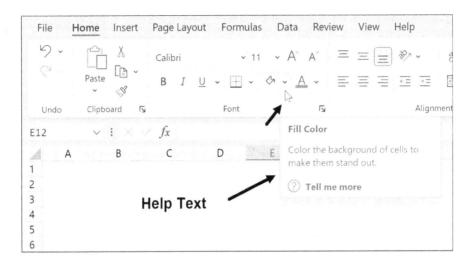

Tell Me More is not always available, but usually you will at least get a brief description of what that image will let you do.

Dialogue Boxes

Dialogue boxes are pop-up boxes that contain additional choices. You will often see one if you click on the arrow in the corner of a section of a tab. For example, here I have clicked on the arrow in the corner of the Font section of the Home tab and that has opened the Format Cells dialogue box.

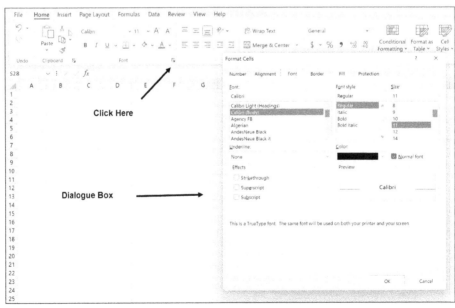

Dialogue boxes often have the most available choices. So if you aren't seeing what you want in the tab choices, then click on that arrow to open the related dialogue box if it exists.

Also, for those who are used to older versions of Excel, dialogue boxes are likely what you're used to working with so using them can sometimes feel more familiar than using the options up top.

You will also sometimes see a dialogue box if you right-click and choose an option from the dropdown menu in the main workspace.

Scroll Bars

When you have more information than will show on the screen, dialogue box, or dropdown menu you can use the scroll bars to see the rest of the information.

The main scroll bars you will see are going to be in the main workspace when there is more data in your rows and columns than can appear on the screen:

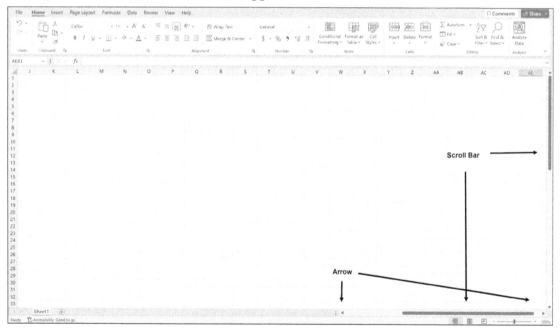

Scroll bars usually appear on the right-hand side or on the bottom of the workspace, dialogue box, or dropdown menu.

In the image above you can see them as darker gray bars. Note that there are also arrows at each end of the scroll bars. And that there is blank space between the arrows and those bars.

The more information involved, the smaller the scroll bars will be and the more space there will be around them.

There are three ways to navigate using the scroll bars.

You can left- click and drag the bar itself. This means, left-click on the bar, hold down the left-click, and move the cursor as you do so. The bar will move and the visible information will change.

If you only want to move a small amount at a time, you can use the arrows. Arrows at the bottom will move one item left or right, arrows on the side will move one item up or down.

You can also, left-click and hold on the arrows to move through multiple items but it will do so one at a time.

The final option is to click into the gray space between the two. One click in that gray space will move you an entire screen's worth. So in the main workspace if I can see Columns A through V and I click in the gray space at the bottom that moves me to Columns W through AR.

In the main workspace, you can only use the scroll bars or click into that gray space to navigate within the area where you have data. But the arrows will let you go past that.

Formula Bar

The formula bar is the long white bar at the top of the main workspace directly below the menu tabs that lets you see the actual contents of a cell, not just the display value.

Here you can see that the value in Cell C1 is 5, but according to what we can see in the formula bar, that value is calculated using the formula =A1+B1, which adds the values in Cells A1 and B1 together:

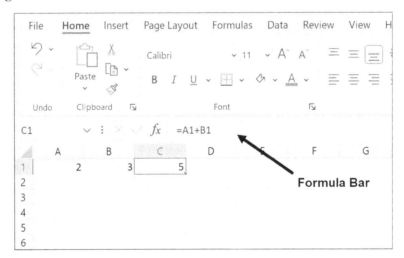

Task Pane

On occasion Excel will open a task pane, which is different from a dialogue box because it is part of the workspace. You can use F1 to see an example of this with the Help task pane which opens on the right-hand side of the workspace.

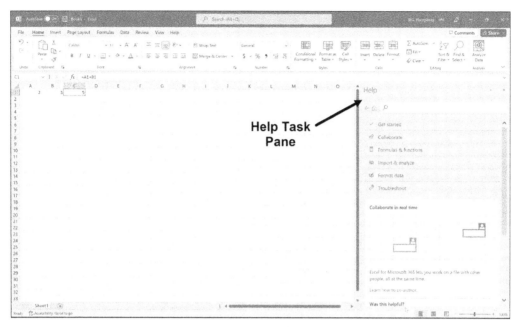

Help Task Pane

They can be closed by clicking on the X in the top right corner.

Absolute Basics

Before we start working in an Excel workbook, I want to cover the absolute basics of opening, saving, closing, and deleting files.

If you're already familiar with Microsoft Word or another Office program or similar, then this will probably all be familiar to you, but I want to make sure it's here for those who aren't.

Open a New Excel File

If you want to start a brand new Excel file, the first step is to open Excel. How you do this will depend on how you have your computer set up and what version of Windows you're running.

One of the first things I do when I get a new computer is I add my key programs to my taskbar. That way when I want to open Excel I can just click on the icon for Excel and open the program.

In Windows 11, a simple click on that green icon with the X will open Excel.

If you aren't set up with that, then you may have an Excel shortcut on your desktop.

Or you can go to the Start menu in the bottom left corner of your computer (if you haven't moved things around), left-click on that blue window icon and it will show you a menu where Excel may be in your pinned apps. If it's not there you can search for it. Or you can go to All Apps and find it there.

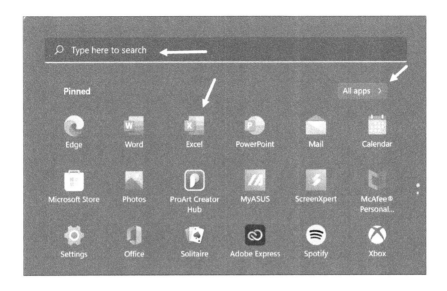

This is Windows 11. Windows 10, you click on the Start menu icon and look for the All Apps listing and then find it that way. They'll probably change it again in Windows 12 or whatever comes next, because they seem to love to do that, which is why I find it once, right-click, and choose to Pin to Taskbar so it's right there when I need it.

Okay. So however you do it, open Excel. If this is your first time in Excel you may have to Activate your account or skip through some screens that want you to activate it. But after you do that, you'll have something like this:

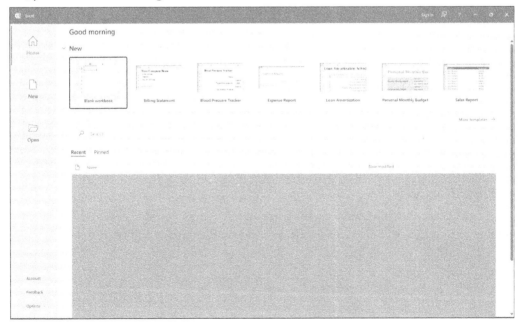

This is the Excel welcome screen. I've grayed out the section with my recent files listed, but otherwise this is what you should see when you first open Excel.

Those appearance settings we talked about before can be changed using Options on the left-hand side, bottom corner.

But if you're there to start a new file, then click on the Blank Workbook choice at the top of the screen.

(You'll see that there are also a number of templates you can choose from, but for what we're going to do in this book you can ignore those for now. If at some point you want to create an expense report, for example, you may want to click on that template and adjust from there.)

You could also click on New on the left-hand side but that just takes you to another screen where you have the Blank Workbook and template choices once more.

Clicking on Blank Workbook will open a new, blank workbook for you that looks like this:

If you are already in an Excel workbook and want to create a new workbook, you have a couple of choices. The easiest is to use Ctrl + N. That will immediately create a new workbook for you.

You can also go to the top of the screen, click on the File option, and then click on Blank Workbook from there.

Open An Existing Excel File

If you already have an Excel file and now want to open that file and work on it, there are a couple of options available.

The first is to find the Excel file wherever you have it saved and double-click on it. That will open the file in Excel and if Excel isn't already open will also open Excel for you.

If you do have Excel open and you've recently used that file, then you should be able to find it in your Recent Files listing on the welcome screen when you open Excel.

You can see in the image below the four most recent files I've opened in Excel and when they were opened last. My screen actually shows eight files and if I scroll down there are two more for a total of ten.

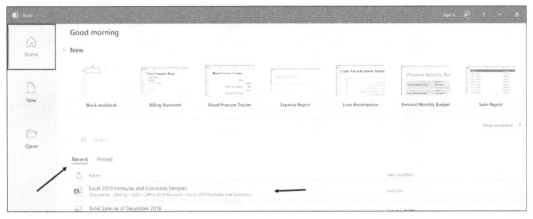

Click on the file name and the file will open.

There may be times when a file is listed in your recent files list but you can't open it from there. This happens if you move the file or change its name outside of Excel.

For a file that you want to open that isn't in that recent files list, click on Open from the welcome screen. You will once more see the Recent Files listing, but there will also be other options. One of those is the Folders option. Click on that and you'll see a listing of any folders that contain files you recently opened.

You can see in the image above that I opened files from the Writing Files and Excel 2019 Formulas and Functions folders today and have opened files from my Desktop, Downloads, Access DB for Writing, and a zip file this week.

This can sometimes be the easiest way to find a file you're looking for if you tend to store your Excel files in just a handful of locations. Click on one of those folder options and you'll see a listing of Excel files that are in that folder. You can then click on that file name to open it.

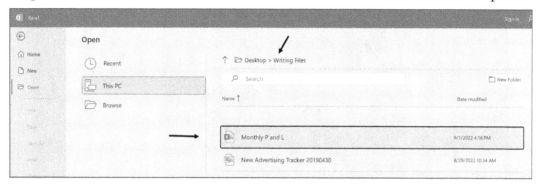

That will often be the best way to find a file. But it doesn't work if the folder the file is in is one you haven't used recently. It also doesn't work if the file you want to open isn't one of the main types of files that Excel can open, namely, .xls, .xlsx, or .csv.

If that's the case, then click on the Browse option instead. This will open the Open dialogue box.

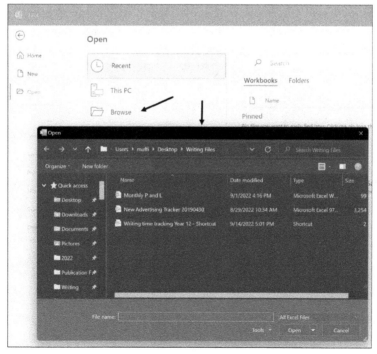

You can then use the options on the left-hand side to navigate to the folder that contains your file and select the file that way.

One of the files I need to open in Excel is a .txt file. By default, Excel will not look for that file type. You can see here that it's not showing any files for me to open.

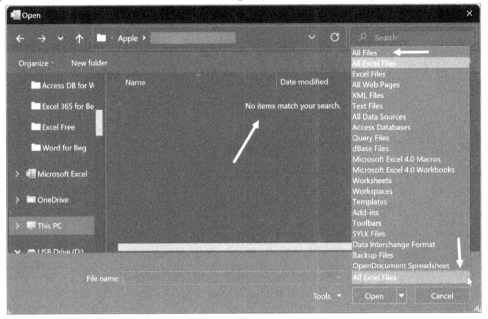

When I need to open one of those Text files, I have to change the file type in the Open dialogue box by clicking on the dropdown menu for file type and changing it to All Files from All Excel Files. Once I do that, I can then see the file I need to open and select that file:

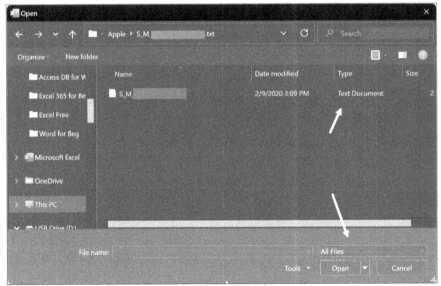

But that's a pretty rare situation, so usually you won't need to worry about that. I just mention it here because for anyone who publishes through Apple, their reports are text files. (That you also have to open with 7-Zip.)

Okay, back to things that matter to most readers instead of just one little subset.

If you already have Excel open and are either working on a file already or are in that main workspace and want to open another file, you can either use Ctrl + O, which will take you to the Open screen, or you can click on File at the top of the workspace and then click on Open.

From there it's the same steps as we just walked through.

Pin A File

If you have a file that you always want readily accessible but that won't stay in your recent files listing because you open enough files that it sometimes falls out of your top ten most recent, then you can Pin that file and it will always be available to you in your Pinned files section.

For example, I have a monthly profit and loss Excel file that I like to review once a month. But it gets lost from my recent files list because when I load all of my sales reports there are more than ten of them. So to make sure I can always find that file, I pin it.

To do this, find the file in your recent files list. Hold your cursor over that listing. You should see the image of a thumbtack appear on the right-hand side, and if you hold your cursor over that image it will say, "Pin this item to the list".

Click on that thumbtack. If you then click onto the Pinned option, that file will be listed there. And it will stay there regardless of what other files you open, so that it's always available to you.

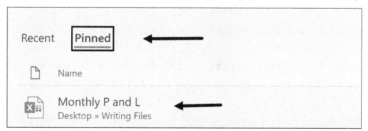

Once you've pinned a file, you can open it by going to your Pinned Files section and clicking on that name.

Close a File

If you ever have an Excel file open and want to close it, you can use Ctrl + W. I personally never remember that particular shortcut, so I instead just click on the X in the top right-hand corner.

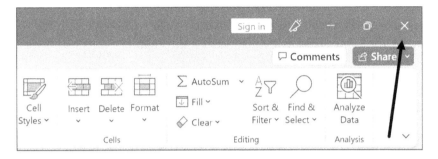

You can also click on File in the top menu on the right-hand side and then click on Close from the list of options on the left-hand side of the File screen.

Save a File

If you've made changes to a file and you try to close it Excel will show you a dialogue box that asks if you want to save those changes.

It gives you three options, Save, Don't Save, and Cancel.

Save will overwrite the existing version of the file. You'll keep the same file name, file location, and file type. All changes you made while that file was open will be saved. Whatever the file was like before that, is gone.

Don't Save will close the file but not save any changes you made to the document while it was open. It will be like you never touched that file.

Cancel will not close the file and also not save the changes. Choose Cancel if you want to save the file as a new version and not overwrite the old version.

If you're trying to close a brand new file, choosing Save will actually open the Save As dialogue box, because Excel doesn't know where you want to save the file or what you want to call it.

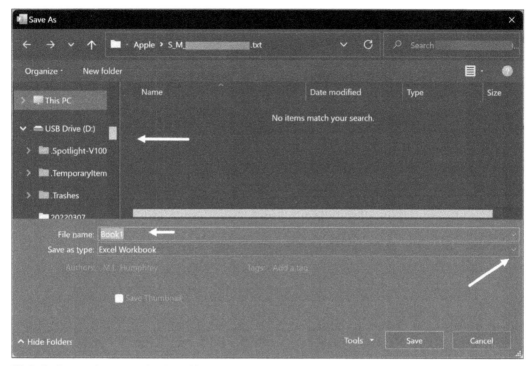

It will default to wherever the last file you opened was saved and the name will be some variation on Book 1. (If you have multiple blank workbooks opened it may be Book 2 or Book 3, etc.)

Type in the new name you want. Use the folders on the left-hand side of the dialogue box to navigate to the folder where you want to save that file. And make sure that the file type is what you want to use. Normally you'll be fine sticking with a file type of Excel Workbook.

But file type is another area where you may run into issues if someone is using an older version of Excel than you are. In that case, change the file type to Excel 97-2003 Workbook.

Be careful doing this, though, because as Excel adds more and more bells and whistles and functionality it makes it more and more likely that the Excel 97-2003 file format is not going to be able to support something you did in your Excel file.

If you're ever looking at file extensions, this is the difference between a .xlsx file and a .xls file. All files before Excel 2007 were .xls files. All files since then are .xlsx. In the past I advised saving to .xls for compatibility reasons, but I think we're far enough along at this point with .xlsx that you don't need to do that by default anymore. And if you're only working on files for yourself or your organization, you absolutely shouldn't need to worry about that.

If that all sounded confusing, don't worry. Just save as Excel Workbook. And if someone ever says, "I can't open that file because I have an older version of Excel," then come back to this section at that point in time.

So that's how you save a file if you weren't being proactive about it and just waited for Excel to remind you to save your file before you closed it.

But it's possible you will want to save that file under a new name or in a new location or as a new file type. Or that you'll want to save as you work so that if your computer crashes you don't lose your work. (Not as much of an issue these days as it was in the past, but it can still happen.)

In that case, let's start with Save first. Save is for a file where you want to save the changes you've made but you don't need to change the name, location, or file type.

The easiest option is Ctrl + S. That will save all of the changes you've made so far and overwrite the former version of the file.

If the file has never been saved before it will take you to the Save As screen under the File tab.

You can also click on the computer disk icon in the top left corner of the screen. Hold your mouse over it and it will say Save (Ctrl + S). Click on that and that too will save any changes you've made so far and overwrite the existing file.

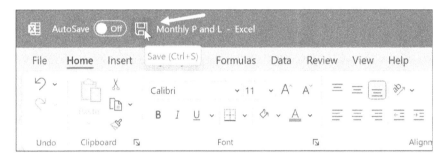

To save the file you're working on under a new name, into a new location, or as a new file type, you need to use Save As. To do that, click on File in the top left corner and then choose Save As.

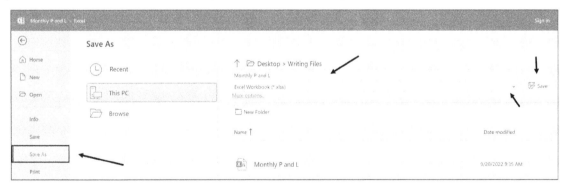

If you just need to change the file name, you can do so right there. Same with the file type. Once done click on Save.

To change the location, click on the Browse option. That will bring up the Save As dialogue box and let you navigate to the new location you want. Clicking on More Options will also bring up that dialogue box.

Keep in mind with Save As that the original file will still exist. So if you want multiple versions of a file, which I sometimes do when I'm building something really complex, that's great. But if what you really wanted was to change the file name or move the file, then you probably don't want to use Save As to do that.

Change a File Name

To change the name of an Excel file you can use Save As as we just discussed but that will leave you with two files. The original file will have the original name and then the newly-saved version will have the new name.

But if you don't need two files, it's better to close the Excel file, go directly to the folder where you have the file saved and change the name there. To do so, click on the file once to select it, and then click on it a second to make the name editable.

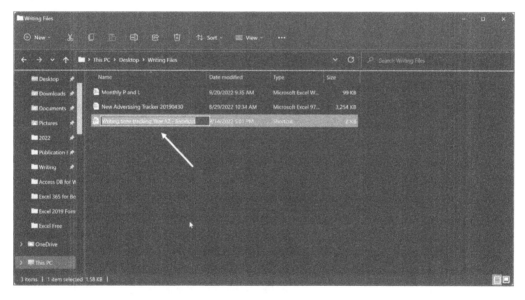

You can see here that I've done that with the third listed file so that the text of the name is now highlighted. I can then click into that field and make whatever change I want to the name. When you're done, hit Enter.

If you change a file name in this way, you will not be able to use the Recent or Pinned file listing to open the file the next time you go to open it in Excel. You will have to open the file directly from where it's saved or use the Browse option.

Delete a File

If you ever want to permanently delete an Excel file. Say, for example, that you did use Save

As but don't need that original file anymore, this has to be done outside of Excel. Close the file in Excel and then go find where you have it saved. Click on the file name once to select it. And then click on the trash can icon at the top of the window. You can also right-click on the file name and click on the trash can from there (for Windows 11) or choose Delete from the dropdown menu (for Windows 10).

File Naming Tip

Before we close out this chapter, I just want to share a file-naming tip I picked up from an efficiency training years ago that's been very helpful for me. I do keep multiple versions of files. For example, when I publish a book there's the original file. And then if I later make an edit because I find a typo or I release a new book in that series that needs to be added to the Also By section, there's another file. Some of my titles have twenty versions because they've been out almost a decade by now.

I want those files to display in an order that lets me quickly find the most recent one. To make that happen, I use a YYYYMMDD naming format.

This book for example would be "Excel 365 for Beginners 20221210". And then if I made an edit on December 15th it would be "Excel 365 for Beginners 20221215". By writing the date in that order–year, month, day–it ensures that when I sort by name, the files sort in proper date order.

(And if I ever for some reason have two on the same day then I add v1, v2, etc. at the end.)

You can use this same trick for folder names as well.

Also, if you have a process that involves multiple files and steps, consider how things will sort there as well. For example, I have put some of my books out as audiobooks. And there are four steps I go through to get to the final file. I have the raw recording, the first pass edit, the Reaper processing, and then the final version. I want to keep all of the raw files together, all the first pass files together, etc. And I want them in order.

So in that case I name the files "Raw 1 Introduction", "First Pass 1 Introduction", etc. By putting the stage of production first that makes sure that the raw files for all fifteen chapters group together. And by using the chapter number next I make sure that the first file in each group is the first chapter.

You will save yourself a lot of headache if you give some thought to your file names up front. And if you don't do so, well, you can always go and rename those files later. Just remember to do it where you saved the files not through Excel.

Okay. Now that we know how to open, close, save, rename, and delete files, let's talk about how to navigate Excel.

Navigating Excel

I want to talk now about how to move around within an Excel worksheet as well as within an Excel workbook and between workbooks.

Move Between Excel Workbooks

Let's start with the easiest one. If you have two Excel workbooks open, the easiest way to move between them is using Alt + Tab. If you have more than two files open just keeping using the Tab key while you hold down the Alt key to cycle through until you reach the one you want.

Alt + Tab lets you cycle through all of your open files or programs, not just Excel.

Items will usually be listed in order of when you last used them, so if you're moving back and forth between two Excel files, even if you have ten items open, those two files should be your first option each time you move. That means just one use of Alt + Tab will take you to the other file.

Another option, is to hold your mouse over the icon for Excel in the taskbar and then choose the file you want that way by clicking on the thumbnail image for the file.

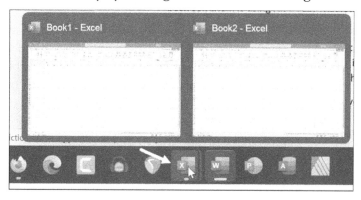

Move Between Excel Worksheets

Within an Excel file it is possible to have multiple Excel worksheets. I usually just click on the name of the worksheet I want at the bottom of the workspace.

You can see which worksheet you are currently on by seeing which worksheet name is white with bolded text.

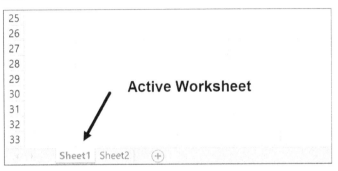

There is also a control shortcut for moving between worksheets that I generally don't use. Ctrl + Page Up will move you one worksheet to the left and Ctrl + Page Down will move you one worksheet to the right. If like on my computer your Page Up and Page Down buttons are combined with your up and down arrows then you may need to use Ctrl + Fn + Page Up and Ctrl + Fn + Page Down.

This does not, as of this moment, cycle through to the start or to the end. Meaning, if you have twenty worksheets and want to get from the first to the last, you would have to use Ctrl + Page Down nineteen times. Just using Ctrl + Page Up isn't an option. (It would be nice if it was, though, so maybe they'll do that someday.)

If you have more worksheets in your file than can be displayed at the bottom of the workspace, there will be little … at the end of the visible worksheet names.

Click on that … to see more worksheets. You can also use those left and right arrows on the bottom left corner of the workspace to move left or right and show more worksheets.

Using Ctrl and left-clicking on one of those two arrows will take you all the way to the first sheet or all the way to the last sheet, depending on which arrow you click on.

You can also right-click on one of those arrows to bring up an Activate dialogue box listing all of your worksheets in your workbook. From there click on the name of the worksheet you want and then click on OK and Excel will take you to that worksheet.

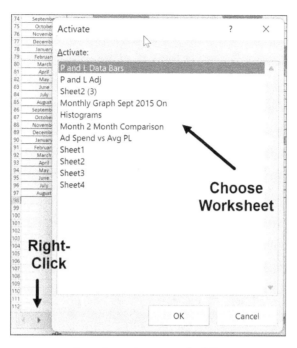

(If you don't want to try to remember those last two, holding your mouse over the arrows will tell you that as well. When in doubt in Excel, try holding the cursor over something because often there will be additional help text that appears.)

Move Within An Excel Worksheet

Any brand new Excel workbook is going to open on Sheet 1 and in Cell A1. To move from there, as we discussed briefly in the terminology section, you have a few options.

You can simply use the arrow keys to move one cell in any direction. So, right arrow moves you right one cell to Cell B1. Or if you used the down arrow it would move you down one cell to Cell A2. And then once you're not pinned into a corner in Cell A1, you can also use the left arrow to go left one cell and the up arrow to go up one cell.

The Tab key will also let you go right one cell. And using Shift and the Tab key will let you go left one cell.

Enter will also move you down one cell. Although, sometimes if you're entering data Enter will actually move you down one row but over to the beginning of where you were entering your data. So, for example, if I put "a" in Cell A1, "b" in Cell B1, and "c" in Cell C1, and then hit Enter that will take me to Cell A2. This can be very useful when entering multiple rows and columns of data directly into Excel.

Page Up and Page Down will take you one full screen's worth of rows up or down. (You may need to use Fn + Page Up and Fn + Page Down depending on how your computer is set up.)

You can also simply left-click into whichever cell you want if it's visible in your workspace.

As discussed more fully in the terminology section, to move greater distances within a file, you can use the scroll bars, the arrows at the end of the scroll bars, or click on the gray space between those arrows and the scroll bars. But be careful using those, because what you see will adjust, but until you click into a cell in the worksheet, you will still be in the last cell you were clicked into or edited.

This has occasionally tripped me up when I have my panes frozen (something we'll talk about later) and then I scroll far down in my data, but forget to click into one of the cells I can see on the workspace and so hit enter and am suddenly back at Row 2 instead of Row 2,354 or whatever.

Also, as mentioned before, according to Microsoft's help, Ctrl + End and Ctrl + Page Down will move you to the end of a range of data or the end of your worksheet, depending on if there's data in the worksheet.

Likewise, to go from somewhere in your worksheet to the top or the left-most edge, you can use Ctrl + Page Up and Ctrl + Home.

For me, with a computer where my arrow keys are combined with my Page Up, Page Down, Home and End keys I just have to use the arrow keys. I don't need to add the Fn key in to this one to get to Page Up, Page Down, Home, and End. So you may need to experiment around a bit to see how your particular computer acts.

Also, the help text on this one seems to differ from how it actually works. The help text says it takes you to the outer range of any existing data, but from testing it, what it actually does is takes you to the end of the next set of data in that particular row or column.

So if Column A has data for six rows and Column B has data for ten rows, depending on which column you're in when you use the shortcut you may go six rows or you may go ten.

If you do use this, and it can be very handy especially when paired with Shift so that you select those cells at the same time, watch out for gaps in your data. If there is an empty column or an empty row, Excel will stop at that gap. You'll need to use the arrow/page up/page down/home/end key again to grab the full range of your data if that happens.

Freeze Panes

If you have a lot of information in a worksheet, Freeze Panes will save you. Because it lets you keep certain information, such as a header row, visible in your workspace while you scroll down to see more data. Without freeze panes you end up with a screen full of data but nothing that tells you what that data is.

Here, for example, is a few rows of data from one of my Amazon reports:

	A	C	E	F	G	H	I	J	K	L
68	2021-01-26	Author A	Amazon.com		70% Standard	1	0	1	4.99	4.99
69	2021-01-26	Author F	Amazon.com		35% Free - Price Match	1	0	1	0.99	0.00
70	2021-01-26	Author A	Amazon.com		70% Standard	2	0	2	4.99	4.99
71	2021-01-26	Author D	Amazon.com		70% Standard	1	0	1	3.99	3.99
72	2021-01-25	Author A	Amazon.com		70% Standard	3	0	3	4.99	4.99
73	2021-01-25	Author B	Amazon.co.uk		70% Standard	1	0	1	3.99	3.99
74	2021-01-25	Author A	Amazon.com		70% Standard	1	0	1	2.99	2.99
75	2021-01-25	Author B	Amazon.com		70% Standard	1	0	1	4.99	4.99

If you wanted to use one of those columns to know the total number of units sold, which one would you use? And which one would show list price of the book? Versus which one shows what a customer actually paid for the book? Some of it is self-explanatory, but not all of it.

This particular report also has 15 columns, which means that I either would need to Zoom Out and make the text smaller to see everything or I'm going to not be able to see the left-most columns when I'm looking at the right-most column.

Which is a problem. I have it hidden right now, but Column B is Title and looking at how much I earned in the second-to-last column doesn't do me much good if I don't know which book it is.

But Freeze Panes lets me solve this issue. Because I can set up this worksheet so that Row 1 is always visible even when I'm on Row 250. And I can also set it up so that my title column is always visible, too.

Like so:

	A	B	N	O	P
1	Royalty Date	Title	Royalty	Currency	
224	2021-01-06	Book Title	2.76	USD	
225	2021-01-06	Book Title	3.96	USD	
226	2021-01-06	Book Title	2.05	USD	
227	2021-01-06	Book Title	5.90	USD	
228	2021-01-06	Book Title	2.76	USD	
229	2021-01-06	Book Title	5.83	USD	
230	2021-01-06	Book Title	2.76	USD	

See how it goes from Row 1 to Row 224? And how it shows Columns A and B and then Columns N and O? All of the other rows and columns are still visible, but I've scrolled down and over to see this information.

So how do you set this up?

If all you want is to freeze the top row of your worksheet or the first column, go to the Window section of the View tab and click on the dropdown arrow for Freeze Panes. Choose either Freeze Top Row or Freeze First Column.

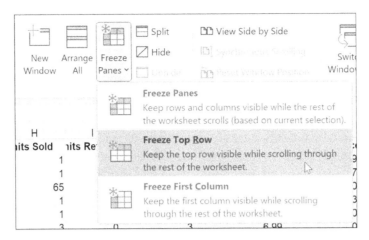

You can do one or the other this way, but not both. If you want to freeze more than one column, more than one row, or columns and rows both at the same time, then you need to first click into your worksheet at the first cell that you are okay *not* seeing.

In other words, below the rows that you want to freeze in place and to the right of the columns that you want to freeze in place.

So in our example worksheet, I want to keep the first row visible and I want book title visible, which is in the second column. That means I need to click into Cell C2.

	A	B	C	E	F
1	Royalty Date	Title	Author Name	Marketplace	Royalty Type
2	2021-01-31	Book Title	Author A	Amazon.com	70%
3	2021-01-31	Book Title	Author B	Amazon.com.au	70%
4	2021-01-31	Book Title	Author C	Amazon.com	70%
5	2021-01-31	Book Title	Author D	Amazon.com	70%
6	2021-01-31	Book Title	Author C	Amazon.fr	70%
7	2021-01-31	Book Title	Author C	Amazon.ca	70%

In the image above you can see that I've shaded the first row gray as well as the two columns on the left gray so that I can make it more clear which data will remain visible.

I can then go to the Freeze Panes dropdown and choose the first option, Freeze Panes, to keep both that top row and the left two columns visible.

Now, honestly I don't care about keeping the date visible, but with freeze panes you don't get to be that specific. So it's everything to the left and everything above the cell you choose. Which means if I want book title I am also going to get date.

(I could hide a column or move a column to fix that, but it's not that big a deal to me.)

To remove freeze panes, just go back to that same dropdown menu. The top option will be Unfreeze Panes now and you can just click on it to remove any freeze panes that are in effect.

Now, one thing to be careful of, that I do more than I should. If you are clicked into Row 1 and have freeze panes in effect and have scrolled down to Row 10,522 but not clicked into any cell in that row or in that part of your data, you are still on Row 1 as far as Excel is concerned. And so if you use your down arrow you will go to Row 2 and the rows you see on your workspace will change to Rows 2 through…37 or so. And then you'll have to scroll all the way back down to Row 10,522 again.

Also, don't try to freeze too many rows or columns at a time. If you freeze the majority of your screen then you'll only be able to scroll maybe one record at a time which is very inefficient.

Hide Columns or Rows

Sometimes when I'm working with data in Excel there will be rows of data or columns of data I really don't need to see at all. So it's not that there's so much information on the screen I can't see it all, it's more that I want what's in Column B next to what's in Column F. Maybe I'm inputting data into those two columns, but there are calculations between the two that I want to stay where they are. So while I'm adding my information I don't need to see the calculation columns, just the columns where I'm putting in information.

When that happens I hide those rows or columns I don't need to see.

To hide a row or column, right-click on the letter or number for that column or row, and choose Hide from the dropdown menu.

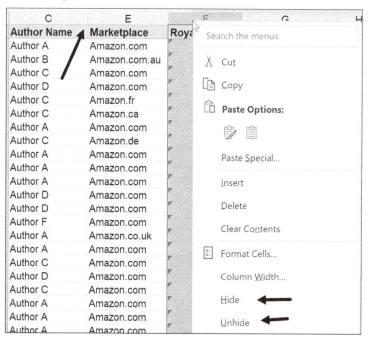

When you hide a column it still exists, so you will see that the letters or numbers skip that missing column or row. It will go from Column C to Column E, for example, if you've hidden Column D like I have in the screenshot above.

To unhide hidden columns or rows, select the columns or rows on either side of the hidden entries and then right-click and choose Unhide.

* * *

Now let's talk about inputting data after which we'll talk about inserting and deleting rows, columns, and cells as well as a bit more about working with worksheets.

Input Data

At its most basic, inputting your data is very simple. Click in the cell where you want to input information and then type. But there are some tricks to it that you'll want to keep in mind.

First, let's take a step back and talk about one of the key strengths of using Excel and that's the ability to sort or filter your data.

For example, I publish books and every month I get reports from the places where my books are published listing all of the sales of my books at those locations.

But what if I only care about the sales of book A? How can I see those if I have a couple hundred rows of information in the report they've given me?

Well, if the site where I sold those books is nice and helpful and they understand data analysis, they've given me my sales listings in an Excel worksheet with one header row at the top and then one row for each sale or for each book.

If they've done that, then I can very easily filter my data on the title column and see just the entries related to title A. Or create a pivot table of that data so I can see all sales for that title grouped together.

If they haven't, then I'm stuck deleting rows of information I don't need to get to the data I want.

Which is all a roundabout way of saying that you can input your data any way you want, but if you follow some key data principles you'll have a lot more flexibility in what you can do with your data once it's entered.

Those principles are:

1. Use the first row of your worksheet to label your data.

2. List all of your data in continuous rows after that first row without including any subtotals or subheadings or anything that isn't your data. Keep all data for a specific item on one row. (So a customer buys something from you on July 1st, have all of the information related to that transaction on one single line if transactions are what you care about. Or have all information related to sales of Widgets on one line per transaction if what you care about is your widgets.)

3. To the extent possible, format your data in such a way that it can be analyzed. (Which means rather than put in a free-text field, try to use a standardized list of values instead. A column that uses a 1 to 5 point ranking scale is better for analysis than a column that uses a free text field where anyone can say anything.)

4. Standardize your values. Customer A should always be listed as Customer A. United States should always be United States not USA, U.S.A., or America.

5. Store your raw data in one location; analyze or correct it elsewhere.

I wrote an entire book on this subject, *How to Gather and Use Data for Business Analysis*, so if you really want to explore this topic, that's where you need to go. In the interim those were just my high-level rules to follow when possible.

Of course, some of the ways in which I use Excel don't conform to those principles. And that's fine.

My budgeting worksheet is more of a snapshot of information than a listing of data, so it doesn't follow most of these rules because it's a report. But my worksheet that lists all vendor payments for the year? You bet it's formatted using this approach.

I bring this up because it's important before you start collecting and entering data into Excel that you think about how you might use that data. Are you just wanting to display this information? Or do you want to analyze it?

When in doubt, assume that you'll want to analyze your information at some point and structure everything accordingly. Here is a good example of data that is formatted in a way that in can be easily analyzed:

	A	B	C	D
1	Customer Name	Amount Paid	Date	Customer Satisfaction Rating
2	Customer A	$ 250.00	January 1, 2020	3
3	Customer B	$ 125.00	February 3, 2022	4
4	Customer C	$ 132.00	June 1, 2021	5
5	Customer D	$ 287.00	July 8, 2020	3
6				
7				

It's not that you can't work with data that isn't set up using the rules above, it's just that it's harder to do.

Okay, now that we have that out of the way, what are some tricks you should know to make inputting or deleting data easier?

Enter Information In A Cell

To enter information or data into a cell in Excel, click into that cell and just start typing or paste in whatever it is you want to enter.

Edit Information In A Cell - F2

If there is already data in that cell and you want to edit it, I find using the F2 key helps. The F2 key will take you to the end of the contents of that cell. And then you can use the arrow keys to move within the contents of the cell and make whatever edits you need to make.

This is useful for when you don't want to completely overwrite what's already in there. For example, I sometimes will forget a closing paren when I enter a formula. Going to that cell, using F2, and then typing that closing paren is the quickest way to fix that issue.

However, not every computer is set up to have F2 be the default. I've had to change that on each new laptop I've bought over the last five years or so. If that's the case and your key that says F2 is actually controlling the volume on your computer, then you'll need to use the Fn key and the F2 key together.

Edit Information in A Cell – Other Options

Another option is to click on the cell and then click into the formula bar and edit the text that way. Once more, you can use the arrow keys to move through what's already there once you're clicked into that cell. Or you can click into the point in those cell contents where you want to make your edit.

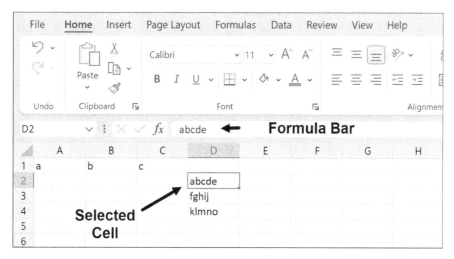

If you are working with formulas and cell references, when you click into the formula bar each cell reference will be color-coded and the corresponding cell in the worksheet will share that color.

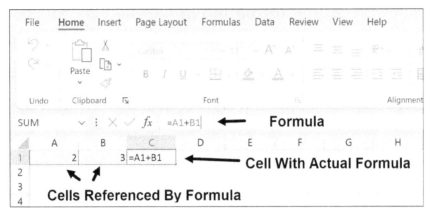

Undo

To undo something when you make a mistake, use Ctrl + Z. Learn this one.. Trust me.

I sometimes think I've done something the right way and as soon as I finish, I realize I was mistaken. Ctrl + Z quickly gets me back to where I was before I made that mistake.

And sometimes undoing what you did (like a bad sort that didn't include all columns) is the only way to safely fix things.

If you don't want to use that control shortcut, you can also click on the Undo option in the Undo section of the Home tab. It looks like an arrow pointing counter-clockwise.

That also gives you the option, if you click on the dropdown arrow instead, to undo multiple steps at once.

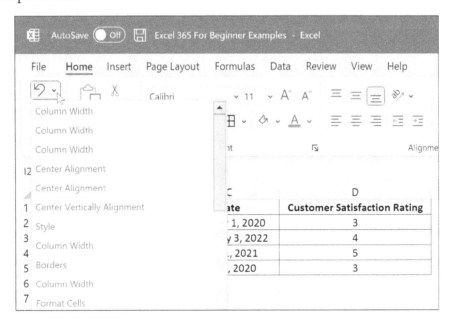

You can see the steps I took to create that data table in the image above. If I click on one of the items at the bottom of that list, Excel will undo every step from that point forward. So if I scroll down and find "Typing 'Customer Name' in A1" and click on that, it erases the table entirely and the worksheet goes back to how it was at that point in time.

Redo

Of course, you may find that you undo something that you didn't want to undo and have to bring it back. That's what Redo (Ctrl + Y) is for. That will bring back one step. But you can also go to the Undo section of the Home tab and click on the dropdown for Redo, which is an arrow rotating clockwise, and then choose from that list to bring back as many steps as you need to.

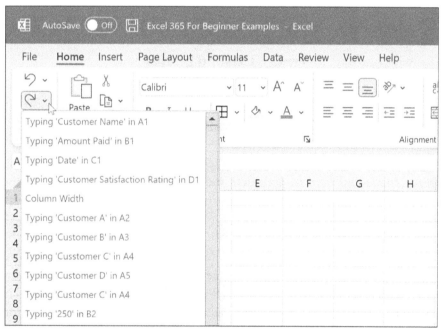

So I would scroll to the end of that list there and choose the very last option to restore my entire table.

Esc

Another handy tool to keep in mind is using the Esc key. Sometimes I will start entering information in a cell and then accidentally click somewhere I don't want to or in some other way get stuck doing something I don't want to be doing. If I'm mid-mistake, I use Esc to back up.

It basically says, "Oops, just kidding, let me stop doing this and go back, thanks." It comes in especially handy when working with formulas when an inadvertent click can change a formula in a way you did not want.

Use Auto-Suggested Text

If you're inputting a lot of data directly into Excel and that data is repetitive, auto-suggested text can save you a ton of time.

What it does is looks at the values you've already entered into a column and suggests how to complete an entry for you.

So if I'm selling Widgets, Whatchamacallits, and Whatsits and I have five hundred rows of data to enter, I don't have to type each full word each time.

I can start to type Widgets, W-I, and Excel will suggest that word for me if I've already used it. Like here:

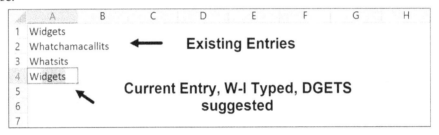

For that fourth entry, all I've typed so far are the W and the I, but Excel looked at the list of entries I already made and tried to complete the entry for me. I can ignore it and just keep typing or I can hit Enter to accept the suggestion. I only had to type two letters instead of seven, which is a great time-saver.

Now, there are some caveats here.

It tends to only look at entries that are connected. Meaning, if I had tried to type W-I in Row 5 but left Row 4 blank, Excel wouldn't make a suggestion. Unless I had a column next to this one that already had continuous entries in Rows 1 through 5. Basically, Excel needs some way to presume that the cell you're entering data into now is connected to the one above it before it will make a suggestion.

Also, what you type has to be unique for Excel to make a suggestion. So when I type W-I, Excel says "Widgets". But if I type "W-H" it's not going to do anything because that could be either Whatsits or Whatchamacallits. I'd have to type W-H-A-T-S or W-H-A-T-C before Excel suggested a word for me.

If you can, keep this in mind when creating your values. Because using Customer A, Customer B, Customer C doesn't save you any time. But using A Customer, B Customer, and C Customer would. (And if you find that funky, you could always later use data manipulation to turn "B Customer" into "Customer B" after you'd saved yourself a bunch of time inputting those entries.)

Excel also doesn't tend to be very good with pulling in rare values. Here, for example, I entered Whatchamacallit as my value for about 440 entries and then tried to type Widgets. I had to type W-I-D-G-E-T before Excel finally suggested Widgets as my value.

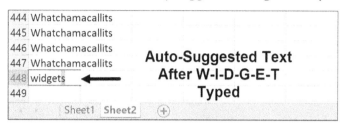

Excel also won't make suggestions for numeric values. So even if you have an entry like 123TRE, it won't even try to suggest a value until that first letter is typed. But once the first letter is typed it will look for a word to suggest.

Again, keep this in mind when coming up with values that you might input. You will save more time if you have TRE123 instead of 123TRE as the customer identifier as long as TRE is somewhat unique and you don't use TRE123, TRE456, TRE789. In which case you'd be better off sticking with 123TRE, 456TRE, and 789TRE.

Despite how confusing I probably just made that sound, it really is helpful when inputting values.

Copy Patterns or Repeated Entries

In the next chapter we'll discuss copying data in detail, but this is more of a tip related to inputting your data, so I wanted to cover it here.

Excel has the ability to recognize patterns. For example, let's say that you wanted to create a data table that shows your income for each month of a year. So you want Column A to have January, February, March, etc.

That is a pattern that Excel can recognize. Which means you do not have to enter all twelve months. You can actually type just January into the first cell, click back onto that cell, and then left-click and drag down from the bottom right corner. Your cursor should look like a little black plus sign as you do this and as you drag past each cell Excel is going to show you the value it predicts for that cell.

Here, for example, I have dragged down to Row 4 and Excel is telling me that will be April. As I dragged past Row 2 it showed February and for Row 3 it showed March.

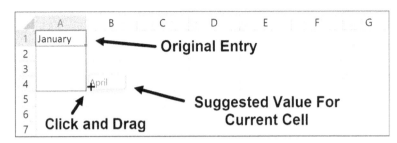

When I let up on that left-click and drag, Excel will then populate all of those fields for me. Like so:

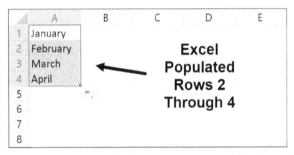

All I had to do was give Excel the start of the pattern. It took it from there.

Now that was click and drag. But if you already have other entries in your data table, then you don't even have to do that. You can double-left click on that bottom right corner and if Excel can see how far to take the entries down it will populate all those rows for you.

Here, for example, I have twelve rows that already have a year entered:

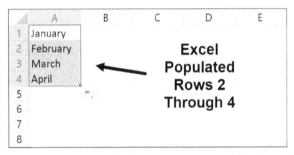

All I have to do is double left-click in the bottom right corner of the cell that says January in it and Excel does the rest for me.

Sometimes, though, you may just want to copy values down instead. For example, when I bring in my monthly sales reports from my various vendors I always add two columns, one for Month, and one for Year. In the first row of my data I put the Month and Year values. I then highlight both of those sells and double-left click in the corner.

Excel does its thing and populates the values for Month and Year for the rest of the entries in that table (which can be hundreds of entries). But it tries to turn them into a series. So January 2020 is followed by February 2021, etc.

	A	B	C	D	E	F	G
1	Month	Year	Date				
2	January	2020	1/2/2020				
3	February	2021	1/2/2020				
4	March	2022	1/2/2020				
5	April	2023	1/2/2020				
6	May	2024	1/2/2020				
7	June	2025	1/2/2020		**Change To**		
8	July	2026	1/2/2020		**Copy Cells to**		
9	August	2027	1/2/2020		**Copy Down**		
10	September	2028	1/2/2020		**First Row**		
11	October	2029	1/2/2020		**Values**		
12	November	2030	1/2/2020				
13							
14			○ Copy Cells				
15			◉ Fill Series				
16							
17			○ Fill Formatting Only				
18			○ Fill Without Formatting				
19			○ Fill Months				

That's not what I want. But it's an easy fix. I can click on the dropdown arrow for that Auto Fill Options that shows at the bottom right side of the series in the workspace and change the option from Fill Series to Copy Cells. That immediately changes all those values to January 2020 which is what I want. It's faster than copying the top entries, selecting all the other cells, then pasting, especially when there are a lot of entries. Although that works, too. (And is discussed in the next chapter.)

The examples I just showed you are for copying a pattern down a column, but it works just as well across a row. So you could write Monday in Cell A1 and then click and drag to the right from the bottom right corner of that cell to get the rest of the days of the week.

Excel can also recognize custom patterns, but you usually have to give it more than one entry for that. And it seems to be better with numbers than letters. So I can enter Customer 123, Customer 124, Customer 125, and then get it to predict Customer 126 and so on, but if I use Customer A, Customer B, Customer C, it can't see that pattern.

So sometimes it will help, sometimes it won't. But when it does help it's very helpful.

Display the Contents of a Cell As Text

Excel tries to be helpful, but sometimes it fails miserably. There's a reason there are numerous jokes on the internet about Excel mistaking things for dates. If you get anywhere close to entering information that it thinks might be a date, it will transform that entry into a numeric date and format it accordingly.

For example, I sometimes want to have "January 2020" in a cell in my worksheet as a label. As soon as I type that into that cell and hit Enter, Excel turns it into a date with a day of the week included.

My text entry of "January 2020" displays as Jan-20 in that cell and in the formula bar you can see it listed as 1/1/2020.

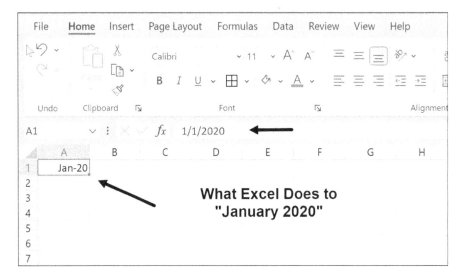

Not what I want.

The other time this happens is if you ever try to start an entry in a cell with a dash (-), a plus sign (+), or an equals sign (=), all of which Excel interprets as the beginning of a formula.

So if I want to use "- Item A" in a cell, I can't just type that in that cell. Excel will get very confused and give me a #NAME? error.

To keep Excel from reacting this way, you can type a single quote mark (') before the contents of the cell. If you do that, Excel will treat whatever you enter after that as text and will keep the formatting type as General. It also won't think that you're entering a formula in that cell that requires it to make a calculation.

For example, if you want to have June 2020 display in a cell in your worksheet, you need to type:

'June 2020

Not just

June 2020

If you want to have

- Item A

display in a cell, you need to type it as

'- Item A

The single quote mark will not be visible when you look at that cell in your worksheet or when you print the data from your worksheet. It is only visible in the formula bar when you've selected that cell. Like so:

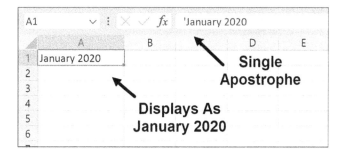

Include Line Breaks In a Cell

Another thing you might find yourself wanting to do is to include text in a cell but have it break across lines. So, for example, you may want an entry that looks like this:

where the A, the B, and the C are all on separate lines. You can't just use Enter because that will take you to the next cell. What you have to do is use Alt + Enter. So hold down the Alt key as you hit Enter and that will create a line break within the cell.

Delete Data

To delete information you've entered into a single cell, simply click into that cell and use the Delete key. You can delete the text in more than one cell at a time the same way. Just select all of those cells and then use the Delete key.

This deletes the contents of the cell, but leaves the cell where it is.

You can also double-click on a cell or use F2 to get to the end of the contents in a cell and then use your computer's backspace key to delete the contents of a cell one character at a time.

Or you can click on a cell and then go to the formula bar and select a portion of the cell contents and then use Delete or Backspace.

Clear Cell Formatting

When you delete the the contents of a cell that does not remove the formatting that's been applied to that cell.

To delete the contents of a cell as well as the formatting, select the cell(s), go to the Editing section of the Home tab, click on the dropdown next to the Clear option, and choose to Clear All.

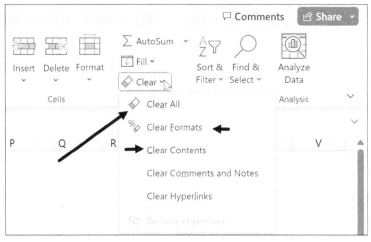

You can also choose to just Clear Formats or Clear Contents using that same dropdown menu.

Find and Replace

Find will locate whatever it is you're searching for. Replace takes that one step further and locates that entry and then replaces it with whatever you designate.

I don't use replace often in Excel, because I'm usually dealing with data entries and I don't want to risk messing those up. But I do use find fairly often to get to a particular entry in a data table.

(Another option, which we'll cover more later, is filtering. That one is best for displaying a subset of your data, especially when find would return more than one result.)

But back to find and replace. Let's walk through an example using replace.

Above I mentioned that typing in A Customer instead of Customer A would let Auto-Suggested text work in your favor. But having entries that say "A Customer" feels awkward. I could enter all of my entries using A Customer and then use Replace to change those over to Customer A. That's one way to fix that after the fact.

Here are some random entries to work with:

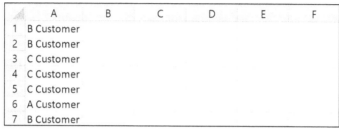

I actually have 51 rows of entries randomly assigned between A Customer, B Customer, and C Customer. I want to change those over to Customer A, Customer B, and Customer C.

Either Ctrl + F or Ctrl + H will open the Find and Replace dialogue box. Ctrl + F will open it to the Find tab, Ctrl + H will open it to the Replace tab.

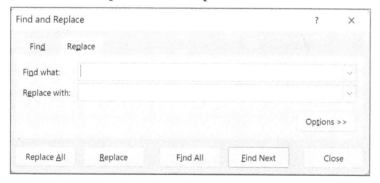

If you don't want to use the control shortcuts or you forget them, you can go to the Editing section of the Home tab and click on the dropdown arrow for Find & Select and then choose either Find or Replace from there.

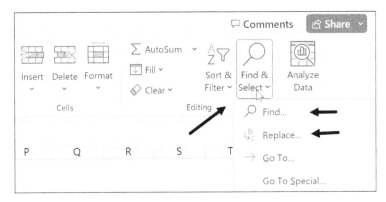

That will also open the same dialogue box.

The entries we're dealing with here are very basic. So we could probably just type A Customer in the Find What field and Customer A in the Replace With field and be fine clicking on Replace All.

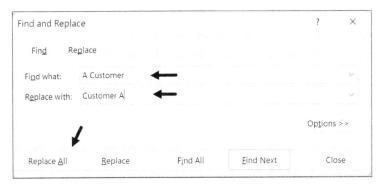

And, sure enough, that worked just fine on the 19 entries in my list that said A Customer. You can see two of those entries here are now Customer A.

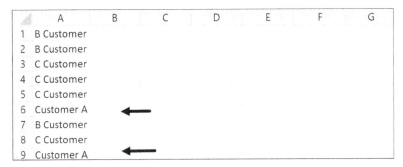

But you have to be careful with Replace. Because it is not, by default case sensitive. And it also does not, by default, look for whole words. So if I'd had entries that were AA Customer, for example, and I did a replace for A Customer, those entries would be changed, too. I would end up with entries that said ACustomer A, which is not what I want.

The way to make sure that Excel only replaces what you want it to replace is to click on that Options button to expand the Find and Replace dialogue box. Here is what that will look like:

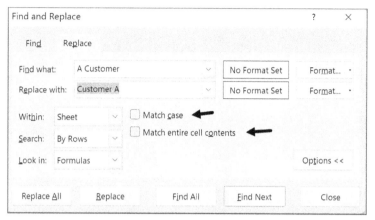

If I check the box for Match Entire Cell Contents, that addresses the issue with AA Customer versus A Customer. And if I check Match Case, that makes sure that if I have a paragraph of text in that worksheet that discusses "how a customer may want to…", I don't inadvertently replace that and end up with "how Customer A may want to…"

Replace in Excel is a fairly blunt tool as it currently exists. It is far more refined in Word where I do use it often. But wherever you use it, be sure you've really thought through what the replacement you're making will actually do to your contents.

When in doubt, you can use the Find option first to see which entries your current criteria capture. Here I clicked over to the Find tab, typed in my text, B Customer, under Find What, and then clicked on Find All. The Value column shows the contents of each cell in its entirety.

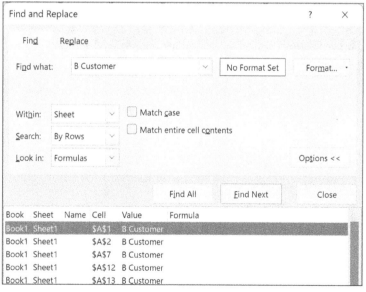

You can click on each entry in that list to go to it.

If you just want to walk through your results, you can use Find Next instead.

Turn Off Scroll Lock

On occasion I will find that navigating in Excel isn't working the way I'm used to. I arrow and things don't move like they should. When this happens, it's usually because Scroll Lock somehow was turned on. The way to turn it back off is to click on the Scroll Lock key on your keyboard.

Unfortunately, I haven't had a computer with a Scroll Lock key in probably a decade, so you have to open a virtual keyboard to do this. Use the Windows key (the one with four squares to the left of your spacebar) + Ctrl + O to open it.

(Another option is to go through your Start menu to Settings and search for keyboard there and then toggle the on-screen keyboard to on.)

The keyboard will appear on your screen. The Scroll Lock key (ScrLk) should be colored when it's turned on. It's one of the right-hand-side options on the keyboard:

Click on it to turn it off and then close the virtual keyboard by clicking on the X in the top corner. Excel will return to acting normally.

* * *

Okay. That's the basics of entering information into Excel. I do still want to talk about how you enter formulas in Excel, but I'm going to save that for its own chapter where we discuss formulas at a very high-level. (For the detailed discussion you'll want to read *102 Useful Excel 365 Functions*.)

Now let's talk about copying, pasting, and moving data around.

Copy, Paste, and Move Data

Now that you know how to enter data into an Excel workbook it's time to talk about how you can move that data around.

Before we dive in on copy, cut, paste, etc. I want to refresh you on how to select cells. It was covered in the terminology section, but in case anyone skipped that...

Select Data

To select one cell, click on it or arrow to it.

To select multiple cells that are next to one another, go to a cell at the outer end of that range, hold down the Shift key, and then use the arrow keys to select your cells. Or left-click and drag with your mouse to select the remaining cells you want. You can select across rows, columns or both rows and columns.

To select multiple cells that are not next to one another, click on the first cell you want, and then hold down the Ctrl key as you click on the other cells you want. You cannot use the arrow keys for this one.

To select an entire column, click on the letter for that column.

To select an entire row, click on the number for that column.

To select multiple rows or columns it works the same as for cells. Shift and arrow or left-click and drag if they're next to each other, Ctrl if they aren't.

Select All

If you want to select all of the data in a worksheet, go to that worksheet and then use Ctrl + A.

If you don't want to use Ctrl + A, you can also click in the top left corner where the columns and rows meet.

* * *

Now that you know how to select cells, rows, columns, or data, we can talk about copy, paste, and moving things around.

Copy and Move Data As Is To One Location

Let's start with copying data from one location to another without any special changes to that data.

When you Copy you leave an original version of the data where it was and you take that exact same data and you put a copy in a different location.

By default that data will transfer with all of its formatting. And if there were any formulas in the data you selected those formulas will move as well. (We'll come back to formulas more in the formulas section.)

So to copy and move data as is, first, select the data you want to copy.

Next, the easiest way to copy is to just use Ctrl + C. (If you only memorize a handful of Ctrl shortcuts, make this one of them.) That will take a copy of your data for you.

Go to where you want to put that data, click into the first cell in that range, and hit Enter.

Here, for example, I have copied the data from Cells A1 through A6 to Cells E1 through E6.

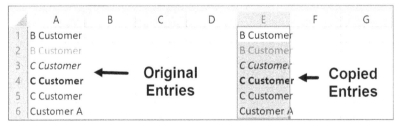

So I selected Cells A1 through A6, used Ctrl + C, went to Cell E1, and hit Enter. All of the text and all of the formatting copied over.

If you didn't want to use a Ctrl shortcut there are a number of other ways to access the copy option. One is to right-click on the selected cells and choose Copy from the dropdown menu.

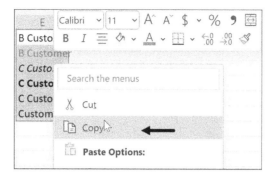

Another is to go to the Clipboard section of the Home tab and click on the Copy option from there.

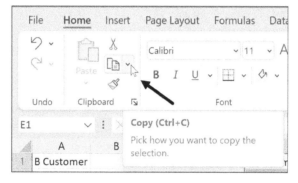

Copy and Move Data As Is To Multiple Locations

If you want to copy and move the same data but to multiple locations, then you'll want to use the Paste function instead of Enter to place the data in each new location.

So copy it the same as before, but when you click into the first cell of the new range use Ctrl + V instead to paste the data. (This is another Ctrl shortcut you should absolutely memorize.)

Look at these copied and pasted entries. It may be a little hard to see, but the copied entries have a dotted line around them:

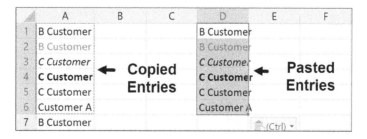

This means that they are still copied even though I pasted them once into Column D, so I can go to another location and paste them again. As long as I use Ctrl + V (or one of the other ways to paste that I'll discuss in just a moment) I can put that copied data into as many locations as I want.

When you are done copying your data, use the Esc key to turn that off. Typing into a new cell will work as well.

Just like with Copy, Paste can also be found by right-clicking on the selected cell(s) or going to the Clipboard section of the Home tab.

Move Data To A New Location

If you don't want to take a copy of your data, but instead want to move that data to somewhere new so that there's just that one copy of the data in the new location only, then you need to use Cut. It works the same as Copy, you select your data, Cut, and then go to the new location, and put the data there.

The control shortcut for this is Ctrl + X. (Another good one to memorize.) And it works with either Enter or Ctrl + V at the new location.

But with Cut you are moving that data and you can only move it once. So both Paste and Enter place the data and you're done.

Here is data I Cut from Cells A1 through A6 and Pasted into Cells C1 through C6:

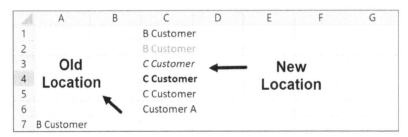

I went to Cells A1 through A6 and selected them, used Ctrl + X, clicked into Cell C1, and used Ctrl + V. Note that there is now no content in Cells A1 through A6. It is only in Cells C1 through C6.

Cutting also takes the cell formatting with it. So if I type a new value in Cell A2 which previously had red text in it, that text is black not red.

You can Cut by selecting the cells and then right-clicking and choosing Cut from the dropdown menu or by going to the Clipboard section of the Home tab. Cut is shown as a pair of scissors in the Clipboard section.

Copying or Cutting Cells With Formulas

If you have formulas in the data you're moving you need to be more careful because the choice to Cut versus the choice to Copy will impact your result, but I'm going to save that for the

Formulas chapter. Just note for now that there is an issue there that you need to be aware of.

Copy and Move Data With Changes

Sometimes you will want to copy just the contents of a cell without keeping any of its formatting. Or you will want to take a list of values in a column and put them into a single row instead. Or maybe you want the results of a formula, but you don't want to keep the formula anymore.

That's where the Paste Special options come in handy.

First, know that you can only use Paste Special if you've copied the contents of a cell (Ctrl + C). These options do not work if you've cut the contents of a cell (Ctrl + X).

To Paste Special, you either need to right-click in the new cell and choose from the Paste Options section in that dropdown menu

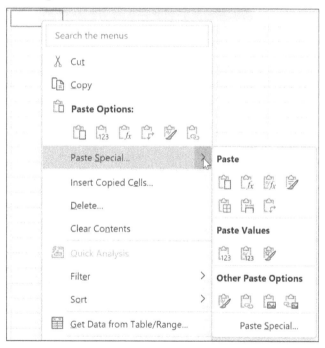

Or you need to click on the dropdown arrow under Paste in the Clipboard section of the Home tab.

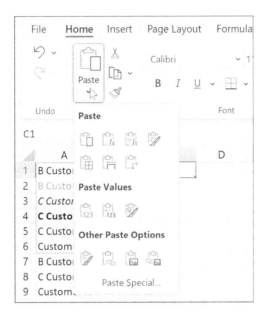

Clicking on Paste Special at the bottom of either of those lists will open the Paste Special dialogue box, but you're rarely going to need that.

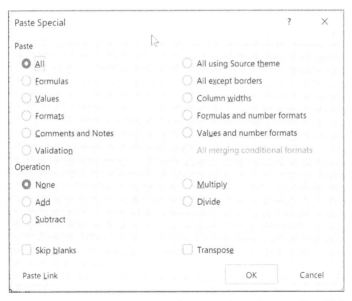

If you use the dropdown menu you can actually see what the result will be by holding your mouse over each option. Here, for example, I have my cursor over Paste Values and you can see that it will paste in the text that I've copied from Column A but without any of the formatting such as bolding, italics, or red text color.

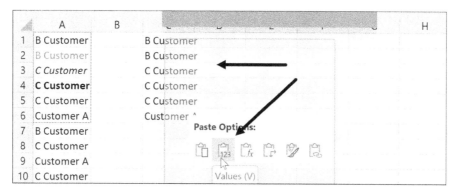

And here is what Paste Transpose looks like in preview:

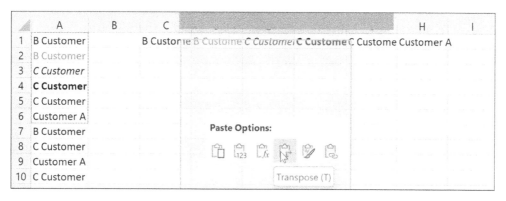

Those are the two paste options I use the most.

Paste Values has a 123 in the bottom corner of the clipboard image and what it lets you do is copy entries and then just paste those values. This is incredibly useful when working with formulas. For example, I would've probably fixed that transform B Customer to Customer B problem using one of two functions, TEXTJOIN or CONCATENATE. But that means I would've been doing so using a formula. And that formula would have depended on the content of cells in two different columns that I would have wanted to delete.

The only way to delete those columns but keep my "calculation" result would be to copy that column with my final calculation and then paste-values so that I keep the result of the "calculation" but not the formula.

It's also useful when you want the contents of a cell, but would prefer to use the formatting in the destination cell(s). For example, if you're copying from one Excel file to another.

Another way I use it is when I've run a set of calculations on my data, found my values, and now want to sort or do something else with my data but don't want to risk having the values change on me.

I will highlight the entire data set, copy, and then paste special-values right over the top of my existing data. (Just be sure to type Esc after you do this so that the change is fixed in place.)

I often do that when dealing with pivot tables. I'll create a pivot table to summarize my data, but then I copy that table and paste-special so that it's no longer a pivot table but just the calculated values.

The Paste Transpose option—the one with two sets of arrows in the bottom corner—is very useful if you have a row of data that you want to turn into a column of data or a column of data that you want to turn into a row.

Like in the screenshot above where you can see that my six entries that were in a column would be in a single row across six columns if I chose that option.

Just be sure before you paste that there isn't any data that will be overwritten when you paste your entries, because Excel won't warn you before it overwrites it.

There are a lot more paste options available, but those are the two main ones I use. I do also use paste formatting, but I do that through the Format Painter option in the Clipboard section of the Home tab. We'll discuss that more when we talk about how to format your data.

* * *

Now let's talk about another way to move around your data which is by inserting cells, rows, and columns. Also, I want to talk about worksheets a bit more, namely renaming them to reflect what they contain and also moving or copying them.

I'm going to start with worksheets, because that's the easiest part.

Rename a Worksheet

To rename an Excel worksheet, double-click on the worksheet name, and then start typing the new name you want to use. If you change your mind, use the Esc key to back out.

You can also right-click on the tab with the name and choose Rename from the dropdown menu.

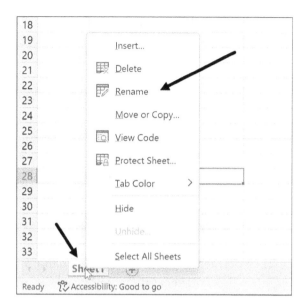

There are rules to naming worksheets. It can't be blank. It also has to be 31 character or less. And those characters cannot include / \ ? * : [or] and the worksheet name cannot begin or end with an apostrophe ('). Also, no worksheet can be named History because behind the scenes Excel already has one of those in each worksheet.

Don't worry too much about those rules. In more recent versions of Excel they just won't let you type those prohibited characters. And if you accidentally leave the name blank it will show a dialogue box telling you there's an error with the name. You just need to click OK on that and type in an actual name. Use Esc to go back to the original name.

Add a Worksheet

To add a new worksheet you can click on the little plus sign next to the last existing worksheet. That will add a worksheet to the right of the last worksheet you were clicked on.

Or you can go to the Cells section of the Home tab, click on the dropdown arrow under Insert, and choose Insert Sheet. That will insert a worksheet to the left of the one you were clicked on before you chose that option.

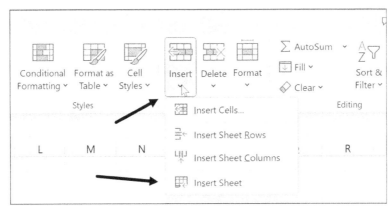

Move a Worksheet

To move a worksheet, left-click on the tab for the worksheet name and drag the worksheet to where you want it. As you move the worksheet there will be a little arrow pointing at the spot between the two worksheets where it would move to.

You can also right-click on the worksheet name and choose the Move or Copy option. That will bring up the Move or Copy dialogue box.

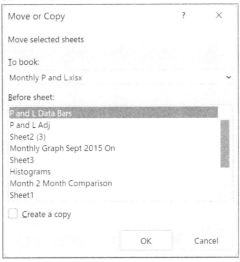

Click on the name of the worksheet you want to place the worksheet *before* and then click on OK. If you want to move a worksheet to another workbook you can do that from the Move or Copy dialogue box as well. Just change the option under To Book using that dropdown. Your available options will be a new Excel workbook or any Excel workbooks that are currently open.

Copy a Worksheet

You can also use the Move or Copy dialogue box to make a copy of a worksheet. I often will do this to put a copy of a worksheet I create in one workbook in a new workbook. To do so, click on the Create a Copy checkbox.

Here I've done so and selected to copy it to a new workbook using the dropdown menu choices. I just need to click OK to make that happen.

If you are moving or copying a worksheet to a new workbook and it includes formulas that reference other worksheets in the old workbook it will continue to reference to the old workbook. So be very careful about that, because if someone doesn't have access to the old workbook, those formulas aren't going to work for them.

(In general, I think it's best to keep everything contained in one workbook when working with formulas, but I know there are situations where that isn't possible. All I can say is, if you're going to have formulas that work across workbooks do so deliberately not just because it was a sloppy error.)

Delete a Worksheet

You can also delete a worksheet. To do so, right-click on the worksheet name and choose Delete from the dropdown menu.

Or you can go to the Cells section of the Home tab, click on the dropdown arrow for Delete, and choose Delete Sheet from there.

If the worksheet was blank, Excel will just delete it. If it contains any data Excel will show you a pop-up window asking you to confirm that you want to delete that worksheet. Be sure you really want to delete that worksheet, because you won't be able to undo it if you change your mind later.

* * *

That was worksheets, now let's talk about inserting and deleting columns, rows, and cells.

Insert a Column or Row

You only need to insert a column or row if you already have data in your worksheet and realize that you want a new column or row in the midst of that data that already exists. (Because, remember, the number of columns and rows in a worksheet is constant. So when you "insert" a column or row what you're really doing is just shifting around your existing data on that column and row map. You're taking data in Column A and moving it to Column B, but the total of columns in the worksheet isn't going to change.)

You have a number of options for this one.

I usually right-click on the letter for the column or number for the row and choose Insert from the dropdown menu.

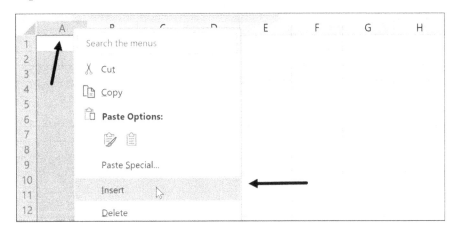

This will, for columns, insert a new column where I right-clicked and shift all of the data that was in that column previously or that was in any column to the right of that column over by one column. So if I right-click on Column B, all data that was in Column B is now in Column C, all data from Column C moves to Column D, etc.

You can insert multiple columns using this approach. Left-click on the column where you want to insert those new columns and then drag until you've selected the desired number of new columns to insert. Right-click and choose Insert from the dropdown. That should insert X number of columns and shift everything to the right.

Here you can see this for rows.

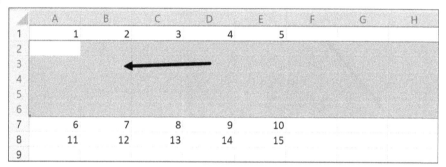

I selected Rows 2 through 6, then right-clicked and chose Insert. That moved the values from Rows 2 and 3 (the numbers 6 through 10 and 11 through 15) down that many rows so that they are now in Rows 7 and 8. Rows are always added above the selection, so everything shifts down.

You can also insert a column or row by right-clicking in a single cell that's in that row or column and choosing Insert from the dropdown menu. Excel won't know whether you want to insert a cell, row, or column, so it will show you the Insert dialogue box.

Click Entire Row or Entire Column and then choose OK to insert a row or column, respectively.

Your final option is to select a row or column or click into a cell in that row or column and then go to the Cells section of the Home tab and choose Insert Sheet Rows or Insert Sheet Columns from the dropdown menu.

Insert a Cell

Inserting a cell works much the same way. Click where you want to insert that cell, right-click, and choose Insert. Or click where you want to insert that cell and go to the Cells section of the Home tab, click on the Insert dropdown arrow, and choose Insert Cells.

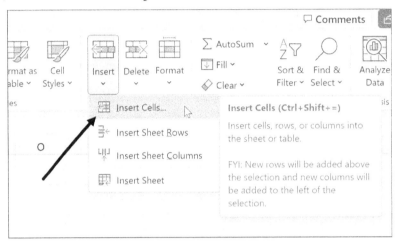

There is one quirk with inserting cells, however, and that's that you have to tell Excel whether to shift things to the right or to shift things down to make room. So you will always see the Insert dialogue box.

If you choose to Shift Cells Right, all data in that row with that cell will move to the right one column. If you choose to Shift Cells Down, all data in that column with that cell will move down one row.

Which you want will depend on the data you already have in your worksheet and why you're adding this cell.

You can insert multiple cells at once, which is what I often do. Just select the cell range first (left-click and drag) and then choose to insert.

Be careful when adding cells into a worksheet as opposed to entire rows or columns. I have, more than once, added say five cells and shifted my data but forgotten that I had other data in that same column or row in my worksheet and accidentally moved my data out of alignment.

So when adding cells, check first to see what is impacted. And check again after to make sure everything looks okay. If you get it wrong, Ctrl + Z, for Undo, is your friend. It will undo what you just did and let you try again. (Ctrl + Y is Redo if you ever undo something and decide that wasn't necessary.)

Delete Rows, Columns, or Cells

Deleting works just like inserting. Select the row, column, or cells that you want to delete and then either right-click and choose Delete from the dropdown or go to the Cells section of the Home tab, click on the dropdown for Delete, and choose your option there.

As with inserting cells, when you delete cells you should see a dialogue box that looks just like the insert one except it's talking about deleting. You will again need to decide whether to shift cells, this time left and up are the two choices.

So look at your other data and decide what to do. You may need to delete a range of cells instead of one single cell to keep everything in alignment.

If you select a range of cells and try to use the Delete key that will just delete your data, but the cells will remain there so none of the rest of your data will move.

Also, be careful with deleting rows, columns, or cells that have data in them. Check any formulas in your worksheet to see if deleting that data impacted those formulas. It will usually show up as a #REF! error.

Here, for example, I had a value in Cell A1 and a value in Cell B1 that were then added together in Cell C1. When I deleted Column A, that removed that value that was being used in the formula so the formula no longer works.

Note also that the value that was in Cell B1 moved to Cell A1 and that my formula that was in Cell C1 moved to Cell B1. Everything shifted one column. (One of the nice things about Excel is that the formula automatically updated to reflect that shift. So the formula now shows A1 not B1 for that second value location.)

Formulas and Functions

We've touched on formulas and functions a couple of times now, but I've set that aside each time. If you really want to dig in on formulas and functions in Excel I wrote a whole book about it that includes over a hundred different Excel functions and how each one works, *102 Useful Excel 365 Functions*.

But formulas are such a key part of working in Excel that I also want to talk about them here. So some of what I'm going to cover here duplicates the introductory material in that book. But it's a higher-level discussion than you get there. And we certainly are not going to cover a hundred functions here.

Cell Notation

Before we can move forward with a discussion of formulas, we need to talk in more depth about cell notation because cell notation is how you tell Excel where your data is for your formula.

I already discussed in the terminology section how each cell is identified by the combination of its Column and Row and that you should think of that as map coordinates. So Cell A1 is the first column, first row of a worksheet.

Within Excel when you are referencing that cell, you leave off the Cell portion. So you just write A1.

You can also reference multiple cells at once. To reference a cell range, so all the cells between X point and Y point, you use a colon to separate the first coordinate from the last. If I write

A1:A25

that's all cells between Cell A1 and Cell A25. If I write

A1:B25

that's all cells in Columns A and B and from Rows 1 through 25.

If you want to reference cells that aren't touching or that don't form a clean rectangular shape, then you need to use commas to separate the cells or ranges.

A1,B2,C3

would be referencing Cells A1, B2, and C3. And

A1:A3,B1:B6

would be referencing the combination of Cells A1 through A3 and Cells B1 through B6.

Excel also has ways of identifying which worksheet those cells are in if you're referring to cells in a different worksheet. This is done by writing the name of the worksheet followed by an exclamation point before the cell reference.

Sheet2!C19

is referring to Cell C19 in the worksheet called Sheet2.

You can also identify which workbook a cell is in using brackets.

[Book1]Sheet3!E11

is referring to Cell E11 in the worksheet called Sheet3 in the workbook called Book1.

I have never bothered to memorize how to reference worksheets or workbooks, because Excel will write that for you if you start a formula and then go to that workbook or worksheet and select the cells you want to use. So I always let Excel do that heavy lifting for me.

You can also reference an entire column using the : like so:

A:A

is referencing Column A and

A:C

is referencing Columns A, B, and C.

Same goes for Rows.

1:1

is referencing all cells in Row 1

1:5

is referencing all cells in Rows 1 through 5.

Okay, now that you have an understanding of how to tell Excel where your data is located, let's define formulas and functions.

Definition of Formulas and Functions

For our purposes I'm going to define a formula in Excel as anything that is started with an equals sign and asks Excel to perform a calculation or task.

(Technically, you can start a formula with a plus or a minus sign as well, but I'm just going to ignore that because unless you're coming from a specific background where you learned to do things that way, you shouldn't do that. Also, Excel transforms those formulas into ones that use an equals sign anyway.)

I define a function as a command that is used within a formula to give instructions to Excel to perform a pre-defined task or set of tasks.

Think of a function in Excel as agreed-upon shorthand for some task.

Examples of Formulas and Functions

A formula in Excel could be as basic as:

$$=A1$$

It starts with an equals sign and is telling Excel that this particular cell where we've written our formula should have the exact same value as Cell A1. The "task" Excel completes here is pulling in that value.

But usually a formula will be more complex than that. For example:

$$=SUM(A1,B1,C1)$$

which could also be written as

$$=SUM(A1:C1)$$

is telling Excel to take the values in the specified cells and sum them together. So if the value in Cell A1 is 2, and the value in Cell B1 is 3, and the value in Cell C1 is 4, then this formula would return a value of 9.

You can also combine multiple functions or calculations within a single formula. Each cell can only hold one formula, but that formula can perform multiple tasks. For example,

$$=ROUND(RAND()*100,0)$$

is a formula that combines three steps to randomly generate a number between 0 and 100. It includes two functions, RAND and ROUND, as well as one mathematical calculation.

RAND generates a random number between 0 and 1. The *100 part takes that result and turns it into a value between 0 and 100. ROUND takes that result and rounds that number to a whole number.

How to Create a Formula

The basic rules of building a formula are to (a) start with an equals sign, (b) always use an opening paren after a function name, and (c) if you use an opening paren make sure that it's paired with a closing paren.

Functions always require opening and closing parens, but you can also have opening and closing parens when doing pure math, too. So

$$=234*(123+345+(2*3))$$

is a perfectly valid Excel formula that is telling Excel to multiply 2 times 3 and then add that to 123 and 345 and then take that total and multiply it times 234. It's straight out of math class.

Functions normally require additional inputs, but not always. In our example above with ROUND and RAND, RAND is a function that does not use other inputs. It just has an opening paren followed by a closing paren.

But ROUND does have inputs. And everything between that opening paren after ROUND and the closing paren at the end of that formula are those inputs. In the case of RAND the first input is the number to be rounded. In this case, that was the randomly generated number times 100. The second input is how many places to round that number to. Since I wanted a whole number that was 0.

For each function you use, Excel will help you with which inputs are required. If I type

$$=ROUND($$

into Excel, the minute I type that opening paren it tells me what the inputs are that are required for that function. Like so:

If that isn't enough information for me, because maybe I'm not familiar with the function, I

can click on the function name in that little display box and it will open a dialogue box or Help text on the function that gives more information.

Formulas do not have to start with a function or a calculation.

$$=A1+SUM(B1:B5)$$

is a perfectly legitimate formula that takes the value in Cell A1 and adds that to the values in Cells B1 through B5.

Your Result

After you enter your formula in your cell, hit enter or leave the cell by arrowing, using the tab key, or clicking away. That will be when Excel tries to calculate your result.

The cell where you entered your formula will then display the result of the formula.

The formula can still be seen and edited via the formula bar. So if you click back on that cell you will see the value in the cell, but the formula in the formula bar. Like so:

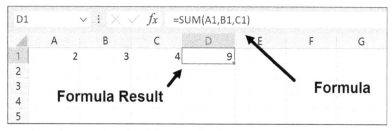

Here you can see that the result of adding Cells A1, B1, and C1 was 9 and that the formula used for that was

$$=SUM(A1,B1,C1)$$

You can also double-click into the cell with the formula or into the formula bar and Excel will color code each cell reference within the formula and within the worksheet so that you can make sure that the right cells were referenced in the formula.

It's a little hard to see in print, but Cells A1, B1, and C1 are each shaded a different color which corresponds to the color they are in the formula bar. This makes it easy to see which cell is being used in which part of a formula. That becomes especially helpful when dealing with very complex formulas.

Be careful moving away from a cell that has a formula in it. The best bet is to exit the cell using Esc. Otherwise sometimes Excel will try to select a new range of cells to use in the formula instead of just leaving the cell. This is especially an issue when using the arrow keys.

When you exit a cell that contains a formula, the cell will return to showing the calculated value not the formula.

Basic Math Calculations

Now let's talk about how to perform some basic math calculations in Excel.

Addition

If you want to add two numerical values together in Excel, you can use the plus sign (+) to indicate addition.

Here I'm adding 2 to 3:

$$=2+3$$

If those values were already showing in other cells, let's say Cells A1 and B1, you could write the formula to reference those cells instead:

$$=A1+B1$$

If you use cell notation, like in the second example there, then any change you make to the values in Cells A1 and B1 will also change the result of your formula because your formula is no longer performing a fixed calculation, like 2+3, but is instead performing a conditional calculation based on what's in Cells A1 and B1.

If you have more than two numbers to add together you can keep using the plus sign, so:

$$=A1+B1+C1$$

would add the values in Cells A1, B1, and C1. But it's better at that point to use the SUM function which will add all values included in the function. So:

$$=SUM(A1:C1)$$

adds the values in Cells A1, B1, and C1 together.

$$=SUM(A:A)$$

adds all the values in Column A.

$$=SUM(1:1)$$

adds all the values in Row 1.

If you ever forget how to write a cell range or to refer to an entire column or row, just start your formula, like this:

$$=SUM($$

and then go select the cells you want. Excel will write the reference for you and then you just need to close out the function with the closing paren.

Subtraction

To subtract one number from another you use the minus (-) sign. There is no function that will make this one easier, because the order of the values matters. Two minus three is not the same as three minus two.

However, you can combine the minus sign with the SUM function. So:

$$=A1-SUM(B1:D1)$$

is the equivalent of

$$=A1-B1-C1-D1$$

Multiplication

To multiply numbers you can use the asterisk (*) sign. Or you can use the function PRODUCT. All of the following will get the same result:

$$=A1*B1$$

$$=PRODUCT(A1:B1)$$

$$=PRODUCT(A1,B1)$$

Division

To divide two numbers you use the forward slash (/). There is no corresponding function because, again, order matters. Two divided by three is not the same as three divided by two. So:

$$=A1/B1$$

is the value in Cell A1 divided by the value in Cell B1.

* * *

To summarize:

Calculation	Numeric Symbol	Function	Examples
Addition	+	SUM	=A1+A2 =SUM(A1:A2)
Subtraction	-		=A1-A2
Multiplication	*	PRODUCT	=A1*A2 =PRODUCT(A1,A2)
Division	/		=A1/A2

A Quick Tip

Often when I just need to see the sum of values in a range of cells, I won't even write a formula or function. I'll just select those cells and look in the bottom right corner of my workspace. By default Excel displays the average, count, and sum of a range of selected cells in the very bottom right corner of the workspace.

(You can right-click where the values are displayed and also choose to have it display minimum and maximum values.)

Where To Find Functions

To find the functions available in Excel, you can go to the Formulas tab. There is a section called Function Library that lists various categories of functions. Mine shows Recently Used, Financial, Logical, Text, Date & Time, Lookup & Reference, Math & Trig, and then there's a dropdown for More Functions that shows the categories Statistical, Engineering, Cube, Information, Compatibility, and Web.

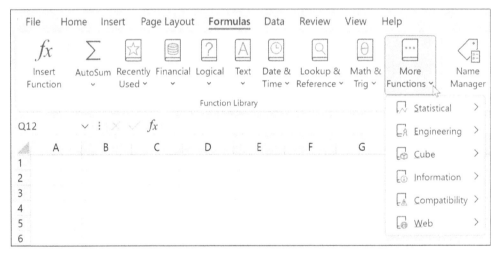

Click on the dropdown arrow under any of the categories and you'll see a listing of functions that fall under that heading. But, unless you know what you're looking for, that listing probably won't help you much because the functions are named things like ACCRINT and IFNA.

You *can* hold your cursor over each of the names and Excel *will* provide a brief description of the function for you, but for some of the lists that's a lot of functions to look through.

Each description also includes a Tell Me More at the end of the description. If you click on that option, the Excel Help task pane should appear. You can then click on the category for that function and choose the function from the list you see there to see further discussion of the function and examples of how to use it.

The level of detail provided varies by function. Sometimes it is very useful to read the Help section for a function and sometimes…it is not.

The approach I normally take instead is to click into the cell where I want to add my formula and then use the Insert Function option available on the far left-hand side of the Formulas tab.

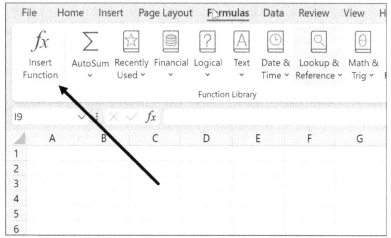

That brings up the Insert Function dialogue box.

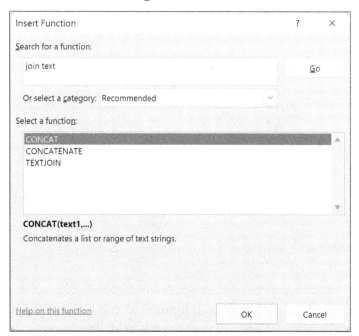

In the top section where it says "Search for a function" you can type what you're looking to do and then click on Go like I have above with "join text". (Be sure that the category dropdown right below the search box is set to All unless you know for sure what category your function falls under. After you click on Go that will turn into Recommended like it did in the image above.)

Excel will provide a list of functions that it thinks meet your search criteria. Sometimes this list is very far off, so don't just accept the first choice blindly.

You can left-click on each of the listed functions to see a brief description of the function directly below the box where the functions are listed. In the image above, that's showing for the CONCAT function.

You will also see in the description for each function a list of the required inputs for that function. For CONCAT that's at least one text entry.

If you need more information on a function, you can click on the "Help on this function" link in the bottom left corner of the dialogue box which will bring up help specific to that function.

Otherwise, you can just click on the function you want and choose OK, which will insert the function into whichever cell you were clicked into before you chose Insert Function. Excel will also open a Function Arguments dialogue box that lists the inputs your function needs and provides a location for you to input those values so that Excel can build your formula for you.

Here is the Function Arguments dialogue box for the TEXTJOIN function:

If you use the dialogue box, click into each input field and either input numeric values, cell references, or select the cells you want to use for each field. As you do so, Excel will show you a sample result based upon the inputs you've chosen at the bottom of the dialogue box next to Formula Result.

If you use the dialogue box, when you're done, click OK and the calculated value will appear in your cell.

If you don't want to use the dialogue box, close it out by clicking on OK and then OK on the error message that will appear.

This will give you the function in your cell in a formula format but without any of the required inputs, like so:

=TEXTJOIN()

Your cursor will be in the empty space between the opening and closing parens and you can then manually add the inputs at that point. Excel will show you which inputs are required and in which order.

If you X out the dialogue box instead, you'll just have a blank cell with no function or formula started.

* * *

That's about all I want to cover on how to write formulas and functions in this book. You can do a lot with basic addition, subtraction, multiplication, and division in Excel. And you now have an idea of where to look if you want to get fancier than that. And, of course, the third book in this series, *102 Useful Excel 365 Functions*, is almost two hundred pages long and covers over a hundred of the most useful functions in Excel.

But the other thing we need to cover when it comes to formulas is what makes them really powerful, and that's how you can copy formulas so that they apply to multiple cells.

Let's do that now.

Copying Formulas

The way in which formulas copy in Excel is key to what makes them so powerful. That's because you can write a formula once, copy it, and paste it to thousands of cells, and Excel will automatically adjust that formula to each new location

It's fantastic.

Let's say, for example, that I want to calculate total cost based upon units sold and price per unit for a thousand rows of data. Here are what the first few rows look like:

	A	B	C
1	Units	Cost Per Unit	Total Cost
2	2	$1.65	
3	4	$1.32	
4	3	$6.95	
5	6	$7.80	
6	9	$4.90	

I have units in Column A, cost per unit in Column B, and I want a total cost for each row in Column C.

The formula for Cell C2 in that first row is:

$$=A2*B2$$

Now, here's where the beauty of Excel comes in. I click on Cell C2 where I wrote that formula and then I double-left click in the bottom right corner of that cell and Excel copies my formula down for me.

(I could also use Ctrl + C, select the cell range and then use Ctrl + V or Enter to copy and paste my formula.)

Here's what I now have:

	A	B	C
1	Units	Cost Per Unit	Total Cost
2	2	$1.65	$3.29
3	4	$1.32	$5.28
4	3	$6.95	$20.84
5	6	$7.80	$46.81
6	9	$4.90	$44.11
7	3	$0.82	$2.47

Let's go to the Formula Auditing section of the Formulas tab and click on Show Formulas so we can see what Excel did for us.

	A	B	C
1	Units	Cost Per Unit	Total Cost
2	2	1.6452643749914	=A2*B2
3	4	1.3203471105506	=A3*B3
4	3	6.9475273087147	=A4*B4
5	6	7.80121230326684	=A5*B5
6	9	4.90149762880339	=A6*B6
7	3	0.824543582413774	=A7*B7

As Excel copied that first formula from Cell C2 down to Cells C3, C4, etc. it changed the formula. When the formula was copied one cell down from the original the cell references were updated to also reference cells one down.

So the original formula in Cell C2 used

$$=A2*B2$$

but when that was copied down to Cell C3 Excel changed that to

$$=A3*B3$$

Each cell reference in the formula adjusted relative to the original position.

Which is great for our thousand rows of data. It means we can write that formula once and copy it down and it works for all thousand rows of data.

Perfect.

But there are going to be times when you don't want Excel to adjust your formula for you. When that happens you need to either use fixed cell references or cut the formula and move it instead of copy and paste it. Let's start with fixed cell references.

Fixed Cell References

Let's take this scenario we've been working with and add a fixed 5% tax that needs to apply to every transaction. Here's our new data table:

	A	B	C	D	E	F	G	H
1	Units	Cost Per Unit	Total Cost	With Taxes		Tax Rate	5%	
2	2	$1.65	$3.29	$3.46				
3	4	$1.32	$5.28					
4	3	$6.95	$20.84					
5	6	$7.80	$46.81					
6	9	$4.90	$44.11					

Column D is calculating for that first transaction the total cost when we include a 5% tax. The formula is:

$$=C2*(1+G1)$$

where C2 is the cost before tax and G1 is the tax rate. If I copy that down to the other cells right now, Excel will adjust the cell references for both C2 and G1. I want it to do so for C2, but not for G1. I want every formula in my worksheet to continue to reference that tax rate in Cell G1.

To tell Excel to keep a cell reference fixed, I need to use dollar signs ($). That tells Excel, don't change this one. Keep it as is. And since I want to refer to that one specific cell, then the way to write that is:

$$=C2*(1+\$G\$1)$$

That means don't change the column or the row from G1 when you copy this.

Once I make that change to my formula, I can copy that formula down to all my other rows and have no issue.

	A	B	C	D	E	F	G
1	Units	Cost Per Unit	Total Cost	With Taxes		Tax Rate	0.05
2	2	1.6452643749914	=A2*B2	=C2*(1+$G$1)			
3	4	1.3203471105506	=A3*B3	=C3*(1+$G$1)			
4	3	6.9475273087147	=A4*B4	=C4*(1+$G$1)			
5	6	7.80121230326684	=A5*B5	=C5*(1+$G$1)			

Here you can see that I've double-clicked on Cell D4 to confirm that the formula is still referencing my tax rate in Cell G1. Perfect.

You can fix either the column reference for a cell, the row reference for a cell, or both. Just use the $ sign in front of whichever part of the cell reference you want to fix.

Moving a Formula

What happens if you're perfectly happy with a formula as written, but you just don't want it to display in the cell it's currently in? Sometimes, for example, I'll write a formula below a table of data and then later decide that I'd rather have all calculations off to the side of the table instead of below it.

I can't just copy that formula, because when I copy the formula and move it, all the cell references will change.

The way to get around this is to Cut the formula instead. So click on the original location, Ctrl + X, go to the new location, Ctrl + V. Esc. Or Ctrl + X, go to the new location, Enter.

If you just want the text of the formula as it exists right now but you don't want to move the original calculation, click on the cell, go to the formula bar, use Ctrl + A to select all of the text, use Ctrl + C to copy the selected text, Esc to exit that cell, click on the new location, and then use Ctrl + V to paste the text. (This is, for example, how I've copied the formulas into this book from the sample Excel worksheets where I wrote the formulas.)

* * *

Okay. Now that we've covered inputting your data and formulas, let's talk about how to make your data presentable. Because raw data in Excel is not pretty.

Formatting

If you're going to spend any amount of time working in Excel then you need to learn how to format cells, because inevitably your column won't be as wide as you want it to be or you'll want to have a cell with red-colored text or to use bolding or italics or something that isn't Excel's default.

That's what this section is for. It's an alphabetical listing of different things you might want to do to format your data in Excel.

You can either format one cell at a time by highlighting that specific cell, or you can format multiple cells at once by highlighting all of them and then choosing your formatting option. In some cases, you can also format specific text within a cell by clicking into a cell, selecting that text, and then choosing your formatting option.

There are basically four main ways to format cells or text in current versions of Excel.

First, you can use the Home tab and click on the option you want from there.

Second, you can use the Format Cells dialogue box. Either right-click from the main workspace and select the Format Cells option from the dropdown menu or use Ctrl + 1 to open the dialogue box.

Third, you can right-click from the main workspace and use the mini formatting menu that appears above or below the dropdown menu.

Finally, some of the most popular formatting options can be applied using control shortcuts. For example, Ctrl + B to bold text, Ctrl + I to apply italics, and Ctrl + U to apply a basic underline.

Okay, let's dive right in.

Align Text

By default, text within a cell is left-aligned and bottom-aligned. This won't be noticeable at the default row height and column width, but is definitely noticeable if you change either of those enough.

The easiest way to apply alignment to a cell is to go to the Alignment section on the Home tab. There are two rows of lines there on the left-hand side that visually show your choices. The top row contains Top, Middle, and Bottom alignment choices. The second row contains Left, Center, and Right. You can choose one option from each row.

In the screenshot below I've clicked on Cell B2 where I've chosen Middle Align and Center. You can see those options selected in the Alignment section of the Home tab.

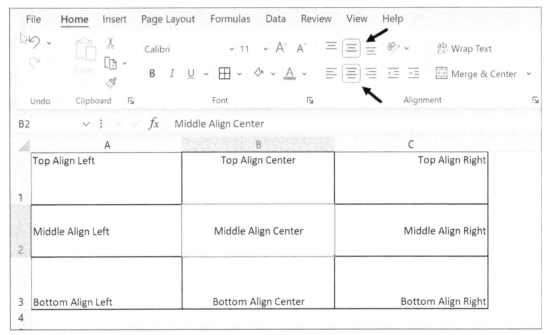

You can also see examples in Cells A1 through C3 in the screenshot above of all nine combinations.

The second-best choice for applying alignment is to use the Alignment tab of the Format Cells dialogue box. The Horizontal and Vertical alignment dropdown menus will give you the same choices as well as a few others that you're unlikely to use.

The mini formatting bar includes an option for centering your text, but that's the only alignment option it includes.

Angle Text

You can choose to angle your text in various ways using the dropdown menu under the angled "ab" with an arrow under it on the top row of the Alignment section of the Home tab.

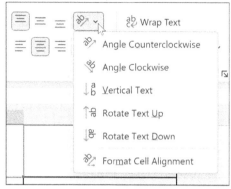

It has a handful of pre-defined options for changing the direction of text within a cell. You can choose Angle Counterclockwise, Angle Clockwise, Vertical Text, Rotate Text Up, and Rotate Text Down.

(It also offers another way to access the Alignment tab of the Format Cells dialogue box by clicking on Format Cell Alignment at the bottom of that dropdown menu.)

The Format Cells dialogue box lets you specify an exact degree for angling your text. So if you want to angle text at say a 30 degree angle, you'd need to do that in the Format Cells dialogue box. You can either enter that value in the Degrees field or click on a point in the Orientation box.

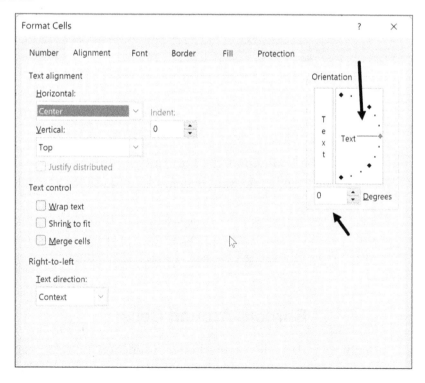

Bold Text

You can bold text in a number of ways. For each option below, select the text within a cell that you want to bold or the entire cell or cells first.

My default is to use Ctrl + B.

Another quick option is to click on the large capital B in the Font section of the Home tab.

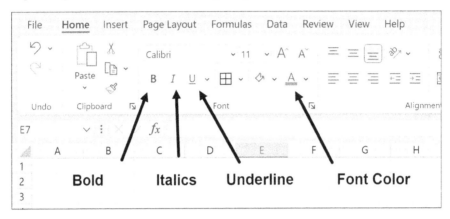

Or you can choose the capital B from the mini formatting toolbar.

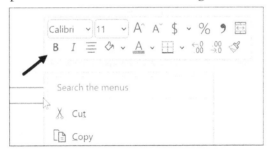

Your final option is to go to the Font tab of the Format Cells dialogue box and choose Bold from the Font Style options listing. If you want text that is both bolded and italicized, choose Bold Italic.

To remove bolding, you use the same options again (Ctrl + B or click on the capital B). If the selected text is only partially bolded when you do so, Excel will bold everything first so you'll have to do it twice. You can also go to the Format Cells dialogue box and change the Font Style to Regular.

Borders Around Cells

Placing borders around your data allows for better distinction between each cell and is something I do almost always when I create a data table. It's also very helpful when you print data from Excel, because that background grid that you see when working in Excel isn't actually present when you print.

Let me show you.

Here are those alignment choices pictured above as seen in Excel with no border around the individual cells. You can see that there is a faint line around each cell, right?

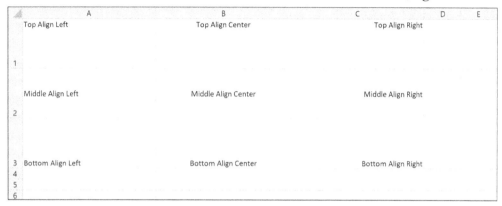

Here is the print preview of the first two columns of that image:

Top Align Left	Top Align Center
Middle Align Left	Middle Align Center

Note how the borders are no longer showing on the page? That's because the default cell borders that you see when working in Excel do not print. You have to add your own borders if you want your data to print with borders around it.

For the final comparison, this is that same information in print preview with a border added:

Top Align Left	Top Align Center
Middle Align Left	Middle Align Center

(Print preview, which we'll discuss in the chapter on how to print, is the best way to see how your data will actually appear when printed without wasting paper actually printing the document.)

There are three main ways to add borders around a cell or set of cells.

The easiest is also the newest.

If all you want is a simple basic border around a range of cells, go to the Font section on the Home tab and click on the dropdown arrow for the Borders dropdown option. It's a four-square grid with an arrow next to it that's located between the U used for underlining and the color bucket used for filling a cell with color.

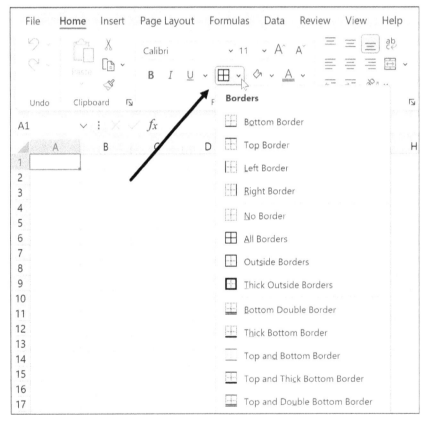

Go to the bottom of the dropdown menu and choose Draw Border Grid:

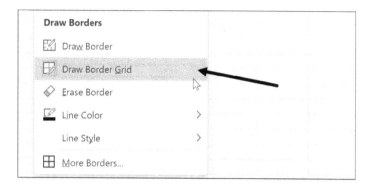

Click on it and then select the cells that you want to apply borders to.

Excel will apply the default line color and line style around all four edges of each cell you select. When you're done, use the Esc key to turn it off or click on the Border icon in the Font section of the Home tab.

For me, with the computer I'm working on and in Excel 365 as it exists in December 2022, the default line thickness isn't as dark as I would prefer it to be. I find myself wanting to change that line thickness to something I can see better on the screen.

But…

And here's where it gets weird, that line thickness is just fine in print preview. And when I choose the darker line that looks best to me on the screen, it's way too thick in print preview.

Now, I don't know if this is because of the computer I'm using which has better graphics than computers I've used in the past, or if this is part of the new streamlined appearance they rolled out with Office 2021.

But it's something to check on your own computer. Because if I were in an office environment where I was designing worksheets that others had to use and print, I'd need to be very careful that I didn't set the appearance of my worksheets to what I visually prefer since those settings will not print well.

Let me show you what I'm seeing. This is what the thick line option looks like on my worksheet:

Not bad, right? But this is what it looks like in print preview:

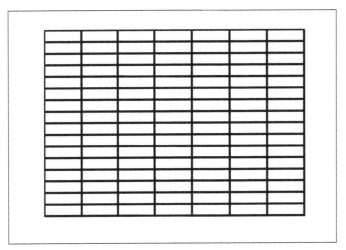

Horrible. That thick border is best for outlining a table, not for interior lines.

Which is all to say, if you're going to add borders to a document in Excel using Excel 2021 or Excel 365 and that document will be printed, be sure to look at that document in print preview before you print or provide it to others and adjust your borders accordingly.

Okay. Now, how do you adjust those lines from the default?

Go to the bottom of the Borders dropdown menu and choose one of the options from the Line Style secondary dropdown menu:

To change the line color, use the Line Color secondary dropdown menu.

The key, though, is that you need to change your line style or line color *before* you apply any borders to your cells.

That means since I don't like the default line style anymore that step one for me is to choose my line style from the dropdown. Step two is to then choose Draw Border Grid from the dropdown. Step three is to select the cells I want to add a border to. Step four is to hit Esc when I'm done.

Excel will keep that changed line style as the current default as long as that file is open.

If you have specific edges of cells where you want a border, you can use the Draw Border instead of the Draw Border Grid option. Simply select it and then click on the edge of a cell where you want to place a border line.

Draw Border when used on a range of cells at one time will apply a border around the perimeter of those selected cells but leave the inner cell borders alone.

So here, for example, I used Draw Border Grid with the default line style, highlighted my cells, and then changed the line style to the thickest option, chose Draw Border, and highlighted those exact same cells again.

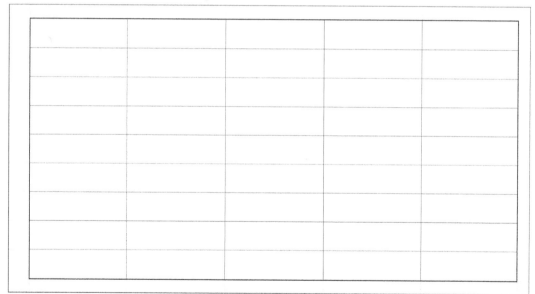

That combination gave me a table with interior lines that were thin and a dark exterior border.

Be sure each time that you choose Draw Border Grid or Draw Border that you see a pencil shape before you start highlighting your cells. There were a few times I clicked on that option and it didn't turn into the pencil for me so didn't work.

Also, hit Esc when you're done to turn off that pencil.

That is the easiest way I think to draw a table in current versions of Excel. But there are a couple other ways to do it.

That same Border dropdown menu has a number of choices at the top that you can use. With those options, though, you first need to select the cells you want to format and then choose the option you want from the dropdown.

All Borders is one I've used often as well as Thick Outside Borders. But if you use both together like I could have to create the table in the screenshot above, be sure to apply them in the right order. All Borders first, Thick Outside Borders second.

The other option for applying borders is to select your cells and then go to the Border tab of the Format Cells dialogue box either by clicking on More Borders at the bottom of the borders dropdown menu or by right-clicking on the selected cells and choosing Format Cells from that dropdown. Here is that Border tab:

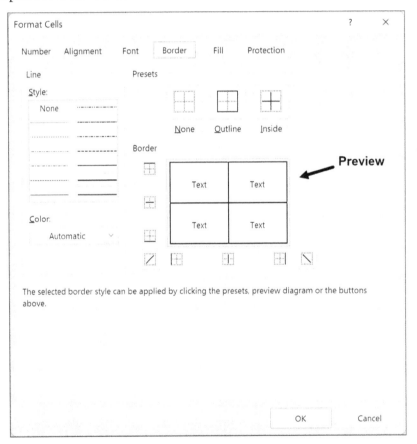

The image in the Border section of the dialogue box that shows four cells with Text in them, will show the current formatting for the selected cells.

To change that formatting, choose your line style and color on the left-hand side and then either click on the presets (none, outline, inside) above the preview or on the individual border thumbnails around the perimeter. You'll see the preview update as you click on each option.

The Format Cells dialogue box is the only way I know of to place a slanted line in a cell.

As I've done a few times in the examples above, you can combine different line styles and line colors in the same table. You just need to think through the order of applying them and make any color or line style choice first before trying to apply it to your entries.

Here is an example where I'm using three different line styles (thick, medium, and dotted line) as well as two line colors. Each of those had to be applied separately with changes to the style and/or color made before I chose the line position.

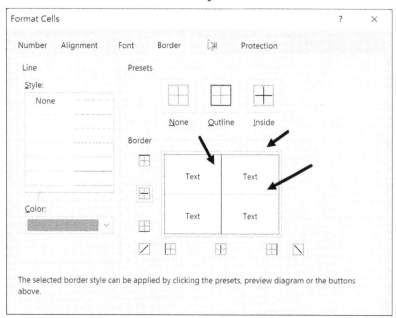

If you're in the Format Cells dialogue box and want to clear what you've done and start over, you can select None from the Presets section. The corresponding option in the dropdown menu is No Border. This does not, however, reset your line style and color choices, so if you changed those you'll need to manually change them back before you draw new borders in that worksheet. (Or close the worksheet and reopen it to reset to the default choices if you're not sure what they are.)

Color a Cell (Fill Color)

You can color (or fill) an entire cell with any color you want. I do this often when building tables. I will add fill color to the header rows of my tables and also to any columns that are either labels or non-input columns.

Like here with this example of the MAXIFS function where the header rows in each table have a green fill color, the cells with calculated results have a gray fill color, and the cells with the text of the formulas used have a blue fill color.

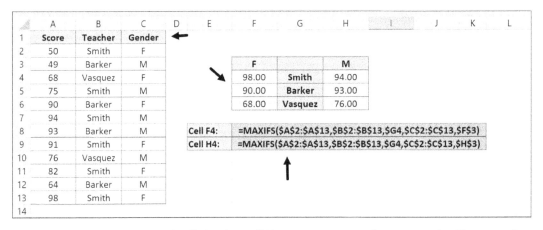

To add fill color to a cell(s), highlight the cell(s) you want to color, go to the Font section of the Home tab, and click on the arrow to the right of the paint bucket that by default has a yellow line under it.

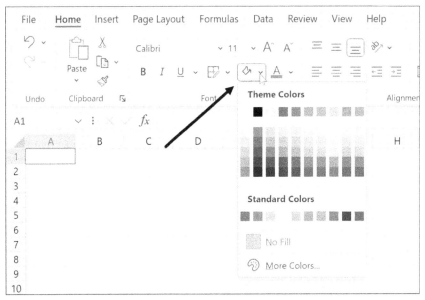

This should bring up a colors menu with 70 different colors to choose from, including many that are arranged as complementary themes. If you want one of those colors, just click on it.

(If you just wanted the default yellow color you could click on the paint bucket image without needing to bring up the dropdown menu. After you choose a color that option will change to show the last color used, so you can always click on the image to apply whatever color is shown without needing to use the dropdown menu.)

For more color options or to specify a specific color, click on More Colors at the bottom of the dropdown menu to bring up the Colors dialogue box.

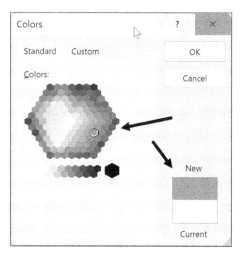
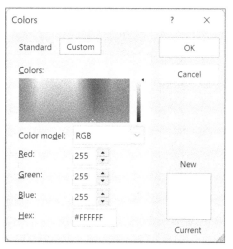

The first tab of that box, Standard, has a honeycomb-like image in the center that includes a number of colors you can choose from by clicking into the honeycomb. Shades of black, white, or gray can be selected just below that.

When you select a color it will show in the bottom right corner in the top half of the rectangle there under the heading New.

The second tab is the Custom tab. Click on it and you'll see a rectangle with a rainbow of colors that you can click on to select a color.

It also allows you to enter specific RGB, HSL, or Hex code values to get the exact color you need. (If you have a corporate color palette, for example, they should give you the values for each of the corporate colors. At least my employers always have.)

RGB is the default option, but you can change that in the dropdown menu.

Or you can enter a specific Hex code at the bottom if you have that.

On the Custom tab, you can also use the arrow on the right-hand side to darken or lighten your color.

If you like your choice, click on OK. If you don't want to add color to a cell after all, choose Cancel.

If you add Fill Color to a cell and later want to remove it, select the cell, go back to the dropdown menu, and choose the No Fill option.

Column Width

If your columns aren't the width you want, you have three options for adjusting them.

First, you can right-click on the column and choose Column Width from the dropdown menu. When the box showing you the current column width appears, enter a new column width. (I don't use this one often because I'm not a good judge of how wide I need to make a column in terms of a specific numeric value.)

Second, you can place your cursor to the right side of the column name—it should look like a line with arrows on either side when you have it in the right spot—and then left-click and drag either to the right or left until the column is as wide as you want it to be.

Or, third, you can place your cursor on the right side of the column name and double left-click. This will make the column as wide or as narrow as the widest text currently in that column. (Usually. Sometimes this one has a mind of its own. But it almost always works with shorter text entries.)

To adjust all column widths in your document at once, you can highlight the entire worksheet (Ctrl + A or click in the top left corner) and then apply one of the above options. A double-left click on any column border will adjust each column to the contents in that column. (Usually. See comment above.) Manually adjusting the width of one column or setting a Column Width using the dropdown menu, will apply that width to all columns in the worksheet.

Currency Formatting

Currency has two main formatting options, Currency and Accounting, but there are a number of other choices available as well.

To format cells using one of the currency options, highlight the cell(s) you want formatted, and then go to the Number section of the Home tab, and either click on the $ sign (which will use the Accounting format) or click on the dropdown arrow for General and choose Currency or Accounting.

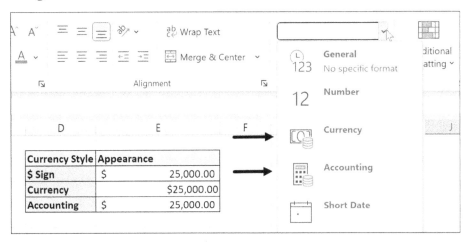

As you can see in the image above, the main difference between the two options is where they place the $ sign relative to the numbers. The Currency option places the $ sign right next to the number, the Accounting option left-aligns the $ sign and right-aligns the numbers.

The $ sign option in the Number section of the Home tab has a dropdown menu where you can choose other common currencies. Also, if you just want your currency to display as whole numbers you can click on the Decrease Decimal option twice, which is located in that same row.

If those options aren't enough for you, you can go to the Number tab of the Format Cells dialogue box and then either use the Currency or Accounting category:

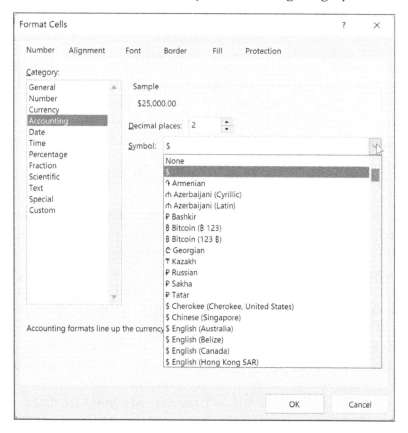

That gives a much larger range of currencies to choose from. The Currency category also includes multiple choices for how to distinguish negative values.

You can also use Ctrl + Shift + $ to apply the Currency format to a selected cell or range of cells.

Date Formatting

Not only does Excel sometimes like to format things as a date that aren't but it also sometimes has a mind of its own about how to format dates. Here are a few examples:

Input Value	Excel Default Displayed Result	Excel Short Date
3/6	6-Mar	3/6/2022
January	January	January
January 2020	Jan-20	1/1/2020
3/6/20	3/6/2020	3/6/2020

In the first column you can see the text I entered. In the second column you can see what Excel did with that text. The third column is the date, when applicable, that Excel assigned to what I'd entered.

So that first entry 3/6, Excel automatically interpreted as the date March 6th (for me, here in the United States with U.S. settings) but rewrote it as 6-Mar and added the current year to the date, which was 2022 when I was writing this so stored that date as March 6, 2022.

The second one, January, it left alone and did not turn into a date.

The third, January 2020, it converted into a date, rewrote as Jan-20, and stored as January 1, 2020.

The fourth, 3/6/20, it reformatted slightly, and treated as March 6, 2020. (Again, for me, here in the United States where month is written first.)

This demonstrates a key thing you need to remember about Excel and dates. It will always insist on having a month, day of the month, and year for every date. If you don't provide that, Excel will do it for you. And it is over-eager to turn anything that may possibly be a date into a date.

The other thing to know is that once Excel decides something is a date, you can't really change that with formatting. So with that first entry there I tried to change that to a Text format and it showed it as the number 44626 which is how Excel really stores dates behind the scenes. (As the 44,626th day since Excel's start date.)

Which means that if Excel ever turns an entry of yours into a date and you didn't want it to, the best thing is to Undo and then retype the entry using that single apostrophe at the start of the cell to keep Excel from converting the entry on you.

But let's say you did want that to be a date. How can you control the date format that Excel applies to your date?

Click on the cell with your date in it, go to the Number section of the Home tab, click on the dropdown menu which should show General by default, and then choose either Short Date or Long Date from there. You will be able to see examples of what that date will look like when chosen:

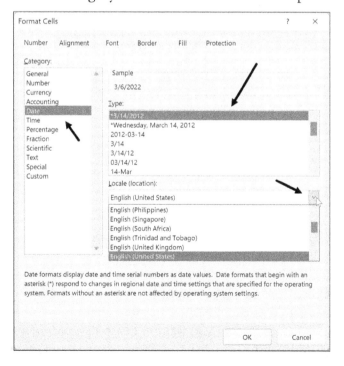

Usually, Short Date will be the one you want.

But if neither of those work for you, go to the Number tab of the Format Cells dialogue box, and click on the Date category. There will be about a dozen options to choose from there.

Note that there is also a Locale dropdown menu that lets you choose formats used in other countries. For example, here in the United States 3/6 is March 6th, but in many other parts of the world 3/6 is June 3rd, so if you're going to use that Short Date format understand that it is a regional format that may be misinterpreted by others on a printed document. (I believe Excel adjusts the display for the local country settings, so it won't be an issue when looking at the Excel file, but be careful there just in case.)

You can also use Ctrl + Shift + # to apply a date format that uses day, month, and year. For me the format was 2-Jan-20 for January 2, 2020.

Font Choice and Font Size

The current default font choice in Excel is Calibri and the default font size is 11 point.

You may have strong preferences about what font you use or work for a company that uses specific fonts for its brand or just want some variety in terms of font size or type within a specific document. In that case, you will need to change those settings.

There are a few ways to do this. Each requires selecting your text or cells first.

Once you've done that, option one is to go to the Font section on the Home tab and select a different font or font size from the dropdown menus there by clicking on the one you want.

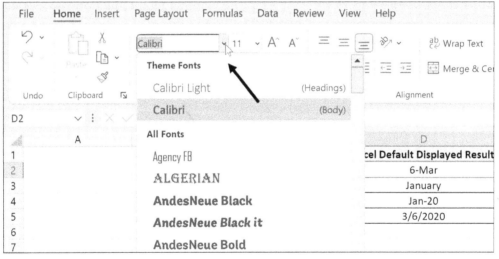

Which fonts are available in the font dropdown will depend on which fonts you have on your computer. Most people have a number of fonts already available. I have a large number of additional fonts so you may see different fonts listed there than I do.

Excel shows your theme font at the top and then the rest of your fonts are shown in alphabetical order below that. You can either use the scroll bar on the side to scroll down or you can start typing the name of the font you want to get to that part of the list.

Each font will display in the list using that font. You can see this in the screenshot above where Agency is a very different font from Andes Neue and Algerian.

The font size dropdown only has the most common sizes listed. It lists 8, 9, 10, 11, and 12 pt but then starts jumping up in numbers. If you have a specific font size you want that isn't listed, you can just type it in.

You also have the option to increase or decrease the font one listed size at a time by clicking on the A's with little arrows that are shown next to the font dropdown box. The bigger of the two, on the left, increases the font size. The smaller one decreases the font size.

All of these options are also available in the mini formatting menu if you right-click in the main workspace after selecting your cells.

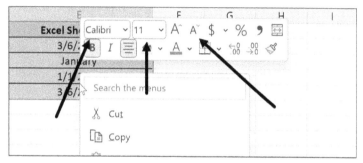

Your other option, which really doesn't give you any additional functionality, is to use the Font tab of the Format Cells dialogue box.

Font Color

The default color for all text in Excel is black, but you can change that if you want or need to. (For example, if you've filled a cell with a darker color you may want to change the font color to white to make the text in that cell more visible.)

You have three options. All require selecting the text or cells first.

After that, the first option is to go to the Font section on the Home tab and click on the arrow next to the A that by default will have a red line under it. (Or click on the A if you want the color shown.)

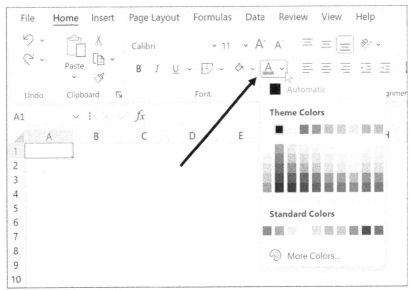

You can then choose from one of the 70 colors that are listed, and if those aren't enough of a choice you can click on More Colors and select your color from the Colors dialogue box. (See Coloring a Cell for more detail about that option.)

Second, you can use the mini formatting menu.

Third, you can use the Color dropdown in the Font tab of the Format Cells dialogue box.

Indent Text

If you want your text within your cell to be indented from the edge of the cell, you can increase the indent to make that happen by selecting the cell, going to the Alignment section of the Home tab, and clicking on the Increase Indent option that's located to the left of the Merge & Center option.

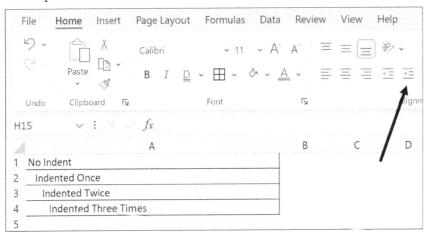

You can see how that would impact text placement in the screenshot above.

To decrease the indent, use the Decrease Indent option located to the left of the Increase Indent option.

You can also use the Indent field in the Alignment section of the Format Cells dialogue box. It will accept a whole number for the number of times to indent the text.

Italicize Text

To italicize text, highlight the text selection or cells containing text you want to italicize, and then use Ctrl + I or click on the slanted I in the Font section on the Home tab or in the mini formatting menu.

You can also change the Font Style option in the Font tab of the Format Cells dialogue box to Italic or Bold Italic.

To remove italics from text or cells that already have it, select that text and then use Ctrl + I or click on the slanted I in the Font section of the Home tab or the mini formatting menu. You may have to do this twice if you select text that is only partially italicized since Excel will apply italics to the entire selection first.

You can also remove italics by changing the Font Style back to Regular in the Format Cells dialogue box.

Merge & Center

Merge and Center is a specialized command that can come in handy when you're working with a table where you want a header that spans multiple columns of data. (Don't use it if you plan to do a lot of data analysis with what you've input into the worksheet because it will mess with your ability to filter, sort, or use pivot tables. It's really for creating a finalized, pretty-looking report.)

What it does is merges the cells you select and then centers your text across those merged cells.

You can merge cells across columns and down rows. So you could, for example, merge four cells that span two columns and two rows into one big cell while keeping all of the other cells in those columns and rows separate. But what I usually am doing is just merging X number of cells in a single row.

If you're going to merge and center cells that contain text, make sure that the text you want to keep is in the top-most and left-most of the cells you plan to merge and center. Data in the other cells that are being merged will be deleted. (You'll get a warning message to this effect if you have values in any of the other cells.)

To use this option, first select all of the cells you want to merge.

Next, go to the Alignment section of the Home tab and choose Merge & Center. This will combine your selected cells into one cell and center the contents from that left-uppermost cell across the selection.

Like so:

In the screenshot above I've merged and centered the text "House Sale Price" across Columns C through G in Row 2. I've also merged and centered the text "Commission to Realtor" across Rows 4 through 7 in Column A. (You'll note that I also changed the alignment of the commission text.)

That is the option I use most often, but there are additional choices available if you click on the dropdown arrow for Merge & Center. You can also choose to Merge Across (which will merge the cells in each row of the selected range separately and will not center the text) or to Merge Cells (which will merge all of the selected cells but won't center the text).

If you ever need to unmerge merged cells you can do so by selecting those cells and then clicking on the Unmerge Cells option from that dropdown.

You can also merge or unmerge cells by using the Merge Cells checkbox in the Alignment tab of the Format Cells dialogue box.

Merge & Center is also an option in the mini formatting menu. It's located in the top right corner of the menu. Clicking on it for previously merged cells will unmerge those cells.

Number Formatting

In addition to date and currency formatting, which we already discussed, you can apply other basic number formatting to your cells.

The first option is to use the Number section of the Home tab. The second option is to use the mini formatting menu. And the final option is to use the Format Cells dialogue box.

There are three default number styles in the dropdown menu on the Home tab that you may want to consider. If you already have values entered, the dropdown menu will show you a sample of how each one will look.

Here, for example, I used 10000 as my entry and you can see how General, Number, and Scientific would display that number:

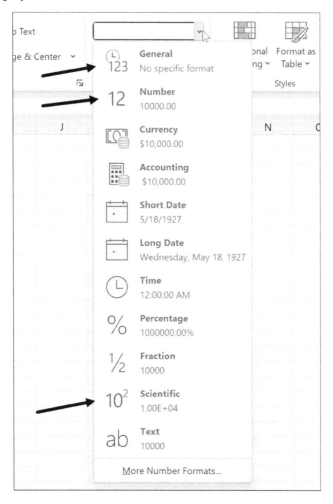

I often prefer to use the Comma Style option that's available below the dropdown and is just shown as a big comma because that one includes a comma for thousands where Number does not:

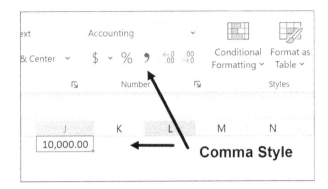

It is also available in the mini formatting menu.

Ctrl + Shift + exclamation mark (!) will give a similar but not identical result to the Comma Style option. (The spacing within the cell is different.)

And, as with all other number formatting options, there is a more detailed option in the Number section of the Format Cells dialogue box, in this case using the Number category.

You can also use the Increase and Decrease Decimal options in the Number section of the Home tab or in the mini formatting menu to change the number of decimal places for your values, just be sure to do that after you've applied your number format, not before.

Percent Formatting

To format numbers as a percentage, your first option is to highlight the cell(s), and click on the percent sign in the Number section of the Home tab or the mini formatting menu. This will convert the value to a percent with no decimal places.

Your second option is to use the dropdown menu in the Number section of the Home tab and choose Percentage from there. This will format the value as a percentage, but also include two decimal places.

Your final option is to use the Percentage category in the Number tab of the Format Cells dialogue box which will let you specify the number of decimal places to use.

With any of the above options, be sure that your numbers are formatted correctly or it won't work properly. In other words, 0.5 will translate to 50% but 50 will translate to 5000% so you want your entries pre-formatting to be .5 not 50 if you're looking for 50%.

(You can fix this by dividing those entries by 100, copying that result, and then pasting special values over the original values.)

Row Height

If your rows aren't the correct height, you have three options for adjusting them.

First, you can right-click on the row you want to adjust, choose Row Height from the dropdown menu, and when the box showing you the current row height appears, enter a new row height.

Second, you can place your cursor along the lower border of the row number for the row you want to adjust until it looks like a line with arrows above and below. Left-click and hold while you move the cursor up or down until the row is as tall as you want it to be.

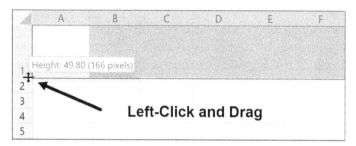

Third, you can place your cursor along the lower border of the row, and double left-click. This will fit the row height to the text in the cell. (Usually. Sometimes in the past it would not work with really large amounts of text and the only option was to manually resize the row height.)

To adjust all row heights in your document at once, highlight the entire worksheet (Ctrl + A or click in the top left corner) first and then use one of the options above. Entering a specific row height or clicking and dragging will keep all rows the same height. Double-left-clicking will resize each row to its contents. (Theoretically.)

Underline Text

Underlining text works much the same way that bolding and italics work.

For a basic single-line underline select the text or cells with text that you want to underline and then use Ctrl + U or click on the underlined U in the Font section of the Home tab.

You can also use the Underline dropdown in the Font section of the Format Cells dialogue box.

There are other underline types such as a double underline. For that, use the dropdown arrow next to the underlined U in the Font section of the Home tab or choose one of the options in the Format Cells dialogue box which includes single accounting and double accounting options as well.

To remove underlining from text or cells that already have it, highlight the text and then use one of the above options again. If you applied a special underline type, then using Ctrl + U or clicking on the underlined U in the Font section will first change the underline to a single underline, so you have to do it twice to completely remove the underline.

Wrap Text

Wrap text is an essential one to learn if you want to use text in your worksheet and be able to see all of the text in that worksheet without expanding the width of your columns to make that happen.

To Wrap Text in a cell, select the cell(s), go to the Alignment section of the Home Tab, and click on the Wrap Text option in the top row.

Or you can go to the Alignment tab in the Format Cells dialogue box and check the box for Wrap Text in the Text Control section.

Here is an example of a FINRA regulation in the left-most column and then an analysis column next to it. The content of the cells in Rows 1 through 3 are the same as those in Rows 6 through 8. In Column A, Rows 2 and 3 did not wrap the text but Rows 7 and 8 did.

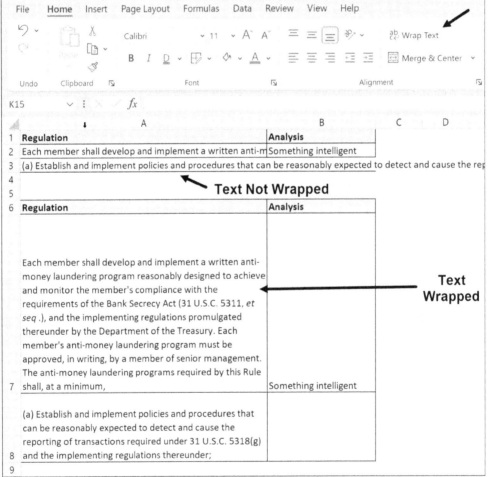

Note a few things. In the example at the top where the text is not wrapped, the text stops at the next column when there is content in that next column. You can see that in Cell A2. But when there isn't text in that next column, the text is visible on the screen. You can see that in Cell A3.

But when text is wrapped, like in Cells A7 and A8, the text moves to a new line when it reaches the border with the next column and as long as the row height is high enough, you can see the full text in that cell, regardless of what text may or may not be in any other column.

It also just looks much better when it's contained to the cell it belongs to.

(Excel does seem to have a maximum row height which will limit the amount of text you can display in one cell, so if you have any cells with lots of text in them, check to make sure that the full contents of the cell are actually visible. You may have to manually adjust the row height or it just may not be possible to see all of the text.)

* * *

Okay. That was our alphabetical discussion of the various formatting options, but before we move on to sorting and filtering, I wanted to cover a couple more formatting tricks.

Copy Formatting From One Cell To Another

I find this one incredibly useful, although I use it more in Word than in Excel.

If you already have a cell formatted the way you want it, you can use the Format Painter located in the Clipboard section of the Home tab to sweep the formatting from that cell to other cells you want formatted the same way.

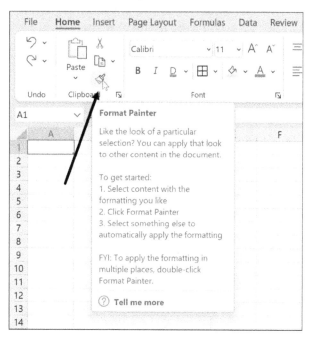

The help text sort of says it all.

First, select the cell(s) that have the formatting you want to copy (if the formatting is identical, just highlight one cell).

Next, click on the Format Painter. Double-click if you have more than one place you want to apply that formatting.

Finally, click into the cell(s) you want to copy the formatting to.

The contents in the destination cell will remain the same, but the font, font color, font size, cell borders, italics/bolding/underlining, and text alignment and orientation will all change to match that of the cell that you swept the formatting from.

If you double-clicked, use Esc or click on the Format Painter again to turn it off when you're done.

You can also find the Format Painter tool in the mini formatting menu.

You need to be careful using the Format Painter because it will change all formatting in your destination cells. So, if the cell you're copying the formatting from is bolded and has red text, both of those attributes will copy over even if all you were trying to do was copy the bold formatting. (This is more of a problem when using the tool in Word than in Excel, but it's still something to watch out for especially if you have borders around cells.)

Also, the tool copies formatting to whatever cell you select next, which can be a problem if the cell you're copying from isn't next to the one you're copying to. DO NOT use arrow keys to navigate between the cells. You need to click directly on the cell you're transferring the formatting to.

Remember, Ctrl + Z is your friend if you make a mistake. But if you format sweep and then undo, you'll see that the cell(s) you were trying to format from are surrounded by a dotted border as if you had copied the cells. Be sure to hit the Esc key before you continue to turn that off.

Clear Formatting

I don't use this often, but it can be handy if I had a lot of formatting in a worksheet and deleted the contents but the formatting is still there and I don't want it anymore.

To clear formatting, select the cells where you want to do this (or the entire worksheet with Ctrl + A), and then go to the Editing section of the Home tab and click on the dropdown arrow under Clear.

The Clear Formats option will remove all formatting from the selected cells. Clear All will remove contents and formatting at the same time.

* * *

Okay, that was formatting. We have three more topics to go: Sorting, Filtering, and Printing. And then we're done with this introduction. Yay. The end is in sight.

Sorting and Filtering

Two of the most common and basic ways I analyze or use data in Excel is by sorting or filtering. (The other option I use frequently is PivotTables, which are covered in the next book in this series.)

Sorting

Sorting allows you to display your information in a specific order. For example, by date, value, or alphabetically. You can also sort across multiple columns, so you can, for example, sort first by date, then by name, then by amount.

To sort your data, select the data, including your header row if there is one, and all columns of related information.

And do be sure that you select *all* columns of your data. Because this is one of those areas where if you choose the first five columns out of ten and sort those five, there's no way to return things to an order that matches those five columns that were sorted with the ones that weren't.

So you have to be a little careful here because sorting is one of the ways to irretrievably break a data set.

If you set your data up with the first row as the header and all of the rest as data with no subtotals or grand totals, the best thing to do is just use Ctrl + A or click in the top left corner of your worksheet to select all of the cells in the worksheet. Excel will then figure out the limits of your data from there.

If you have a table of data that starts lower down on the page or that has a summary row or that is followed by other data, be sure to only select the cells in the data set that you want to sort, because Excel will sort everything you select whether it makes sense to do so or not.

(I often mess this up and end up sorting my data so that my summary row is included, for example, so instead of seeing my best-selling title at the top I see a value for all sales of all books instead. It's not the end of the world if that happens, but it is mildly annoying and something to fix before anyone else sees your data.)

Once you've selected your data, go to the Editing section of the Home tab. Click on the arrow next to Sort & Filter, and choose Custom Sort.

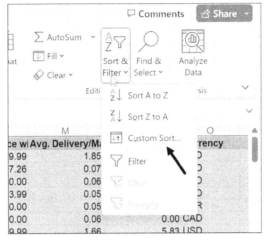

(The Sort A to Z and Sort Z to A options are ones I try not to use simply because that gives a little too much control to Excel about how it sorts the data. It seems to default to sorting by values in the first column when you choose that option, but I'm not always clear on where it goes from there and I've had it not work for me. Also, I often am not interested in sorting by the first column, so I just default to Custom Sort from the beginning. Less thought required.)

You can also go to the Sort & Filter section of the Data tab and click on the Sort option there. That's the one I tend to use.

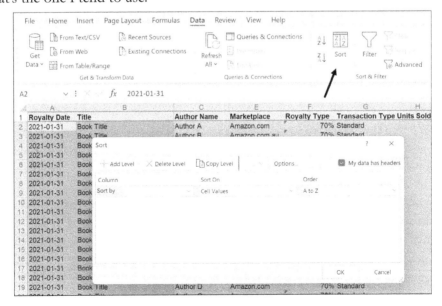

Either option will open the Sort dialogue box that you can see in the screenshot above.

The first thing you need to do is tell Excel whether or not your data has headers. It will guess the answer, but review to make sure it got it right.

If your data does have headers that box in the top corner that says, "My data has headers" should be checked.

If you indicate that there is a header row, it will not be included in your sort and will remain the first row of your data. Also, the Sort By dropdown will use the text in that first row for the dropdown menu choices. Like so:

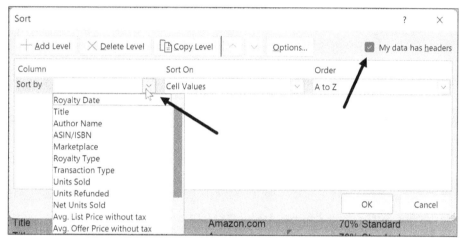

If you don't have a header row, the listed field name choices for Sort By will be the generic column names (Column A, Column B, etc.) and all of your selected data will be sorted, including the first row. Which makes sense to have happen if, for example, you are sorting a subset of your data.

When might you do this?

I have a worksheet that tracks my advertising spend where I need to do this because when I input the advertising spend I just do it in the order it's shown on my reports. However, when I'm matching that spend up to sales to see if my ads were profitable it's easier to do that if I sort alphabetically by title. But I only want to do that for the current month. That worksheet tracks advertising spend back to 2013. I only select the rows for the current month and then sort by title.

So it can happen that you don't have a header row to include for your sort.

The next step is to choose your sort order.

Decide what the primary criteria you want to sort by is and then choose that column from the Sort By dropdown menu.

After you've done that, choose what to sort on for that sort option. For a basic sort, like mine above where I want to sort by title, you'll generally leave this alone because you want to sort by the values in each cell.

There are also options to sort by cell color, font color, and conditional formatting icon which will only be useful to you if you've manually applied color to certain entries or used conditional formatting to do so. (Conditional formatting is covered in the next book in this series.)

Finally, you have to specify the Order that will be used for your sort. The choices there are going to depend on the type of data.

For text use A to Z to sort alphabetical or Z to A to sort reverse alphabetical. I also sometimes use the Custom List option when I have a column with the months of the year or the days of the week in it because Excel already has those set up.

For numbers it's Smallest to Largest or Largest to Smallest.

For dates it's Oldest to Newest or Newest to Oldest.

The default choices are A to Z, Smallest to Largest, and Oldest to Newest. But if you want to use a different option you can change this using the dropdown arrow.

If all you want is to sort by one column, then you're done. Click OK and Excel will sort your data.

If you want to then sort by another column, you need to add that second column to the Sort dialogue box.

(For example, maybe you sort first by year, then month, then Customer so that all of the sales for a particular month are grouped together and then within that month the information is sorted by customer name.)

To add a second sort level, click on Add Level and select your next column to sort by and your criteria for that sort.

Here for example, I have four total sort levels:

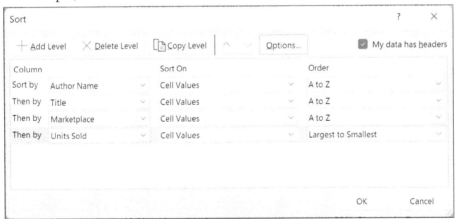

The data will first be sorted by author name, then by title, then by marketplace, and finally by units sold in reverse order from largest to smallest.

If you add a level you don't need, like I just did here with units sold which should only have one value per marketplace, title, and author, click on it and then choose Delete Level from the top of the dialogue box.

Also, if you have multiple levels but decide that they should be sorted in a different order, you can use the arrows at the top to move the selected sort level up or down.

The default for sort is to sort top to bottom, so down a column, but you can click on Options to sort left to right or to make your sort case-sensitive. (Something I rarely need, but have used once or twice.)

If you change your mind about sorting your data, click Cancel or the X in the top right corner of the dialogue box. Otherwise, when you're done with your sort options, click OK and Excel will sort your data.

If you get a sort that has a mistake in it, use Ctrl + Z to undo and try again. Don't try to fix a bad sort, just undo it and start over.

Filtering

The other thing I do often is filter my data. Sometimes I just want to look at a quick subset of a data table. For example, all of the sales for Author A. The data in the table is just fine, I don't need to summarize it in any way, I just want the rest of the entries hidden while I look at that subset.

Filtering allows you to do that as long as your data is set up the right way. (Ideally, a header row at the top, rows of data below, no subtotals or blank lines or blank columns.)

To turn on filtering for your data table, the first step is to click on any cell in the first row of the table and then go to the Editing section of the Home tab, click on the arrow next to Sort & Filter, and choose Filter.

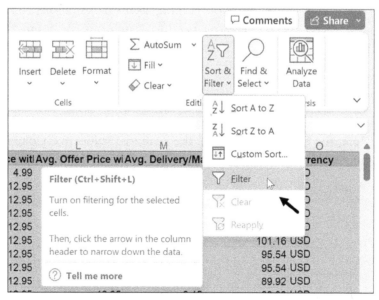

You can also click on Filter from the Sort & Filter section of the Data tab.

(It's possible that Excel will now appropriately apply filtering as long as you've clicked on any cell in the data table or selected the whole worksheet even if you don't click in a cell in the first row of the data table, but in older versions of Excel this could be an issue so I still as a best practice try to click on a cell in the header row before I apply filtering.)

Once filtering has been applied, you should see little arrows in the bottom right corner of each cell in that first row of the data table. If there was a gap in the columns in the table, only the columns on that side of the table will have the filter option. Like here:

F	G	H	I	J	K	L
Royalty Typ	Transaction Ty	Units Sold			Avg. List Price witl	Avg. Offer Price wi
70%	Free - Price Match	65			4.99	0.00
60%	Standard - Paperba	21			12.95	12.95
60%	Standard - Paperba	21			12.95	12.95
60%	Standard - Paperba	19			12.95	12.95
60%	Standard - Paperba	18			12.95	12.95
60%	Standard - Paperba	18			12.95	12.95

I clicked into Cell H1 before I turned on filtering. So all of the columns on that side of the gap have a filter option now. But see that Cells K1 and L1 do not, because Excel doesn't see them as part of the same data table due to that gap.

You can overcome this by selecting the entire worksheet before you apply filtering. If you do that, Excel will apply a filter option to every column in that first row, up to the point where the last column with text is.

From here on out, I'm going to talk about filtering as it exists in Excel 365 as of December 2022. This is one of those areas where you need to watch out for compatibility with older Excel versions. If you are working with someone who has an older version of Excel, I highly recommend that you never share with them a file that has filtering already applied, because there are types of filtering you can do now that you could not do in the past.

Okay, then.

If you click on the arrow for any given column, you should see a list of all potential values in that column. Here, for example, are all of the potential values for Column C in this data table, which contains author names.

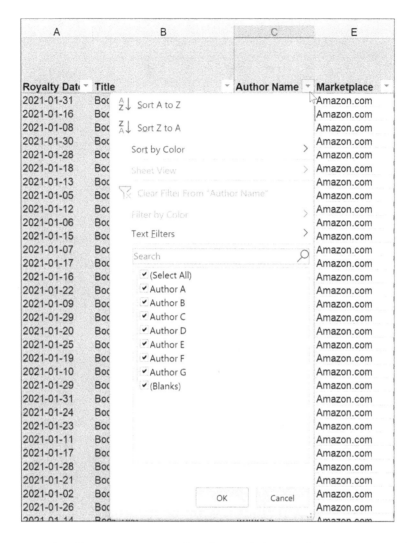

Note that there are checkboxes next to each value and that by default they are all checked.

For really long data sets (tens of thousands of rows) that have a lot of potential values this may not be a complete listing. (It definitely wasn't in older versions of Excel.)

If there are any values you don't want displayed, you can simply uncheck the box next to that value. Usually I want just one out of that list or maybe a few. The easiest way to accomplish this is to click on the box next to Select All. That removes all of the checks for all of the entries. You can then go through and check the boxes for the ones you want to see.

Like here where I now am only going to see results for Author A:

If the list of potential values is really long, you can start to type the name of the value you want to filter by into the Search field to make it appear within the visible list of entries.

Another option is to use filter criteria to narrow down what information is displayed. Depending on the type of data you're filtering and how it's formatted, the option will say Number Filters, Text Filters, Date Filters, etc. In the image above the filter option is Text Filters. It's located directly above the Search field.

Click on the arrow next to the filter name to open a secondary dropdown menu with available choices.

You should see options like "Equals" or "Does Not Equal" or "Begins With" or "Between" etc. The options differ depending on the type of data.

You can use these filter criteria to select only the rows where those criteria are met. So, for example, if I only want to see entries where the number of units sold is greater than 5, I can choose the Greater Than option under Number Filters in the Units Sold column.

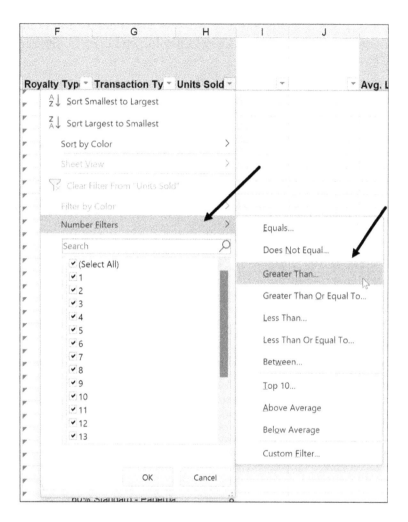

That brings up a dialogue box where I can enter my filter value and then click OK.

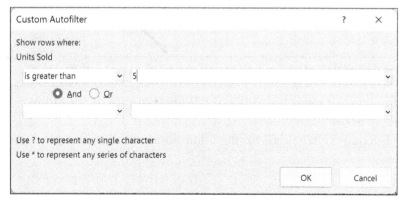

My data will now be filtered to only show those rows that meet the filter criteria I specified.

If you've color-coded cells using font color or cell color, you can also filter by those criteria, using the Filter by Color option.

When cells in your worksheet are filtered, the row numbers in your worksheet will be colored blue or aqua (depending on your theme settings), and you'll see that the row numbers skip since some rows are hidden.

	A	B	C	E
1	Royalty Date	Title	Author Name	Marketplace
3	2021-01-16	Book Title	Author A	Amazon.com
5	2021-01-30	Book Title	Author A	Amazon.com
7	2021-01-18	Book Title	Author A	Amazon.com
8	2021-01-13	Book Title	Author A	Amazon.com
9	2021-01-05	Book Title	Author A	Amazon.com
10	2021-01-12	Book Title	Author A	Amazon.com
11	2021-01-06	Book Title	Author A	Amazon.com

For example, in the screenshot above Rows 2, 4, and 6 have been filtered out. The numbers for Rows 3, 5, 7, etc. are blue.

Columns where filtering is in place will show a funnel instead of an arrow in the corner of the header row like you can see above for Royalty Date and Author Name.

To remove filtering from a specific column, click on that filter image, and select Clear Filter from [Column Name].

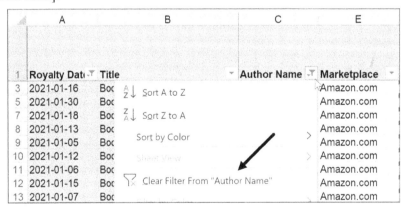

	A	B	C	E
1	Royalty Date	Title	Author Name	Marketplace
3	2021-01-16	Boo	A↓ Sort A to Z	Amazon.com
5	2021-01-30	Boo		Amazon.com
7	2021-01-18	Boo	Z↓ Sort Z to A	Amazon.com
8	2021-01-13	Boo		Amazon.com
9	2021-01-05	Boo	Sort by Color	Amazon.com
10	2021-01-12	Boo		Amazon.com
11	2021-01-06	Boo		Amazon.com
12	2021-01-15	Boo	Clear Filter From "Author Name"	Amazon.com
13	2021-01-07	Boo		Amazon.com

To remove all filtering in a worksheet, go to the Editing section of the Home tab, click on Sort & Filter, and then choose Clear.

To turn off filtering entirely, click on the Filter option in that dropdown once more.

Printing

Alright, so that was the basics of how to work with your data within Excel. But there are going to be times when you want to print your results. Excel can be especially problematic that way, simply because what looks good on the screen doesn't always print well.

Basic printing in Excel is as simple as going to File, Print, (or using Ctrl + P) and then clicking on the Print icon. But don't do that. Take a moment before you do that to check all of your settings and look at your print preview first.

Here is what the Print screen looks like:

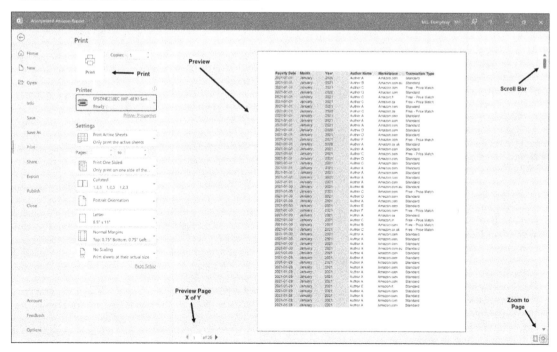

The image of a printer on the top under Print is what you ultimately will click on to print your document.

The preview in the right-hand side of the screen shows you what that document will look like when printed, page-by-page. You can see here how the first page of this document would look if I were to print it right now.

Down below that you can see what page this is and how many total pages will print. There are arrows there for moving between pages. You can also use the scroll bar on the right-hand side to move to the other pages.

In the bottom right corner are options to show margins and zoom to page. Zoom to Page can be useful if you can't read text or see what's on the page well and want to zoom in a bit. But generally I leave those alone.

Now let's look at the print options on the left-hand side:

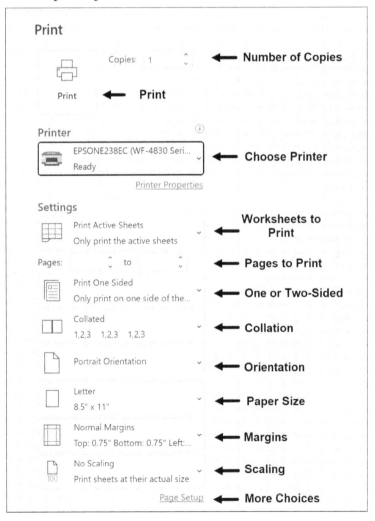

Print

Once you're ready to print your page, you can click on the button on the top left with the image of a printer that says Print to print your document.

Number of Copies

The Copies field is located to the right of the Print button. If you want to print more than one copy, change your number of copies in the Copies field using the up and down arrows or click into the field and type the desired number of copies.

Printer

This should display your computer's default printer, but if you want to use a different printer than that one or print to a PDF, click on the arrow next to the printer name and choose from the listed options. If the printer you want isn't listed, choose Add Printer from the dropdown menu and add the printer.

You generally won't need to click on that Printer Properties link that you can see below the dropdown.

Print Active Sheets / Print Entire Workbook / Print Selection

My version of Excel defaults to Print Active Sheets. This will generally be the worksheet you were working in when you chose to print.

However, you can select more than one worksheet by holding down the Control key and then clicking on another worksheet's name. When you do this, you'll see that the names of all of your selected worksheets are highlighted, not just one of them.

You can also right-click on a worksheet and choose Select All Sheets to select all of the worksheets in your workbook at once. (Be careful doing this because an edit to one worksheet will be an edit to all of them.)

I would only print multiple worksheets together if you're satisfied that each one is formatted the way you want it formatted already.

Also, choosing to print more than one sheet at a time either with Print Active Sheets or Print Entire Workbook, results in strange things happening to your headers and footers if you use those. For example, your page numbering will be across worksheets.

If you mean each worksheet to be a standalone report with numbered pages specific to that report, then you need to print each worksheet separately.

As I just alluded to, the Print Entire Workbook option prints all of the worksheets in your workbook.

Print Selection allows you to just print a highlighted section of a worksheet.

(Or worksheets. I happened to have three worksheets selected at once and when I highlighted the first twenty cells in one of those worksheets, the selection it was ready to print was those twenty cells in each of the three worksheets. So again, be careful that that makes sense to do.)

The dropdown also has an Ignore Print Area option which you could use if a worksheet has a print area set and you want to print everything on the worksheet not just the print area. (A print area lets you permanently specify which cells in a worksheet should be printed instead of the default of all cells with data in that worksheet.)

Pages

Just below the Print Active Sheets section is a row that says Pages and has two boxes with arrows at the side. Using this section, you can choose to just print a specific page or a subset of pages rather than the entire worksheet. To figure out which page(s) to print, look at the print preview.

For a single page use the same page number in both boxes. For a range of pages, put the first page of the range in the first box and the last page of the range in the second box.

In Excel you can only do a range of pages unlike Word where you can print a series of non-adjacent pages.

Changing the values in this section will NOT update your print preview.

Print One Sided / Print on Both Sides (long edge) / Print on Both Sides (short edge)

This option will only be available if you have a printer chosen that can do this.

The default is to just print on one side of the page. If you have a printer that can print on both sides of the page you can change your settings to do so either on the long edge or the short edge.

You generally will want the long edge option if your layout is going to be portrait style and the short edge option if your layout is going to be landscape style. (See below.)

Collated / Uncollated

This only matters if what you're printing has more than one page and if you're printing more than one copy.

In that case, you need to decide if you want to print one full copy at a time, x number of times, or if you want to print x copies of page 1 and then x copies of page 2 and then x copies of page 3 and so on until you've printed all pages of your document.

In general, I would choose collated, which is also the default, which prints one full copy at a time.

Portrait Orientation / Landscape Orientation

You can choose to print in either portrait orientation (with the short edge of the page on top) or landscape orientation (with the long edge of the page on top). You can see the difference in what will print on each page by changing the option in Excel and looking at your print preview.

Which option you choose will depend mostly on how many columns of data you have.

Assuming I'm dealing with a normal worksheet with rows of data across various columns, my goal is to fit all of my columns on one page if possible.

Sometimes changing the layout to landscape allows me to do that because it allows me to have more columns per page than I'd be able to fit in portrait mode.

If I have just a few columns of data, though, but with lots of rows I'll generally stick with portrait orientation instead.

You'll have to decide what works best for you, your specific data, and where the printed document will be used.

Letter / Legal / Statement / Etc.

This is where you select your paper type. Unless you're in an office or overseas, chances are you'll leave this exactly like it is. I'm sure my printer could print on legal paper, but I don't have any for it to use so it's a moot point for me.

In an office you may have the choice of standard paper, legal paper, and even other larger sizes than that. Just make sure whatever you choose is in fact an available option for you.

Normal Margins / Wide Margins / Narrow Margins / Custom Margins

I would expect you won't use this, but if you need to then this would be where you can change the margins on the document. The normal margins allow for .7" on each side and .75" on top and bottom. If you have a lot of columns and need just a little more room to fit it all on one page, you could use the narrow margin option which uses .25" margins on the left and right.

I generally use the scaling option to do this instead.

No Scaling / Fit Sheet on One Page / Fit All Columns on One Page / Fit All Rows on One Page / Custom Scaling

I use this option often when I have a situation where my columns are just a little bit too much to fit on the page or my rows go just a little bit beyond the page.

If you choose "Fit All Columns on One Page" that will make sure that all of your columns fit across the top of one page.

You might still have multiple pages because of the number of rows, but at least everything will fit across one page.

Of course, depending on how many columns you have, this might not be a good choice. Excel will make it fit, but it will do so by decreasing your font size. If you have too many columns you're trying to fit on one page your font size may become so small you can't read it.

So be sure to look at your preview before you print. (And use Landscape Orientation first if you can.)

Fit All Rows on One Page is good for if you have maybe one or two rows too many to naturally fit on the page.

Fit Sheet on One Page is a combination of fitting all columns and all rows onto one page. Again, Excel will do it if you ask it to, but with a large set of data you won't be able to read it, so be careful making this choice.

I usually end up going with Custom Scaling. If you click on that option it opens the Page Setup dialogue box to the Page tab where you can go to the Scaling section and choose to Fit To X pages by Y pages. So maybe I have a report that is five pages long right now with only one row on that last page. I can use scaling to make this 1 page wide by 4 pages long and that will bring that last row up onto my fourth page and give me a cleaner print out than if I just left it as is.

Same with if I have a report that is currently fifteen pages long because the last column extends to the next page so I have ten pages with most of my information spread across two pages wide and five pages long but then I have another five pages with just that last column. I can set this to 2 pages wide by 5 pages long and bring that last column onto the second page.

(If you need it, play around with the setting and you'll see how it can help.)

Page Setup

The Page Setup link at the very bottom gives you access to even more options through the Page Setup dialogue box. We just talked about custom scaling. This is another way to reach that setting. You can also:

1. Center Horizontally or Vertically

On the Margins tab there are two check boxes that let you center what you're printing either horizontally or vertically or both. I will often choose to center a smaller data table horizontally. If I don't do that, it tends to look off balance.

2. Header/Footer

If you want to set up a header and/or a footer for your printed document, you can do so here. The dropdown boxes that say (none) include a number of pre-formatted headers and footers for you to use.

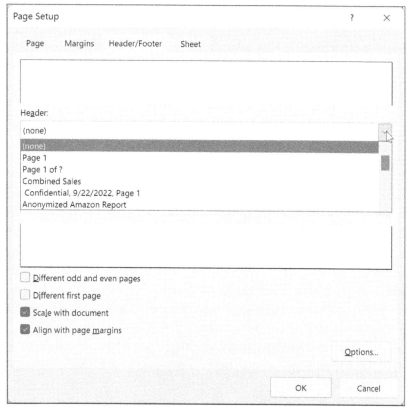

You can see here options for including the page number, worksheet name, and workbook name, for example. Each one shows an example of the actual text that will be included.

Not visible above, because the buttons are hidden behind the dropdown, are options for customizing the header and footer.

3. Sheet

The sheet tab has a couple of useful options, but I'm going to show you a different way to set these options because I find it easier to set them when I'm in the worksheet itself.

* * *

Page Layout Tab

If you exit out of the print option and go back to your worksheet, you'll see that one of the tabs you have available to use is called Page Layout. There are certain attributes that I set up here before I print my documents. Let's walk through them.

(First, though, note that you can change margins, orientation, and size here just as easily as in the print preview screen.)

1. Print Area

If you only want to print a portion of a worksheet, you can set that portion as your print area by highlighting it, and then clicking on the arrow next to Print Area and choosing Set Print Area.

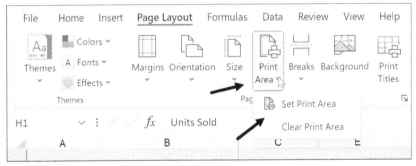

Only do it this way (as opposed to highlighting the section and choosing Print Selection) if it's a permanent setting.

Once you set your print area it will remain set until you clear it. You can add more data to your worksheet but it will never print until you change your print area, clear the setting, or deliberately override it when you choose to print.

I use this when I have a worksheet that has either a lot of extra information I don't want to print or where the formatting extends beyond my data and Excel keeps trying to print all those empty but formatted cells.

2. Breaks

You can set where a page break occurs in your worksheet. So say you have a worksheet that takes up four pages and you want to make sure that rows 1 through 10 are on a page together and then rows 11 through 20 are on a page together even though that's not how things would naturally fall. You can set a page break to force that to happen.

To insert a break, click on the cell where you want to insert the page break and then click on the dropdown for Breaks and choose Insert Page Break. You'll see a line appear on the worksheet to indicate where the page break is.

You can also use that dropdown to Reset All Page Breaks or remove a specific page break.

Personally, I find page breaks a challenge to work with, so I usually try to get what I need some other way.

3. Print Titles

This one is incredibly valuable. When you click on it, you'll see that it brings up the Page Setup box and takes you to the Sheet tab.

The first valuable thing you can do here is set the rows you want to repeat at the top of the page.

Say you have a worksheet with a thousand rows of data in it that will print on a hundred pages. How do you know what's in each column on each page? You need a header row. And you need that header row to repeat at the top of each and every page.

"Rows to repeat at top" is where you specify what row(s) is your header row. Click in that box and then select the row number(s) in your worksheet that you want to have repeat at the top of each page and Excel will write the cell notation for you. (This is why I do this in the worksheet itself instead of from the Print screen.)

The second valuable thing you can do here is set a column(s) you want to repeat on the left-hand side of each page. I need this one less often, but I do still sometimes use it.

Say, for example, that you had a list of students, one per row, and their test scores across fifty tests, and that when you printed that information it printed across two pages. Without listing the student's name in the left-hand column on every page, you wouldn't know whose scores you were looking at after the first page. But you can set that name column to repeat on each page.

To do so, click in the box that says "Columns to repeat at left", and then select the column(s) you want to repeat. Excel will once more write the cell notation you need for you in that field.

If you feel comfortable enough with cell notation you could do this from the print screen, but I never do.

You can repeat more than one row or column on each page, but if you do that, be careful that you don't end up selecting so many rows or columns to repeat that you basically just print the same thing over and over and over again. (Think of this as the printer equivalent of freeze panes if that helps.)

Okay. That's it. Let's wrap this up with a quick conclusion and then you're ready to dive in with using Excel.

Conclusion

As I explained at the beginning, this book was not meant to be comprehensive. Pick up one of the comprehensive books on Microsoft Excel and you'll see that it's two inches thick with small type.

Excel is insanely powerful, but most people don't need all of that. What I gave you here in this book is 95% of what you'll need day-to-day.

You can fill in the gaps as you go along using Excel's help function or online searches, or you can continue on with me in one of two directions if you want. (Or both, I won't mind.)

The next book in this series, *Intermediate Excel 365*, covers more advanced topics like pivot tables, charts, and conditional formatting that can be very valuable when analyzing data.

The other option is *102 Useful Excel 365 Functions*. That one covers exactly what you think it would: how to work with formulas and functions in Microsoft Excel. I've tried in that book to call out the functions I think are most useful. And I've mentioned a number of functions in passing that relate to those functions or are alternate versions of those functions.

For example, I talk about TEXTJOIN in there which allows you to join text strings. But I also cover the older functions that would let you do this, CONCATENATE and CONCAT.

But you don't have to stick with me and buy another book on these topics, because Excel has excellent help available. (The advantage my books give is they focus in specific areas and keep out the noise, so they provide a path to follow. But if you don't need the path, then you don't need a book. Anyway.)

You can open Help in Excel using F1. Or, as of now–this has changed over time–help is available by going to the Help tab at the top of the screen and then clicking on Help from there.

Either option in current versions of Excel will open a task pane on the right-hand side of the workspace that has a search bar as well as a number of help topics available.

I often find it easier to click on Tell Me More which is available when you hover over specific options, like here with Format Painter.

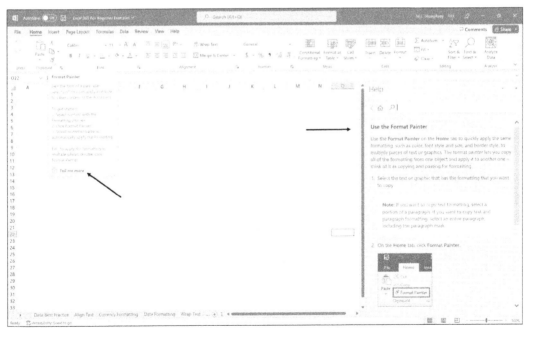

That always goes straight to the help topic for that particular option.

I will also often do a web search and then click on the link that goes to support.microsoft.com. So I might say, "microsoft excel copy formatting" and then click on the link that shows that it came from microsoft.

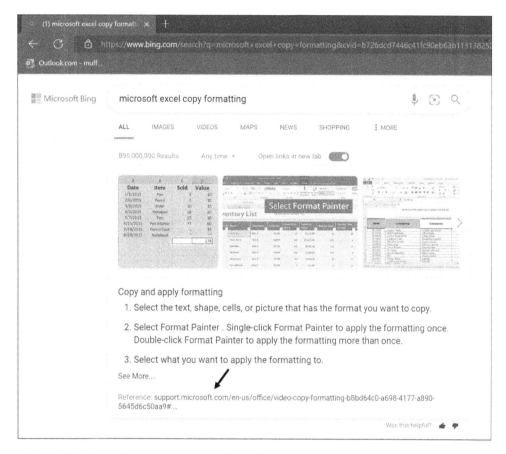

I've noticed in the last six months or so that at least the search engines I'm using give a fairly detailed preview of search results these days so that I don't even have to click through to a website sometimes to see the information I need. (Which is kind of crap for anyone who relies on ad revenue they generate from their website (which I don't), but that's the world for you. Always evolving, sometimes not in favor of the people who provide the value.)

Anyway. The Microsoft built-in help and website are both very good for when you need to know *how* to do something. "How do I copy an entry?", "How do I paste an entry?", "How does X function work?", etc.

For questions about "is this possible" they're less helpful. For that you either need to find someone who made a blog post or video doing what you want to do, or you need to wade into a tech forum somewhere and ask the experts how to do it.

You're always welcome to reach out to me with a question, too. Just know that if you start asking me to do your work for you, I'll quote you my (very expensive) consulting rates. I'm happy to clarify something or point you in the right direction, but "please build this complex calculation for me" is a step beyond that.

I will help with reasonable questions because I want you to understand this stuff, but also please respect that I can't do your work for you.

Also, know that there is no question that I will mock you for asking. I once had to train 90-year-old ladies on how to use a computer system so I know that people can be perfectly intelligent and simply struggle because something is new to them.

I try to keep in mind when I write these books what it's like to be new to Excel, but I sometimes miss something. For example, to click on the X in the top right corner to close things. Or to click on OK to be done with a dialogue box. These are things that are ingrained in me from decades of working with computers that I sometimes forget that other people don't know.

So ask what you need to ask because if I failed to teach you, that's on me.

Okay, that's it. I hope you now understand how powerful Excel can be. Don't be afraid to make mistakes. Ctrl + Z and Esc are you two best friends to get out of trouble. When all else fails, close the file without saving and come back to it.

If you're working with data for work maybe check out *How To Gather and Use Data for Business Analysis*, which is based on my lessons learned from working on data projects in a corporate setting. It talks about how to get data that you can effectively use for analysis.

If you want to understand how to apply basic math in Excel to budgeting then check out the *Juggling Your Finances: Basic Excel Guide*. It walks through Excel from the perspective of using addition, subtraction, multiplication, and division to calculate your basic financial status. (And is a companion to *Budgeting for Beginners* which explains how to use that information to improve your finances.)

You can find links to both of those at https://mlhumphrey.com/business-and-personal-finance/ and links to all of my Microsoft Office books (there are so many) at https://mlhumphrey.com/microsoft-office-all-links/.

And if there's something you need that I haven't written, let me know, I might write it. I wrote *Mail Merge for Beginners* because someone said they needed a book on that and I figured it was pretty easy for me to put it together for them.

Also if you tell me and I write it, chances are I'll send you a free ebook copy as a thank you. No guarantee I'll write it, but if I do…you get your question answered and I have another book out there that people may need. Win-win.

Okay. Good luck with it. Don't be scared. You can do this.

SHORTCUTS

The below tables contain various useful Excel shortcuts, most of which were discussed in the chapters of this book. The header row for each table shows which key to use and then the Task column tells you what that will accomplish. For example, Ctrl + N will open a new Excel file.

Ctrl +	Task
N	New File
O	Open File
S	Save File
C	Copy
V	Paste
X	Cut
Z	Undo
F	Open Find and Replace Dialogue Box to Find tab
A	Select All
P	Print
W	Close Current Workbook
B	Bold/Unbold Selected Text
I	Italicize/Remove Italics From Selected Text
U	Underline/Remove Underline From Selected Text
1	Open Format Cells Dialogue Box

Ctrl +	Task
End	Go to Last Column of Blank Worksheet OR Go to Last Column In Data Range OR Go to Next Column to the Right With Data
Home	Go to First Column of Blank Worksheet OR Go to First Column in Data Range OR Go to Next Column to the Left with Data
Down Arrow	Go to Last Row of Blank Worksheet OR Go to Last Row In Data Range OR Go to Next Row Down That Contains Data
Up Arrow	Go to First Row of Blank Worksheet OR Go to First Row In Data Range OR Go to Next Row Up That Contains Data
Right Arrow	Go to Last Column of Blank Worksheet OR Go to Last Column In Data Range OR Go to Next Column to the Right With Data
Left Arrow	Go to First Column of Blank Worksheet OR Go to First Column in Data Range OR Go to Next Column to the Left with Data

Alt +	Task
S	Refresh Pivot Table
H	Access Menu Options, Use Alt + Letter(s)/Number(s) to Select Task to Perform
Tab	Move Between Open Programs in Windows

Ctrl + Shift	Task
$	Format as Currency
#	Format as Date
!	Format as Number with Comma For Thousands
%	Format as Percent
Right Arrow	Select All Cells in Range To Right
Down Arrow	Select All Cells In Range Downward
Right and then Down Arrow	Select All Cells in Range Across and Down

Other	Task
Esc	Exit a Cell, Back Out of a Function, Close a Tool, General Escape Option
Tab	Move to the Right One Cell
Shift + Tab	Move to the Left One Cell
Windows Key + Ctrl + O	Open On-Screen Keyboard

PowerPoint 365 for Beginners

POWERPOINT 365 ESSENTIALS - BOOK 1

M.L. HUMPHREY

CONTENTS

CONTENTS (CONT.)

Introduction

PowerPoint is a great tool if you need to present information. And it's an essential tool to learn in a number of corporate environments. I'm almost twenty-five years into my corporate career and I've yet to work for an employer who didn't use PowerPoint. These days there are sometimes other, similar options available, but PowerPoint is still that gold-standard program.

And the nice thing about mastering PowerPoint is that most of the other programs out there are based upon the same principles and concepts, so master one, you're pretty close to understanding the others.

But before we get started, we need to discuss what this particular book covers and one little issue you need to keep in mind. This book is written using PowerPoint 365 as it existed in October 2023.

All Microsoft 365 programs are a bit of a moving target because they continuously update, so your version of 365 may differ slightly.

The basics tend to stay the same so it shouldn't prevent you from learning how to use PowerPoint, but there will be changes over time.

For example, I have a different recommendation in this book about using presentation themes than I did in the original *PowerPoint for Beginners* or in *PowerPoint 2019 Beginner*. The October 2023 version of PowerPoint 365 has changed just enough to warrant that.

So I can't guarantee for you that they won't shift things again in the future. That's the risk you take using 365.

Still, the basics tend to be the basics. And the more beginner-level a book the more stable things should be. Just know that with 365 it's not set in stone the way that versions like PowerPoint 2019 are.

Another thing to be aware of is the issue of backwards compatibility. That's the ability to work with those who have an older version of the same program. If you use a tool that was just released, chances are anyone with an older version of that same program won't have the same experience you do. So when you work with a wide range of users, it is best to stick to core functions and keep it simple.

This is probably most important when collaborating with someone on creating a presentation, but it may also come up if you travel around a lot and have to present in a wide variety of settings. If you're using their computer, they may not have the same version of PowerPoint you do.

Limit yourself to the basic functionality of PowerPoint and you should be pretty safe, but it's something to be aware of. And if backwards compatibility is something you really need to keep in mind, then you may be better off learning from *PowerPoint for Beginners* or *PowerPoint 2019 Beginner*, which were written using older versions of PowerPoint. Or maybe even saving your files as .ppt files instead of .pptx files, although that may be more than you need to do.

Just keep it in mind. You should be fine, but I mention it so you're aware that it's a potential issue.

Finally, I'm going to assume here that you have worked in Word or Excel and know the basics of formatting text, etc. I will cover those topics again here just not at the same granular level of detail. If you're brand new to all Office programs, I'd recommend starting with Word first.

Okay then, let's get started by talking about how to change the appearance of PowerPoint.

PowerPoint Appearance

All of the screenshots in this book are going to be made using the Colorful theme in PowerPoint. It will look like this on the main screen when you're looking at a blank presentation:

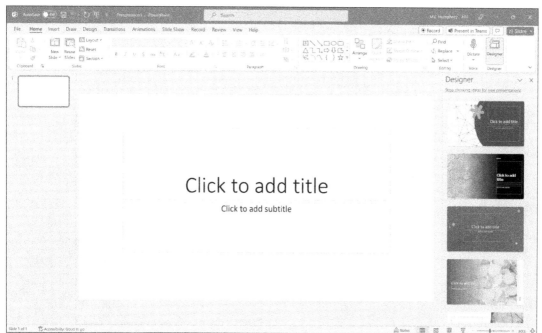

Note the orange color at the top. Also note that the background is light gray and the tasks have a white or lighter gray background behind them.

This is the Dark Gray theme:

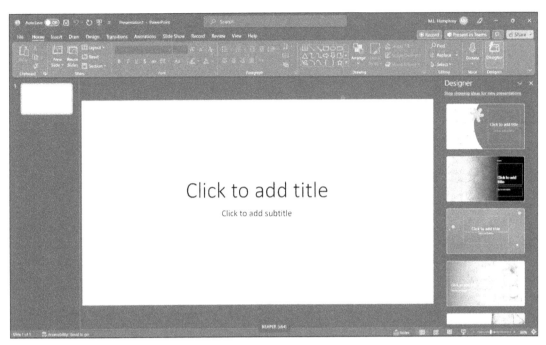

Note that the top and areas around the slide are now dark gray and the main section of options is a lighter dark gray. And that the text in those sections is white.

Another option is the Black theme which looks like this:

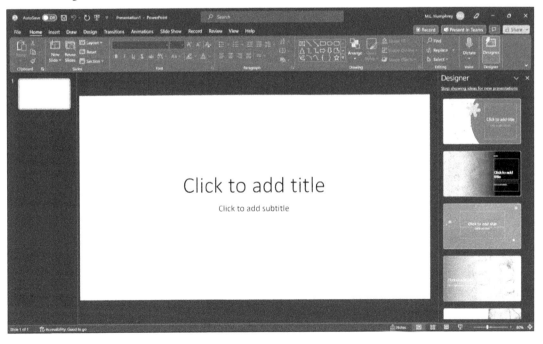

With this one, the top and surrounding areas are black and the options area is a darker gray or lighter black and the text is white.

Finally, there is a White option which looks like this:

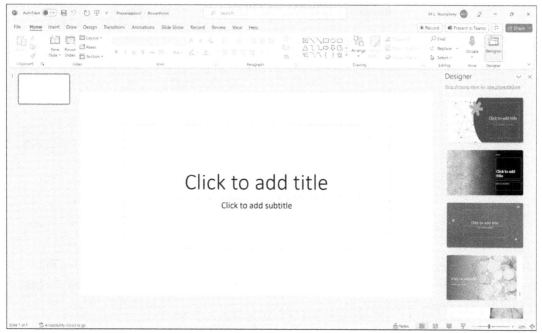

It's much the same as the Colorful option but doesn't have the orange strip across the top.

Those are the options available within PowerPoint itself, but your system settings can also impact the appearance of PowerPoint, too.

If you want your version of PowerPoint to match my screenshots, use either the White or Colorful themes, and the default system settings for Windows.

If you work with other settings, it may mean that at times I tell you something is one color when it's actually a different color for you. Do what makes you most comfortable, just keep that difference in mind.

Your office theme in PowerPoint can be changed from the Welcome screen. This should appear by default when you open PowerPoint, but if it doesn't it can also be found by clicking on the File tab from an open presentation. (Don't worry if you don't know how to do either of those, we will cover both in the Absolute Basics chapter and you can then come back here if you want to change your settings.)

The first way to change your Office Theme is to go to the Options setting at the bottom left corner of the Welcome screen and click on it:

That will open the PowerPoint Options dialogue box. On the General tab under the section Personalize Your Copy of Microsoft Office, there is a dropdown for Office Theme where you can choose the theme you want:

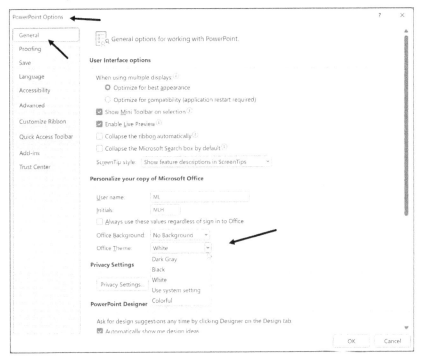

Your other option is to click on Account in the bottom left corner of the Welcome screen. That will bring up the Account page which will also have a dropdown option for Office Theme:

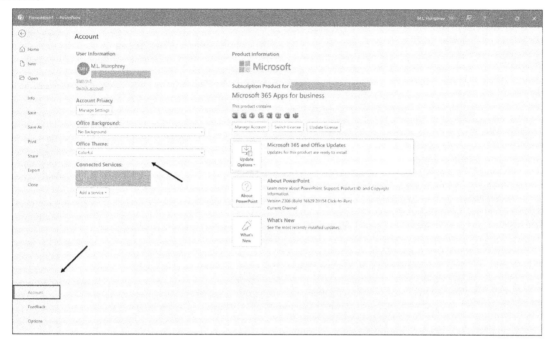

Click on that dropdown arrow and choose the theme you want to use.

Easy enough. Now let's cover basic terminology so that we're on the same page about what to call things.

Basic Terminology

Most of the terminology I use is consistent with Microsoft's Help and what others use, but some of it may be unique to me, so even if you think you know these terms, it's a good idea to at least skim this section anyway.

Tab

I refer to the menu options at the top of your PowerPoint workspace as tabs. This is because in older versions of Office when you selected an option at the top of the screen it looked like a file tab. In more recent versions of Office they've eliminated that appearance so that now the selected tab is simply underlined.

Here you can see the default tab options in PowerPoint:

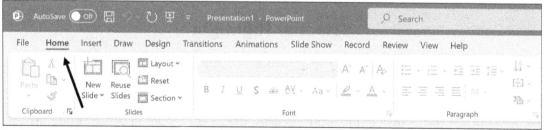

The Home tab is currently selected which you can see because it is underlined. The other tab options listed there are File, Insert, Draw, Design, Transitions, Animations, Slide Show, Record, Review, View, and Help. At times in PowerPoint there will be additional tabs visible when you have certain objects selected.

Each tab has its own set of available options that are grouped together in sections.

For example, as you can see here, the Home tab includes the Clipboard section that has tasks such as copy, paste, and format paint. It also has a Slides section that includes tasks such as add a new slide, reuse a slide, change a slide layout, etc.

When instructing you on how to do something, I will tell you to go to X section of Y tab and then click on Z task. So, for example, go to the Slides section of the Home tab and click on the dropdown arrow for New Slide.

Click

If I tell you to click on something, that means to move your cursor over to that option and then use the mouse or trackpad to either left- or right-click. If I don't say which, left-click.

Left-Click / Right-Click

Left-click simply means to use the left-hand button on your mouse or to press down on the left-hand side of your track pad. (For me on my track pad, it's the bottom of the track pad, but I think some have those buttons at the top instead.)

A left-click is generally used to select something.

Right-click simply means to use the right-hand button on your mouse or to press down on the right-hand side of your track pad.

A right-click generally brings up a dropdown menu of additional options.

Left-Click and Drag

If I ever tell you to left-click and drag this just means to go to that selection, left-click and hold down that left-click while moving your mouse or cursor until you've selected all of the text, images, etc. or until you've moved that selected object to where it needs to go.

Select or Highlight

Before you can make changes to your text, such as size, font, color, etc. you need to select the text you want to edit. If I ever tell you to select text, that means to go to one end of that text, and then left-click and drag to the other end so that the text is highlighted. Like here where I have selected the text "bullet point" in the second row:

- This is a bullet point
- This is another bullet point
- This is another one

Selected text should be shaded like in the image above.

Another way to select text is to click at one end of the text you want to select, hold down the Shift key, and then use the arrow keys to select the text you want. An arrow to the right or left will select one letter at a time; an arrow up or down will select all letters between that point and the same point in the line above or below.

You can select multiple sections of text by selecting the first one normally and then holding down the Ctrl key as you left-click and drag to select the next section of text.

To select an object in PowerPoint, left-click on it. When an object is selected, there will be circles around the perimeter of the object, like this:

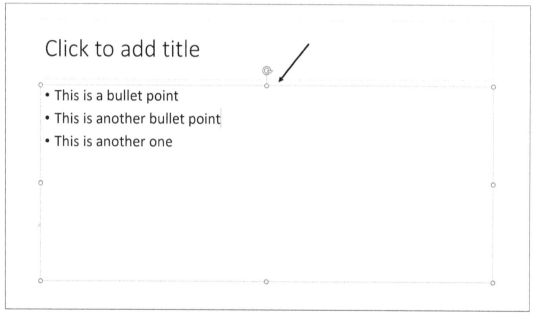

You can see that the second text box in the image above, which contains the bullet points, has been selected, because there are white circles at each corner and in the middle of each edge. Compare that to the text box above that which includes the "click to add title" text where just a faint outline is visible.

We are not going to do much with objects in this book, but I did want to mention it so you know what it looks like.

To select more than one object, click on the first object and then hold down the Ctrl key as you click on the others one at a time.

Ctrl + A, which is a control shortcut which we will define in a moment, can be used to Select All. If you are clicked into a specific text box and you use it, you will select all of the text in that text box. If you are not clicked into a specific text box, then Ctrl + A will select all of the objects on the page.

Dropdown Menu

Often there will be additional choices available if you right-click somewhere in PowerPoint. For example, if you are clicked into a text box of a presentation slide and you right-click, you will see this list of choices that let you cut, copy, paste, etc.:

I refer to this additional set of options as a dropdown menu even though sometimes it will actually drop upwards instead of downwards.

Dropdown menus can also be seen if you left-click on any of the arrows for the options under the tabs in the top menu section. For example, here is the Layout dropdown menu from the Slides section of the Home tab:

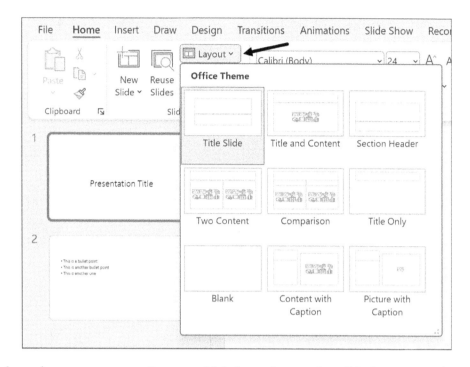

I clicked on the arrow next to Layout which brought up nine slide layouts to choose from. Anytime you see a little arrow like that next to a listed task or below it, that means there are more choices available.

Expansion Arrow

Another way to see more options in that top menu is to click on the expansion arrows that are sometimes visible in the bottom right corner of various sections. You can see one in the corner of the Clipboard section in the image above, for example. Clicking on an expansion arrow will either open a dialogue box or a task pane.

Dialogue Box

The old-school way for Office programs to show you additional options was to use dialogue boxes. Dialogue boxes appear on top of the workspace and can be left-clicked and dragged around. They are usually where you can find the most comprehensive set of options.

If you click in the bottom left-corner of the Font section of the Home tab, you can see the Font dialogue box, for example:

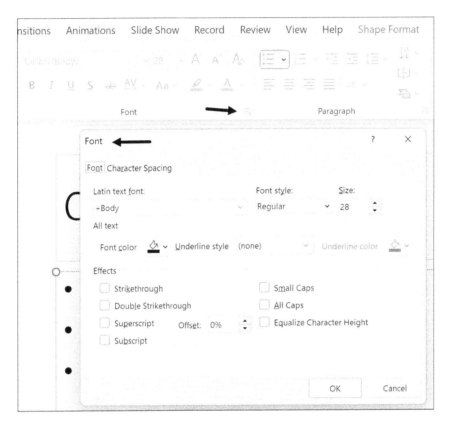

The Font section of the Home tab, which is visible in the background of this image, has options for font, font style, font size, font color, underline, and more. But the Font tab of the Font dialogue box includes those options as well as other options like double strikethrough, superscript, subscript, small caps, and all caps.

To close a dialogue box, click on the X in the top right corner.

Task Pane

In newer versions of Office, they tend to use what I refer to as task panes. These are separate work spaces that are visible to the sides or sometimes below your main work area.

To see an example of a task pane, right-click on a slide and choose the Format X option. It's likely going to be Format Text Effects or Format Shape depending on where you clicked.

This will open a task pane on the right-hand side of the workspace, like this one for Format Shape:

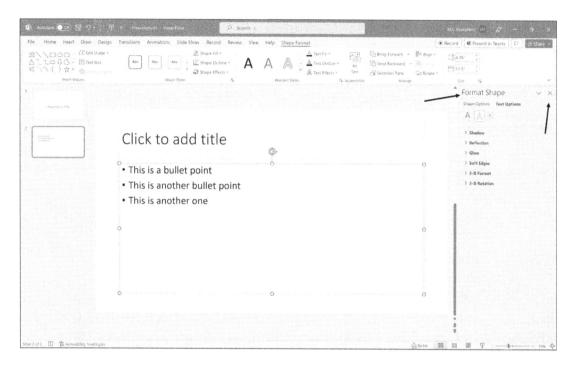

Task Panes usually have multiple sections. You can see above that this one has Shape Options and Text Options. Text Options is currently selected and has three available options to choose from, each one represented by an image with an A on it. The middle one of those is currently selected and that gives the choices of applying Shadow, Reflection, Glow, Soft Edges, 3-D Format, or 3-D Rotation to the text on the slide.

To close a task pane click on the X in the top right corner.

You can also left-click and drag to undock a task pane and move it around if you don't like the default location. To re-dock a task pane, left-click and drag to the side until it once more becomes a part of the workspace. Be careful doing this, because the task pane will reopen wherever you left it last.

Note in the picture above that there is also a sort of task pane on the left-hand side of the workspace, too, for thumbnails of the slides in the presentation. But that area can't be closed or moved. You can resize it, though, by holding your mouse over the inner margin until you see an arrow that points left and right and then left-clicking and dragging the border of the pane until it's your desired width. Note that doing this will impact the size of your slides in your main workspace, too.

You can resize any task pane that way. Just find the inner edge of the pane and then left-click and drag.

Mini Formatting Menu

If you were working in PowerPoint and following along with me, then you've also noticed something I call the mini formatting menu. It's not something I use much because it didn't exist when I was learning all these programs, but I did recently find that it came in handy when I was working on a smaller screen where the top menu options were minimized or hidden.

To see the mini formatting menu, either select some text or right-click in the main workspace. If you right-click, the mini formatting menu will appear above or below the dropdown menu of choices. If you select text it will likely appear above your text, like this:

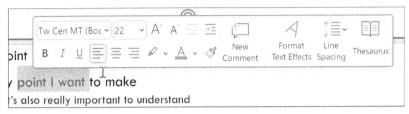

The left-hand side of the mini formatting menu includes the most common text formatting options like font, font size, font color, etc. and is fixed, meaning those options are always there.

The right-hand side of the mini formatting menu is dynamic. It will have default options like those you see here until you start working in PowerPoint, at which point those options will change to be ones you used recently.

That dynamic nature is why I don't use it often, because I'm never sure if the option I want will be there. But for basic formatting, especially if working on a smaller screen or in a tab other than the Home tab, the mini formatting menu may be the best choice.

Scrollbar

To navigate between slides in a large presentation and or through a large list of options in a dropdown menu, you will need to use scrollbars.

Here I've zoomed the main workspace so that you have scrollbars visible on both the right-hand side and the bottom. (Usually a full slide is visible so you won't have a scrollbar on the bottom.):

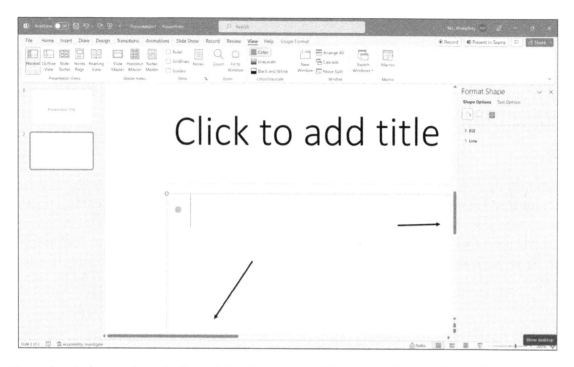

Note the dark gray bars indicated by the arrows. Those are the scrollbars. Or what I call scrollbars.

You can left-click and drag the bar itself to move quickly. In a dropdown menu, like the one for fonts, you will be able to see the choices as you do this.

In your main workspace, you will not see where you are until you let up on the left-click. But if you are scrolling down through your presentation slides it will show a small box that says "Slide X of Y" where X will change as you scroll.

(For me, scrollbars are not the best way to navigate through a presentation. I prefer to click on the slide thumbnails on the left-hand side of the workspace. But I do often need to scroll through that section when I have more than a handful of slides. That scrollbar though lets me see the slides as I do so.)

Another option for working with scrollbars is to click in the lighter-gray space around the actual bar. This will move you in that direction. So if you click in the light gray space above the right-hand scrollbar it will move you up, for example. Or if you click in the light gray space to the left of the bottom scrollbar it will move you left.

If you don't want to move that much at a time, you can also click on the arrows at the very ends of where those bars are. If you use the single arrows to navigate through your slides they will move you one line at a time if you're zoomed in or a slide at a time if you're zoomed out. The double arrows in the bottom right corner of the slide section will move you up or down one entire slide at a time regardless of zoom level.

Slider

Some options in PowerPoint use a slider, which is a horizontal bar with a perpendicular line along the bar that marks the percent value currently being used. You can see in the bottom right corner of your PowerPoint workspace the slider for your zoom level, for example. Click along that bar to change the value.

Control Shortcut

A control shortcut is when you hold down the Ctrl key (or sometimes another key) and then the specified letter to perform an action. So if I write Ctrl + C, that means hold down the Ctrl key and the C at the same time.

I will always write the shortcuts using a capital letter, like I just did, but you don't need to use the capitalized version of a letter. Just hold down that combination of keys at the same time.

Undo

This isn't really a definition, but I want you to learn it as soon as possible. If you ever do something and then regret it, Ctrl + Z will undo the last thing you did. For a more in depth discussion on using Undo and its counterpart Redo, see the Other Tips and Tricks chapter.

* * *

Okay, now let's walk through the absolute basics of working in PowerPoint, including how you open, save, and delete PowerPoint files.

Absolute Basics

Open PowerPoint

There are a number of ways to open PowerPoint. One of the easiest is to double-click on a PowerPoint file. That will open the file and PowerPoint at the same time.

Another is to go to the Start menu (bottom left corner of my screen but may be different for you) and left-click. That will bring up a large dropdown menu with pinned or recently used programs, like here where you can see PowerPoint in that first row:

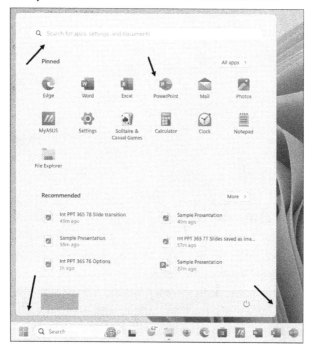

If it's there, just left-click on it.

Otherwise, use the search bar above that to find it. (As of now. They're always changing those options around a bit but the general concept stays the same. You should always see common programs and there should always be a search option somewhere.)

What I like to do is pin my most-used programs to my task bar. In the image above you can see the PowerPoint icon on the right at the bottom of the screen. Every time I need to open PowerPoint I just click on that.

To pin a program to your task bar, right-click on the icon from the start menu and choose Pin To Taskbar. You can also click and drag a shortcut to the program down to the taskbar.

Start a New Presentation

If you open PowerPoint without going through an existing PowerPoint file, you should by default open to the Welcome screen:

To start with an absolutely blank presentation that's just white slides with black text, click on that Blank Presentation option under New at the top of the screen.

If you're brand new to PowerPoint, I'd recommend doing this and then choosing a presentation theme from the Design tab, because those themes are easier to work with and provide a template for a more basic presentation. However, on the Welcome screen PowerPoint does also provide a number of fancier pre-formatted themes you can choose from. You can see six of those in the screenshot above.

There's also a More Themes option at the far end of that row. Click on that to see even more choices:

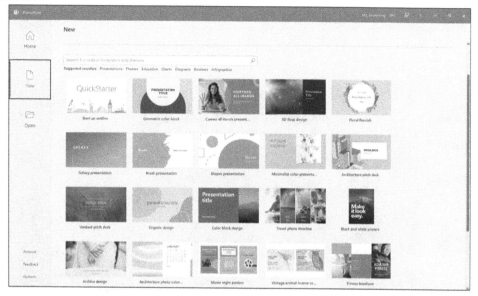

(In the image above, I scrolled down a bit to show more of the templates.)

Here we have twenty options to choose from as well as some Suggested Searches options up at the top that will give you even more choices.

To use one of those templates, click on the applicable thumbnail. PowerPoint will open a dialogue box that talks about the intended use for that particular presentation theme. Click on Create if you want to use it:

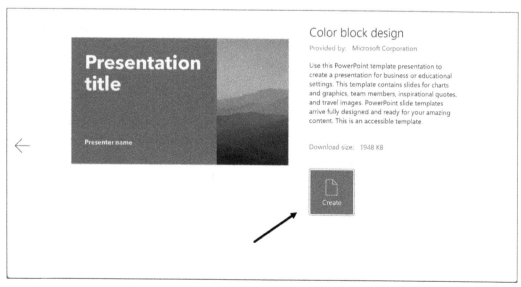

Office will then download the template for you and then open a presentation that has a number of slides visible and pre-formatted using that theme:

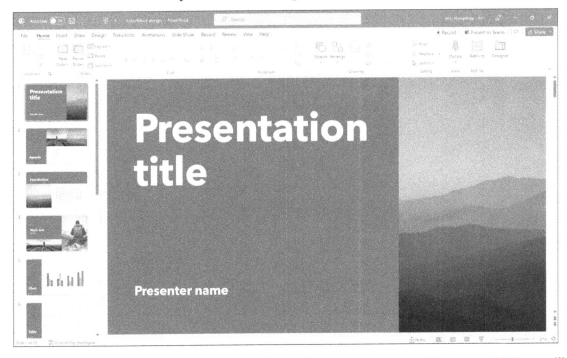

From there you can customize the presentation using your own text and images, which we will spend most of the rest of this book discussing.

If you didn't want to use that template, while you still have that dialogue box up and before you click on Create, as long as you were working from the More Themes screen you will have arrows on the left or right side of that dialogue box that you can use to move through the other template options.

* * *

If you already have a presentation open, the easiest way to start a new presentation is to use Ctrl + N. That will open a plain black and white presentation. You can then either go to the Design tab and choose a theme from there or click on one of the cover slide images in the Designer task pane that will open on the right-hand side of the workspace:

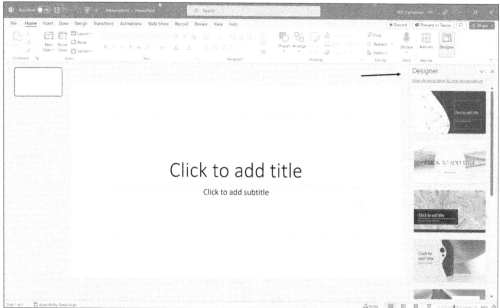

Note that the choices on the right-hand side in the Designer task pane are just a cover slide and not a fully-built template. So by default the accompanying slide layouts are going to be pretty generic. Most just have a colored background, as you can see here on the left-hand side menu of Layout choices:

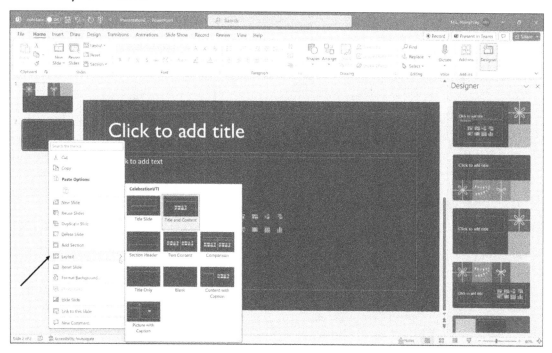

However, you can keep choosing slide layouts from the Designer task pane if you want something more interesting. As you can see on the right-hand side in the image above, Designer continues to suggest various options for each new slide layout.

Your other option for starting a new presentation when you already have one open is to go to the File tab, which will take you to the Welcome screen, and to then choose one of the presentation thumbnails from there as discussed above.

Open an Existing PowerPoint Presentation

There are two basic options for opening an existing presentation. First, go to where the file is saved and double-click to open it. Second, open PowerPoint first and then choose your presentation from there.

For the second option, if you're already working in a PowerPoint presentation, click on the File tab to get back to the Welcome screen. Otherwise, just open PowerPoint.

Your recent PowerPoint presentations will be listed in the center of the screen under Recent. Left-click on the one you want and it will immediately open.

If the file you want is not listed, you can click on Open on the left-hand side of the Welcome screen. This will bring up the Open screen which looks like this:

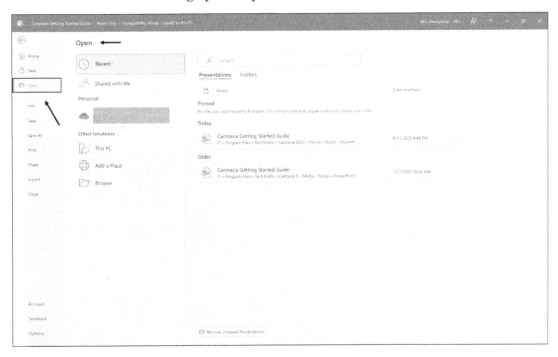

The Open screen will show a listing of your recently-opened presentations and pinned presentations on the right-hand side, but it will also have a section to the left of that where you can search on OneDrive, This PC, or click on Browse for the old familiar Open dialogue box:

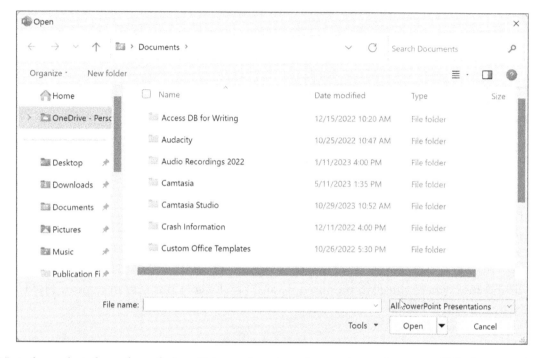

(Note here that the color of that dialogue box is going to depend on your Windows settings. I have changed my background image to a light-colored image which makes this box appear gray. When I have my default background image up instead, this dialogue box is black.)

To use the dialogue box, click on one of the folders in the left-hand side or double-click on a folder in the main section to navigate to where your file is saved. Once there, either double-click on the file you want to open, or click on the file and then click on Open at the bottom of the dialogue box.

The Open screen also has a Folders option up top that you can click on if the file you want is not one you recently opened but is in a folder you recently used. That will display a list of folder names. Click on one to see its contents and then keep clicking through to find your file. You can use the upward pointing arrow next to the file path name above the search box to go back up one level if needed:

Another option for opening a file from within PowerPoint is Ctrl + O which will take you to the Open screen.

Pin a File

If there are any presentations that you always want to be able to access quickly, you can pin them. (You can also pin folders in the same way.)

To pin a file the first thing you need to do is open that presentation. That will put it into your recent list.

Once the file is showing on the Open screen, move your cursor to the right-hand side of that listing near where the date modified is, and you'll see a pin option appear. Hold your mouse over it and it will say, "Pin This Item To The List".

Click on that pin. The file will move to the Pinned section of your files listing and will show with a pin:

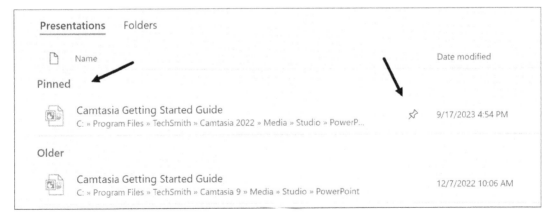

In the Open screen, pinned files are visible at the top of your file listing. In the Welcome screen you need to click on the Pinned option to see your pinned files.

To unpin a file, just click on that image of a thumbtack/pin next to the file name.

To pin a folder, it works the exact same way. Make sure the folder is listed, hold your cursor over that spot, click on the pin, and done.

Save a File

To save a file you have a few options.

Ctrl + S is one of the easiest if you want to keep working on the file. There's also a small icon of a computer disc in the top left corner that you can click on. If the file has already been saved before, that's all you need to do. PowerPoint will save over the latest version of the file using the same name and in the same location.

If the file has not been saved before and you use Ctrl + S or click on that save icon, you will see the Save This File dialogue box:

Save this file   ✕

File name

Presentation title   .pptx

Choose a Location

📁 Documents
C: » Users ×   ⌄

❯   Do you want to share this file?

More options...   Save   Cancel

There will be a default name displayed in the File Name box. It will already be highlighted, so just start typing to give the file the name you want to use instead.

Below that it will have a default location. For me it's my Users file of my C Drive. If that's fine, you just click on Save at the bottom of the dialogue box.

But if you want to use a different location instead, you can click on that dropdown arrow and choose from the listed options. Or you can click on More Options in the bottom left corner. That will take you to the Save As screen:

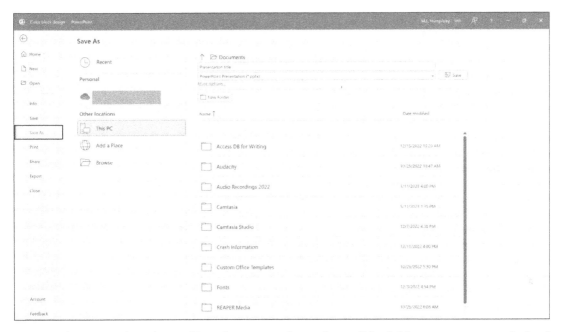

The Save As screen is going to list a larger number of possible folders to save to and also let you change the file type if you need to do that.

You can click on Browse from the Save As screen to bring up the Save As dialogue box which will also let you choose a location, name, and file type.

For most presentations that have been saved before, you'll just save using Ctrl + S or that icon in the top left corner. You can even just close the presentation and when PowerPoint asks if you want to save your changes say yes.

But there are going to be times when you want to save a file with a different name or different format. When that happens, click on the File tab and then click on Save As on the left-hand side of the Welcome screen. From there you can change whatever you need to change.

Do be careful though about changing things this way. If you just wanted to move a file to a new folder, it's better to do that outside of PowerPoint. Same with renaming the file. Let's talk about that now.

Move a File

If you want to just move a file from Folder A to Folder B, that is best done outside of PowerPoint. Close the file, go to the folder where it is saved, select that file, Ctrl + X to cut it from its current location, go to where you want the file to move, and Ctrl + V to place it in that new location.

Keep in mind that if you move a pinned file or a file that was in your recent files list, you will no longer be able to open it from those lists in PowerPoint, because PowerPoint will go to the old location looking for the file and it won't be there anymore. (Same goes for when you change the name of a file.)

Rename a File

If you want to change the name of a file but don't want multiple versions of the file to exist, that should also be done outside of PowerPoint. Find the file where it is saved, click on it to select it, click on it again to make the name editable, and then make your name change. Hit Enter or click away when done.

Delete a File

Deleting a PowerPoint file also needs to happen outside of PowerPoint. Find the file where it's saved, right-click and delete. Or click on it and choose the trashcan or delete option at the top of the dialogue box.

Close a File

Okay. Back to PowerPoint.

The easiest way to close a presentation is to click on the X in the top right corner of the PowerPoint workspace. If you had a single presentation open that will also close PowerPoint.

If you have multiple presentations open that should just close that presentation.

If the presentation you try to close has unsaved changes, PowerPoint will ask if you want to save those changes before closing:

Save your changes to this file?

File name

Camtasia Getting Started Guide   .ppt

Choose a Location

Documents
C: » Users »

More options...   Save   Don't Save   Cancel

Save will save those changes with the same name, file location, etc. and will replace the prior version of the presentation.

Don't Save will close the file without keeping any of your changes from this session.

Cancel will keep the file open. Choose Cancel if you're not sure and want to review the document before closing it or if you want to use the Save As option to save a new version and keep the old one untouched.

To close a file you can also go to the File tab and then choose Close from there.

Or you can use Ctrl + Q to both save and close a presentation or Ctrl + W to just close a presentation.

Personally, I like to be reminded that there were changes made to my presentation before I close it so I'd avoid using Ctrl + Q, because it never fails that you realize you didn't want to save those changes about three seconds after you automatically save them. But it's there if you want to use it.

* * *

Okay. Those were some of the absolute basics of working with files in PowerPoint. Next let's discuss how to choose a presentation theme from within a new presentation and then we'll cover the layout of your workspace.

Presentation Themes

We've touched on these a bit already, but I wanted to devote a full chapter to presentation themes, because as a new user of PowerPoint I highly recommend working with an existing presentation theme. They often come with a variety of slide layouts that are already formatted for you, and they tend to have nice accent elements that a plain, black and white presentation doesn't have.

We already covered the themes available on the Welcome screen, but I don't recommend those for new users. They're a little too fancy and it's a little too easy to get stuck trying to adapt one to what you need as a new user.

Instead, I recommend that new users start with the black and white presentation option and then go to the Themes section of the Design tab:

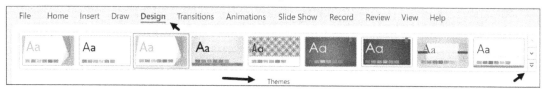

You can see here the current theme as well as eight other choices. In the bottom right corner of that row, there is a downward pointing arrow with a line above it. Click on that to expand your list of choices.

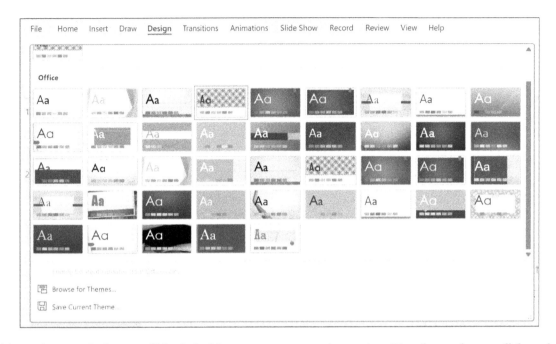

To see how each theme will look, hold your mouse over the option. To select a theme, click on it.

The nice thing about using one of these themes is that moving back and forth between them is relatively easy. You just click on the one you want and everything updates.

Many of the theme choices in this section also have variants. You can find them in the Variants section of the Design tab after you click on a theme.

So here, for example, the Facet theme has a green, a blue, and a pink option as well as a version that uses a dark green background:

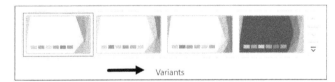

There is also a Colors dropdown that you can find if you expand the variants section. Expand that section and then hold your cursor over Colors and a secondary dropdown menu will appear with a large list of color combinations to choose from.

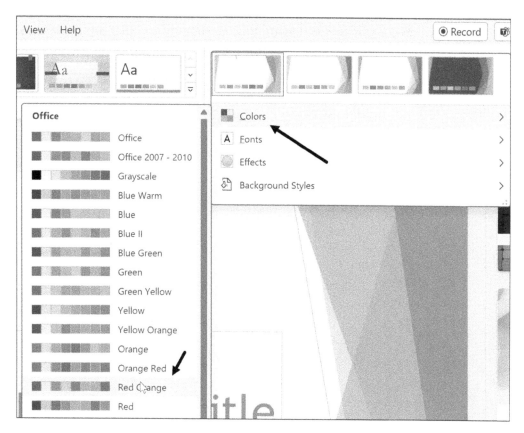

Click on the color combination you want to use. Above, for example, I applied a Red Orange color palette to the Facet theme and you can see in the background that the accents and text changed to match that choice. (In print, maybe not, but in the ebook you can see that.)

For a beginner, I think there's plenty here to work with and it's pretty forgiving, too, so I strongly urge you to use one of these themes for your presentation if you don't have a corporate one you need to use.

The problem I found with using the themes currently listed on the Welcome screen is that when you try to change to a theme in the Themes section of the Design tab, at least for the few I tried, PowerPoint didn't completely change over. It combined the two themes, and not always in a good way.

As a beginner, I wouldn't expect you to be able to unravel that. So to avoid that potential complication, I'd say just start with a blank presentation and then choose an option from the Design tab.

(This is different, by the way, than earlier versions of PowerPoint where the Welcome screen choices corresponded to the Themes options on the Design tab. So it may change back in the future. But for now, save yourself the heartache.)

Also, even though they don't show up by default when you choose a theme, all of these older design choices do come with a variety of built-in slide layouts that use those colors and design elements. Here, for example, Facet has fourteen different slide types for you to choose from.

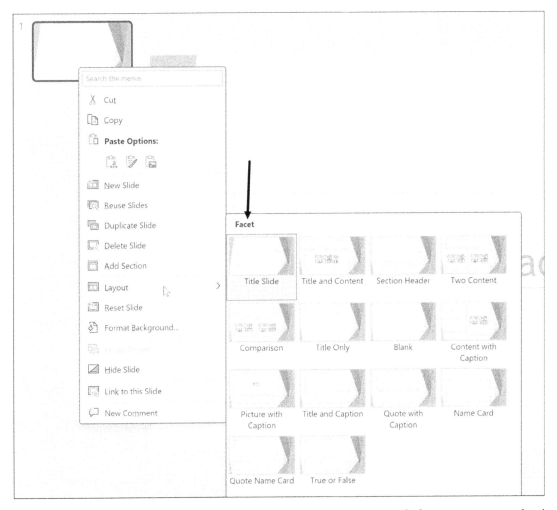

All of those layouts use the same font, color, and accent elements to help you create a cohesive presentation. Is it sexy? Nah, not really. Is it functional? Yes.

Okay. So that's my advice. Open a black and white presentation, choose a theme from the Design tab, and change the color if you want to be adventurous.

But. When you open a black and white presentation, PowerPoint is also going to open the Designer task pane on the right-hand side. Like so:

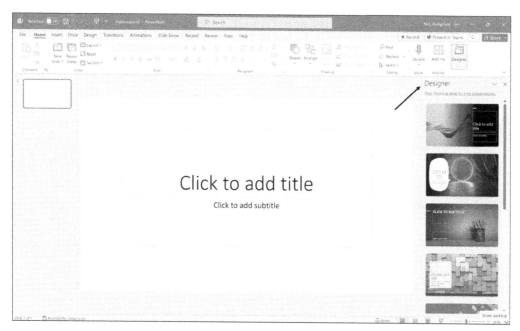

My advice is to ignore it. Click on the X in the top right corner and pretend you never saw it.

But if you're tempted…you can click on one of those options in the task pane and PowerPoint will apply that design to your title slide. If you're lucky it will also offer you some good layout options for other slides in your presentation.

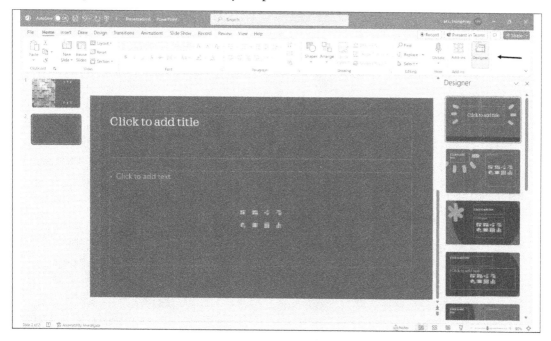

If you're not, you'll get options like this:

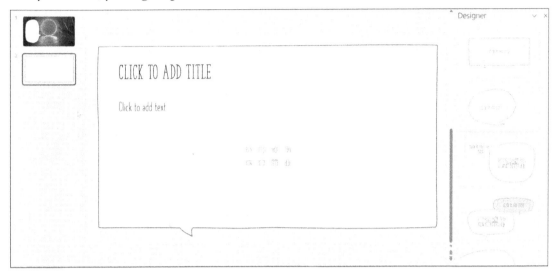

And switching over after you've made that choice is not easy to do. Best to just close the presentation and try to start again instead of try to choose another option.

Now, I understand that you may not be thrilled with using those basic presentations in the Themes section of the Design tab. Another option to make things more interesting, is to start with one of the basic themes, add a new slide (we'll cover how to do that soon), and then open the Designer task pane to see more layout choices than the default. Like these:

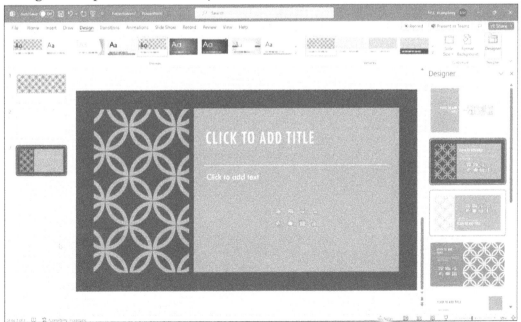

To open the Designer task pane, click on Designer in the Designer section of the Design tab, which you can see in the top right corner of the image above.

I think that gives workable options that are maybe a little more interesting than the default and that still work thematically. You can also switch to a new theme without PowerPoint trying to combine the two designs, although be forewarned that you'll probably have to go through each slide and choose a better layout option.

So that's probably your best call. Start with a blank presentation (Ctrl + N or click on that option on the Welcome screen), apply a theme from the Themes section of the Design tab, choose a variant or color option, if wanted, and then click on Designer to give yourself more choices for your slide layouts.

But only click on Designer after you've added at least one slide to your presentation, don't use it on your title slide.

And one final note. If you move to a new theme after you've added text to your presentation, be sure to check all of your slides. Sometimes there will be a difference in font size or font choice that impacts your appearance. Also be especially careful if you were using a theme that had all caps in the title sections and you move to one that uses upper and lower case. I often find that I didn't properly capitalize my words when all caps was in place.

One more thought. If you are going to print your presentation, try to find a presentation theme that has a white background on the main slides. Like this one:

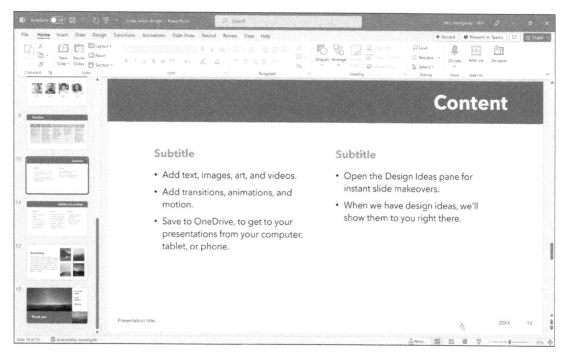

315

It is possible to set your print settings to address slides with dark backgrounds when it comes time to print, but I always prefer that my presentation on the screen match what I've printed.

The reason not to print slides with a dark background is that it takes a lot of ink. And sometimes, depending on the type of printer, a dark background has more chance to smear or smudge or come through stripey.

Also, make sure the theme you choose has layouts that meet your needs. Are there section slides if you need that? Are there image slides? What about the bulleted lists, do they work for you? It's far easier to start with a theme that is set up for your needs than to try to edit it later. And in this beginner book we're not going to cover too much about how to make those sorts of edits, so you're going to be stuck with how the theme is set up.

Okay, now let's look at your workspace.

Your Workspace

This is what PowerPoint looks like using a presentation that has about a dozen slides:

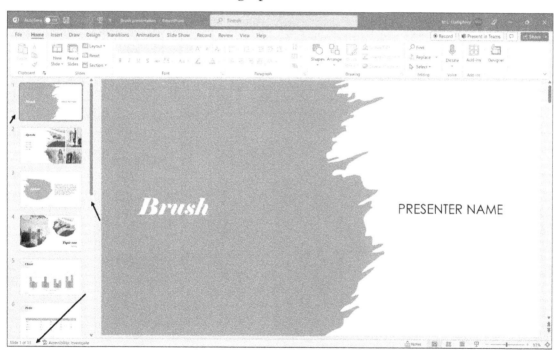

As discussed previously in the definitions section, across the top of the workspace are the tabs, File, Home, Insert, etc. You can click on each of those to see the available options and then click on an option to apply it.

Below that, on the left-hand side of the workspace, are thumbnail images of each slide. You can see six slides at a time at the current size. On the bottom left corner it shows that there are a total of 13 slides in this presentation. The scrollbar for that section is on the right-hand side of the thumbnails, and can be used to move down to see the rest of the slide thumbnails.

To the right of that is the main part of the workspace where you can see the current slide and then to the right of that is another scrollbar.

There is a slider in the bottom right-hand corner of the workspace that will let you zoom in or out on the current slide. My default zoom percentage is 97% which usually lets you see the entire slide while keeping the slide thumbnails visible on the left-hand side. I tend to leave this on the default setting but you can click down there to change your zoom level quickly.

In the image above, I am clicked onto Slide 1. You can see this in the left-hand set of thumbnails where there is a darker border around Slide 1 and the number of the selected slide is also a different color.

To move to a different slide in the presentation, either left-click on a slide thumbnail in the left-hand section, or use the scrollbar on the far right of the currently-visible slide. In that far right scrollbar the double arrows in the bottom right corner will move you one slide at a time regardless of zoom level.

As you work in PowerPoint you may end up opening other task panes which will appear on the right-hand side of the current slide or below it. Or even to the left if you change your settings. But what you see above is the core appearance that you'll see most often.

Now let's walk through what you can do with those slide thumbnails on the left-hand side.

Slide Thumbnails Task Pane

As we just discussed, the left-hand side of your workspace shows thumbnail images of each slide in your presentation. This is where you go to add, delete, or move around your slides in your presentation.

Add a Slide

If you want to add a slide to your presentation, there are a few options available to you.

You can right-click on the slide directly above where you want to add that new slide and choose the New Slide option from the dropdown menu:

That will add a blank slide that corresponds to the template you're using. The layout used will vary depending on the slide that was directly above.

Here I right-clicked on the top slide for this presentation style and chose New Slide and it added a slide in the default layout for this template as Slide 2. But then I also did the same on what is now Slide 3 and it added a new slide in the same layout as Slide 3 as Slide 4:

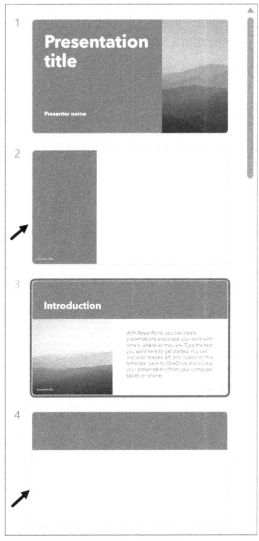

So. The layout you'll see on your new slide is going to vary depending on where you insert the slide and what layout was being used above that. (But, as we'll discuss momentarily, you can easily change that.)

Another option for inserting a new slide is to go to the blank space at the very end of the Presentation Slides Task Pane and right-click on that space. Choose New Slide from there and

PowerPoint will add a slide to the end of your presentation using the same layout as the last slide.

Your final option is to go to the Slides section of the Home tab and click on New Slide. If you use the dropdown arrow under New Slide, you can choose the layout you want:

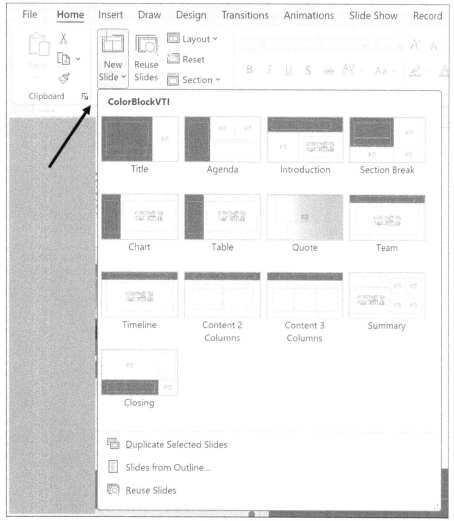

Simply click on your preferred layout from that dropdown. The new slide will insert below the slide you currently have selected in the presentation. If no slide is selected, it will insert at the end of the presentation.

Select Slides

To select a single slide, just left-click on it.

To select multiple slides, left-click on the first slide, and then either hold down the Shift key or the Ctrl key and select the next slide.

Use Ctrl if you want to select one additional slide at a time and also if the slides you want to select are not next to one another.

Use Shift to select a range of slides. With Shift, you left-click on the first slide in the range, hold down Shift, and then left-click on the last slide in the range. All slides between the two slides you clicked on will then show as selected.

Selected slides have a darker border around them and the number of the slide is also a different color. Here I have selected slides 1 through 3:

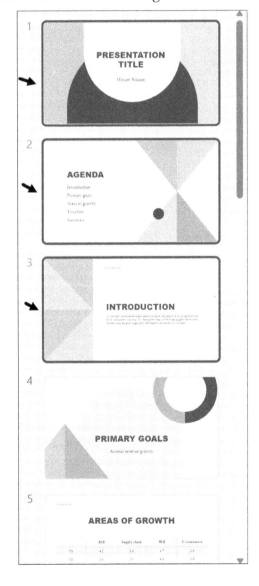

I clicked on Slide 1, held down Shift, and then clicked on Slide 3. (I could have also held down Ctrl and clicked on each individual slide, but Shift saves time when you're selecting a range of slides at once.)

You can combine Ctrl and Shift together to select slides. So maybe you use Shift to select three slides that are next to each other and then Ctrl to select one more slide that isn't next to those three.

To go back to just one slide selected, click on that slide.

You can also click into the gray area at the bottom of the task pane if you don't want any slides selected. The slide you'll see in the main workspace in that case will be the last one in the presentation.

If you want to select all of the slides in the presentation, click into the Presentation Slides task pane, and then use Ctrl + A.

Move a Slide or Slides

It's not a problem if you insert a slide in the wrong location. You can easily move the slide to where you need it. You can also move a range of slides at one time.

To move a single slide, left-click on the slide you want to move, and then hold that left-click as you drag the slide to its new location. Release your left-click when you reach your destination.

Here you can see that I've left-clicked on Slide 18 and am dragging it upward past Slide 17:

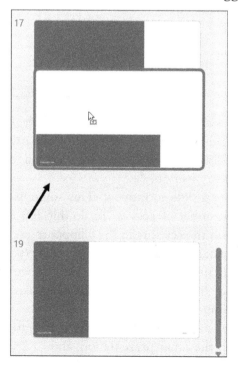

As it reaches a spot above Slide 17, Slide 17 will shift downward to make room for that slide to go above.

To move multiple slides at once, it's basically the same, you just need to select all of the slides you want to move first, and then left-click and drag.

Here you can see that I'm moving two slides (see the red 2 above the outlined slides) and that I've moved those two slides to a spot between the existing Slides 5 and 6 (see the slide numbers on the left-hand side):

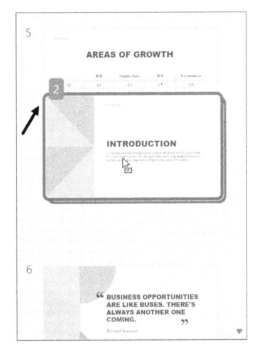

Note that as you moves slides around they will not keep their numbering. The numbering is based on that slide's current position in relation to all of the other slides in the presentation. As soon as you move your slides into their new location, all slides in the presentation will renumber to adjust to their new position.

You can also Cut and Paste a slide to move it. This sometimes is the easier option if you want to move a slide a large number of spaces. To do this, left-click on the slide you want to move, use Ctrl + X (or click on the scissors in the Clipboard section of the Home tab), go to the place in the presentation where you want to place the slide (using the scrollbar on the right-hand side of that task pane if needed), click on the slide above where you want to place the slide, and then use Ctrl + V (or the Paste option in the Clipboard section of the Home tab) to paste the slide into its new location.

Cut can also be used to take slides from one presentation to another. Select the ones you want to move, Ctrl + X, go to the other presentation, and Ctrl + V.

If you want the slides that you paste into the second presentation to use the formatting of that second presentation, then use the Paste dropdown menu in the Clipboard section of the Home tab to choose a different paste option. There are three options to choose from:

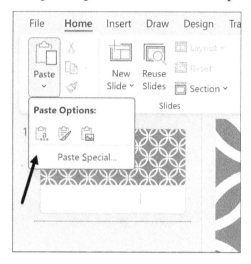

You want the first option, Use Destination Theme.

You can see the description of each paste option if you hold your mouse over the little icon. Right now the Use Destination Theme option looks like a clipboard with an "a" in the bottom right corner with dots under it.

You can also find these paste options when you right-click in the gray space of the Presentation Slides task pane. Either one will work.

Cut, or Ctrl + X, takes a slide from where it is and moves it to a new location. But if you want a copy of that slide to move and want to keep the original where it is, then use Copy, or Ctrl + C, instead. Everything else works the same in terms of pasting the slide into its final location, but Copy will leave the original slide where it was.

In the Clipboard section of the Home tab, Copy is represented by an image of two pieces of paper stacked on one another.

(Note that sometimes Microsoft decides they need to refresh the look of their product and changes the appearance of these icons. But they generally stay in the same location. And in twenty-five years they have yet to change the Ctrl shortcuts. So if you know the Ctrl shortcuts you should always know a way to cut, copy, and paste.)

Duplicate a Slide

PowerPoint also has an option similar to Copy which is Duplicate. You can find it by right-clicking on a slide thumbnail or by using the dropdown under the Copy option in the Clipboard section of the Home tab.

Duplicate takes the slide you currently have selected and puts an exact copy of that slide directly below. So it saves that step of having to paste.

It will copy any text or images, etc. that were on the source slide so if a header is going to stay the same or you have other elements that will repeat from slide to slide, it's very useful.

And you can use it on more than one slide. Just select the slides you want to duplicate first and then choose the Duplicate option and all of the selected slides will be duplicated.

Delete a Slide

To delete a slide, right-click on it and choose Delete Slide from the dropdown. This also works with multiple slides at a time.

Another option is to use the Delete key when you have a slide or slides selected. The Backspace key also works to delete a selected slide or slides.

Reset a Slide

If you make changes to a slide and you don't like them and you want to go back to the default format for that theme, you can reset the slide. Right-click on the slide and choose Reset Slide from the dropdown menu or go to the Slides section of the Home tab and choose the Reset option from there.

When pasting in slides from another presentation, even if you pasted in using the destination theme, you may still want to do this. When I just did this with my pasted slides it brought my text to a left-aligned position instead of centered, for example. If I'd already had slides in this presentation that had been created in the presentation, that difference in alignment would have been noticeable and needed to be fixed.

* * *

Next let's discuss how to choose slide layouts.

Slide Layouts

A good presentation will vary the appearance from slide to slide. Maybe one slide will just contain text but then another will have a chart or two columns of text side-by-side. Presentation themes often have these various layouts built in so that you don't have to try to create one on your own.

To change the layout of a slide, right-click on either the slide thumbnail in the Slide Thumbnails task pane or in the main workspace. Next, go to the Layout option. There should be a secondary dropdown menu that shows you the available layouts for that presentation theme:

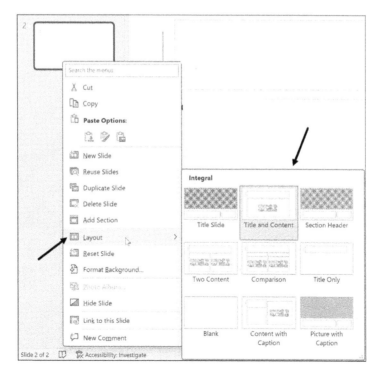

Click on the one you want to use.

You can also do this by selecting the slide and then going to the Layout dropdown menu in the Slides section of the Home tab. Just click on the arrow next to Layout and choose from there.

If you're using the Designer task pane, you can also click on one of the options shown there to apply it. The Designer task pane will not always have suggestions for all slide types, though.

Also, not all themes will have all layouts, so be sure to check what choices you have available before you start working with your chosen theme.

Now that you know how to apply a layout, let's discuss some of the more common choices.

Title Slide

The title slide is the first slide in your presentation. It will usually have a space for a title and a space for a subtitle as well as the design elements for your chosen theme.

Here, for example, is the title slide for the Facet theme:

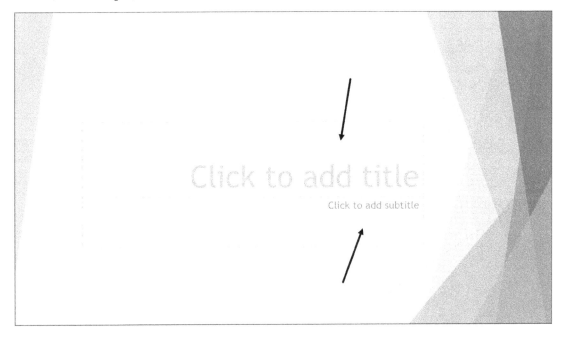

It places the title and subtitle in the center of the slide.

Other themes will place those elements in different locations. For example, the Frame theme places the title and subtitle on the left two-thirds of the slide.

Section Header Slide

Another common slide layout is the Section Header layout. It usually includes fields for a title and a sub-header:

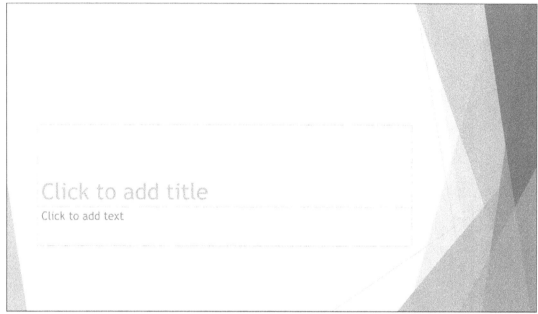

Often-times this will look very similar to the title slide, but maybe the colors on the slide, the font size, or the placement of the text or design elements will differ slightly.

With this theme, the text is on the left of the page instead of centered and the design element in the background is different on the left-hand side.

The Section Header slide is one where you might want to use the Designer to choose different options. In this case there are options with a dark background, like the first and third options here, that make the section stand out more:

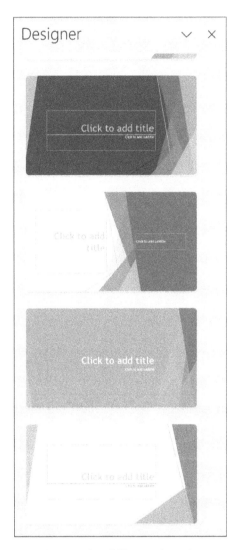

There are also choices that place the text in different locations on the slide, like in the second option.

Remember, if the Designer tab is not visible you can open it by clicking on Designer in the Designer section of the Design tab. Scroll down to see all of your options.

One caution about using the Designer is that the list of slide choices is not going to be the same each time. So if you choose a design that you like for one section header, you'll likely need to duplicate that slide for your next section header to use it again.

Title and Content Slide

The Title and Content Slide is your bread and butter slide. This is the one you will probably use the most. It has a section with the title for the slide, which is usually what that slide is about, and then another section where you can add text or another element like a video, image, illustration, graph, or chart. (We're only going to cover adding text in this book but the Title and Content slide will accommodate any of those other elements, too.)

This theme uses a pretty standard layout with the title at the top and then the text or other element below that. But, as we can see with the Designer choices, that's not the only way to go. Some themes put the title on the left and text on the right like the fourth option here:

Also, if using Designer, be careful, because as you can see here, sometimes the suggested layout doesn't match the type of slide you want, like in the third example there that only has a title.

Two Content or Comparison Slide

A Two Content slide generally has a title section and then two sections with text or other elements side-by-side.

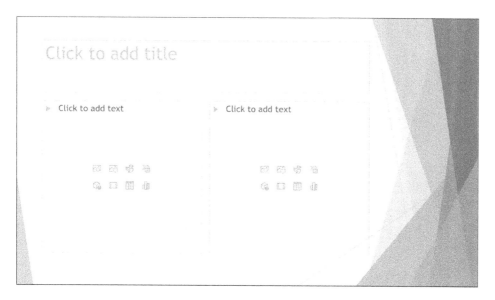

This is one that, at least for this theme, PowerPoint didn't have additional suggestions for in the Designer tab. If I wanted something different then this basic appearance, I'd probably have to build it myself. Not a beginner-level skill.

A Comparison slide layout is much like a Two Content slide, but it has one additional text box above each of the sections in the main body of the slide so you can label those contents.

Content or Picture with Caption

A Content With Caption slide has a title section and an associated text box, and then another box for text or another element like a picture, video, etc.

This is a good one for a high-level description, a descriptive paragraph, and then an image, like this:

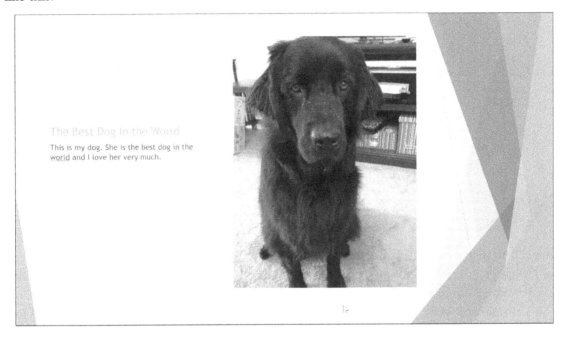

A Picture With Caption slide is similar but may limit the choice for that third box to just a picture as opposed to text or images. Also, the positioning of the three elements may differ between the two different layouts.

* * *

There are a number of other slide types, but the ones above are probably going to be your core group of slides. Once you've selected a theme to work with, you can look at the layout choices and see if any of them will fit for what you want to do. For a basic presentation, you should be fine no matter what theme you choose.

Okay. Now that you know the basics about working with your slides and applying a layout to them, let's talk about how to add and format text, which is usually the core of creating a PowerPoint presentation.

Add, Move, or Delete Text

Add Text

It's very easy to add text to a PowerPoint slide. Find a text box, click on it, and start typing. That's why I recommend using the theme templates, because they already have text boxes for you and they're generally located in good spots on the slide.

So, how do you know where a text box is? Simple. They usually say something like "Click to add title" or "Click to add subtitle". Like here:

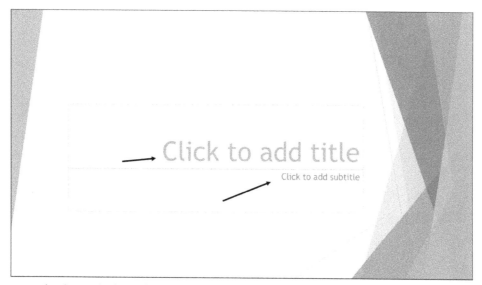

You can see the boundaries of the text boxes with that faint gray line around the edges. The current text color, font, and size is what your text will look like when you click into the box and start typing.

You don't have to replace that text "click to add…" because it will disappear as soon as you click into the text box. (If you already had text in a text box, then, yes, you would have to delete that text to get rid of it, but not this placeholder text.)

When you're done typing your text into the text box, click away from it. The outline of that text box will go away and you'll just have your text. Like so:

All slides work this way. Some, though, are going to have bulleted lists. Like this one:

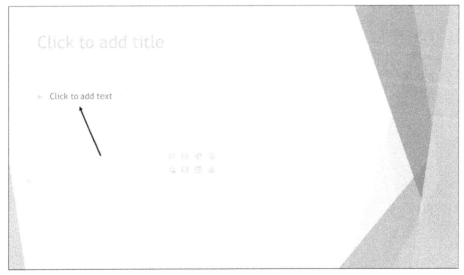

In that case, when you start typing and hit Enter for a new line in that main text box, it will put bullet points at the start of each line. Use the Tab key to indent a line of text and create a multi-level bulleted list. Like so:

> ▷ A Really Important Point
>> ▷ No, seriously, very important
>>> ▷ The most important point of all
> ▷ A Second Really Important Point
>> ▷ But maybe not as important as the first one

To enter this text, I clicked into the text box, typed the first line, hit Enter, used Tab, typed the second line, hit Enter, and used Tab again before I typed the third line of text. That gave me the first three lines.

I then hit Enter and used Shift + Tab twice to move the bullet point back to the first level, and then added that line, Enter, Tab, and then the final line of text.

So with bulleted lists, Tab will move the bullet point in one, Shift + Tab will move it back one. It's easiest to do as you type, but if you need to make adjustments later, click into the line of text right before the first letter, and then use Tab or Shift + Tab as needed.

Another option is to click anywhere on a line and then go to the Paragraph section of the Home tab and use the Decrease List Level or Increase List Level options:

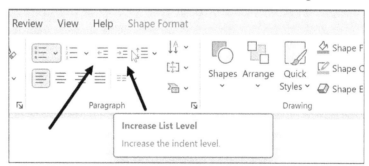

In this template, the various indented text levels had text that was smaller with each indent, but the bullet point remained a green arrow. In other templates the type of bullet point used may change with each level.

As a beginner, I would suggest letting PowerPoint set those shapes and text sizes. These templates tend to be built for use as a presentation that will be shown on a projector screen, so they won't use too small a font size to be visible in that setting. See here how the text in the last three bulleted lines is the same:

> A Really Important Point
>> No, seriously, very important
>>> The most important point of all
>>>> It really is
>>>>> I'm not lying
>>>>>> This is really, really, really important

One final comment, if you're working in a company presentation template and having issues with the bulleted lists not working, that's probably an issue in the master slide of the template, and you'll need someone to fix that or you'll need to switch to a different template or presentation theme. So sometimes it's not you, it's them.

Move Text

You move text in PowerPoint in the same way you would in Word, which I hope you're familiar with already.

Select the text you want to move, and then use Ctrl + X or go to the Clipboard section of the Home tab and click on the scissors to cut the text from its current location. Next, click on where you want to place that text, and then use Ctrl + V or the Paste option in the Clipboard section of the Home tab to place the text.

You can also select the text and then right-click and choose Cut from the dropdown menu, go to where you want to place the text, right-click, and choose Paste from the dropdown menu.

Copy Text

Usually you'll want to move text not copy it, but you can copy using Ctrl + C, the Copy option in the Clipboard section of the Home tab, or by right-clicking and choosing Copy from the dropdown menu. Just select your text first. The text will remain where it is, but you can then also go to a new location and paste that text there as well.

Paste Options

As mentioned above, there is more than one paste option. Either click on the arrow under Paste in the Clipboard section of the Home tab or right-click to see the list of paste options.

We already discussed the first option there, Use Destination Theme. That makes sure the text fits in with what's around it in terms of font, color, etc.

The next one is Keep Source Formatting which will paste the text in but keep it the same color, font, etc. that it was when you copied it.

The third option, Picture, pastes the text in as a screenshot. The text won't be editable at that point. It will be as if you'd taken a photo of that text and dropped in the photo.

The final option, Keep Text Only, will format the text depending on the text that's around it. Here's an example of all four options:

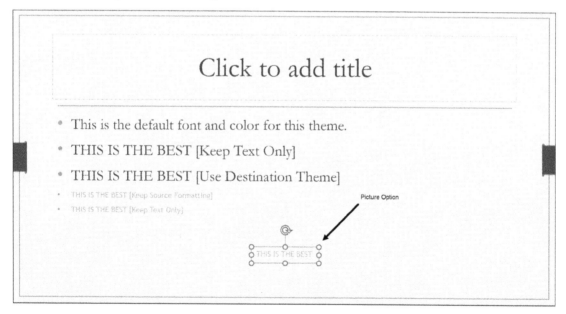

My source text was in green and used the Trebuchet MS font. The presentation I'm pasting into uses the Garamond font in black, like in that first bulleted line there.

In the second bulleted line, I pasted in "THIS IS THE BEST" using the Keep Text Only option. I did the same thing for the last line of text. Note how different they are.

That's because the first line was pasted directly after a line that had black text in Garamond and the second one was pasted directly below a line that had green text in Trebuchet MS.

Each one used the formatting of the text immediately before it.

The third bulleted line in the image above was pasted in using Use Destination Theme. No matter where I pasted that text in within that text box it was going to look like that.

The fourth line is that same text pasted in using Keep Source Formatting. It continues to look like the text I initially copied, which was green and in Trebuchet MS font.

Finally, down there in the center bottom you have a picture of the text I was copying and pasting. I can't edit the text in that last one, it's a picture at this point. And it doesn't position like text anymore either. I have to click and drag that image around to place the text on my slide. But that is a true image of what the source text I started with looked like.

Delete Text

To delete text, select the text, and then use Backspace or Delete.

If you don't select the text first, you can remove text one character at a time. Delete will delete the character to the right of your current position. Backspace will delete the text to the left of your current position.

Delete and Backspace also work on bullet points and the numbers in numbered lists.

Design Principles

Feel free to ignore this section. I have given a number of presentations to various audiences over the years and been on the receiving end of even more, but at the end of the day I have no formal design training, this is just what I've picked up in my finance/consulting/corporate career.

Font Size

For a presentation that is going to be given as an actual presentation, I prefer to keep the font size to 14 pt or higher. You want people to be able to see what is on your slide.

Even though most of the templates will go down to 12 pt, I figure if I'm getting that deep into subpoints, I can probably break the idea down better across a couple of slides.

Note that this rule goes out the window if it's a consulting-style presentation deck that is meant to be printed and handed out. In that case, I'd still recommend 8 pt or above and only use 8 pt for footnotes.

Font Size Consistency

Sometimes PowerPoint automatically adjusts the size of your text to make it visible in your text frame. For example, in the template I've been using for the screenshots for this book it took my text from 36 pt to 32 pt when I tried to have a title section with three lines in it.

Why should you care? Because it can be noticeable during a presentation if five slides are at 36 pt and then one slide is at 32 pt. Or if all of your bulleted points are at 18 pt and 16 pt and then suddenly there's a slide that's at 12 pt.

I will sometimes manually adjust my slides for that lowest common denominator (32 pt or 12 pt in the examples above) to keep the appearance consistent from slide to slide. (We'll cover that soon don't worry.)

Hierarchy of Elements

You want there to be a natural hierarchy among your elements. The font size of the title of a slide should be bigger than the main body text. And any subpoints should be the same or a smaller font size than the main points.

Also, at least in the U.S., the natural tendency is to start at the top and go downward and to start at the left corner and move towards the right. So top-left is usually where you should put whatever you want the audience to see first.

And when placing any other elements, like images or tables, etc. they should be below and or to the right of the text that introduces them.

Font Type

For most of the text in a presentation the goal is for it to be legible. Use workhorse fonts like Times New Roman, Garamond, Arial, etc. Also, if you're in a corporate setting know what the approved corporate font is and use that.

Summary Instead of Detail

When presenting to an audience you don't want to just stare at your slide and read it. You also don't want your audience to be so busy reading your slide that they don't listen to you.

Ideally, to avoid those problems, you will list one line per thought on a slide and then expand on that thought verbally. The text on a slide is more of a framework to work from, not everything you ever wanted to say about the topic.

Now, I will note that consulting presentation decks don't work this way. On those they seem to put every single thought they've ever had and then everyone sits around reading the slide instead of listening. It's almost like a written report in PowerPoint form. Consultants like them because they can still walk through the slides as if they're a presentation and rack up those nice billable hours. (Why, yes, I am jaded.)

Keep It Simple

Later we'll walk through animations and we're going to talk about how to change font colors, etc. But always keep the goal in mind, which is usually to convey information to your audience. If flying, spinning, whirring text helps you do that? Great, use it. If something like that will make your audience stop listening to you, then don't use it.

Same with colors and themes and everything else. Always ask yourself, "Does this help me get the message across?" If not, nix it.

Better to be boring and convey your message than have people talk about all the animations on your slides and forget what the presentation was about.

Contrast

There is a reason that black text on white backgrounds for generic products was so popular at one point in time. Because it works. Black on white, very legible. Very easy to see the words. Red on black? Not so much.

Red on green? Don't go there. Some people are red-green colorblind. Others are blue-yellow colorblind. That means they can't see the difference between certain colors, like blue and purple. So if you put blue text on a purple background, you maybe lose 8% of your audience right there.

Black text on a white background really is the best. Be creative in your headers and design elements, but make sure your main text is as legible as you can get it.

Make It Make Sense

We're not going to cover things like SmartArt in this introductory book, but when I do cover it in the intermediate book one of the things we will discuss is that you need to choose graphics that work for what you're trying to say. If you have connected arrows pointing to the right, your audience will expect that the first element on the left happens before or leads to the next element and so on and so forth. Don't use a graphic like that for unrelated points. Or list the points out of order. None of this:

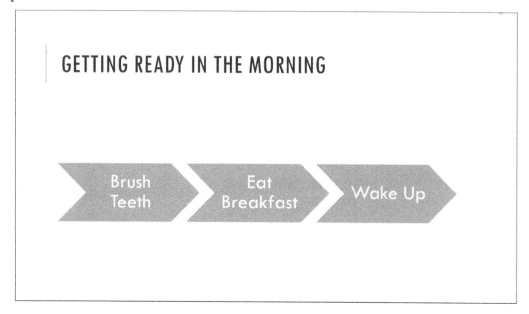

You may brush your teeth before you eat breakfast, but you certainly don't do both of those before you wake up. Right? Always make sure your graphics in your presentation make sense.

$* * *$

Okay. Now let's discuss how to format your text.

Format Text Basics

There are four primary options for formatting text. With each you need to select your text before you try to use it.

The first is control shortcuts for common formatting like bold, italics, and underline.

The second, the one I use most often, is to go to the Font section of the Home tab and choose from the options listed there.

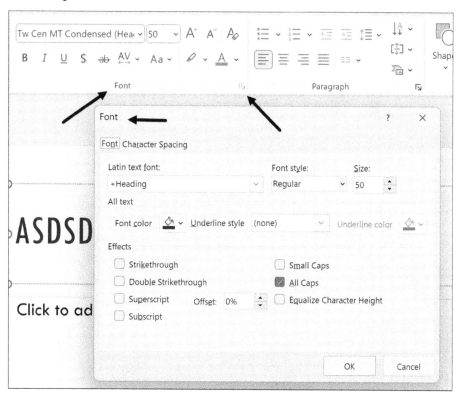

The third is to open the Font dialogue box. To do so, either click on the expansion arrow in the corner of the Font section of the Home tab (see the arrow pointing to the left in the image above) or right-click and choose Font from the dropdown menu.

Both options will open that dialogue box that you see above. Apply the formatting you want from there.

The fourth option is to use the mini formatting menu. If it doesn't appear when you select your text then right-click to bring it up along with a dropdown menu. Choose your formatting option from there.

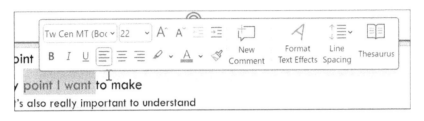

* * *

Now let's walk through all of your formatting options alphabetically. That will make this an easier section to refer back to later.

I am going to assume here that you have already selected the text you want to format, so I don't have to tell you to do that each time. Note that an easy way to select all of the text in a text box is to click into the text box and then use Ctrl + A.

Bold Text

The easiest way to bold text is to use Ctrl + B.

You can also in the Font section of the Home tab or the mini formatting menu, click on the bolded capital B in the second row of options:

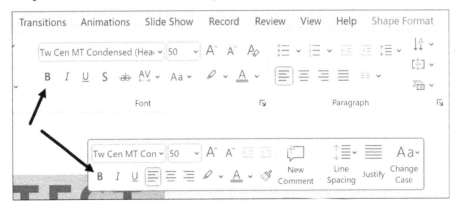

Or in the Font dialogue box you can change the Font Style dropdown to either Bold or Bold Italic, depending on which one you want.

To remove bolding from text, you do the same thing. Select the text and then use Ctrl + B, click on the B in the menu, or change the Font Style in the Font dialogue box to Regular.

If you have text that is both bolded and not bolded and use either Ctrl + B or the B in one of the menu options, you may have to use it twice to get the result you want. It will take all of the text in one direction—bolded or not bolded—and if you were trying to go in the other direction, then you have to use Ctrl + B or the B in the menu one more time. The Font dialogue box does not have this same issue since you're specifically telling Excel which formatting you want to apply.

Font

Fonts are what dictate how your text looks. In the paste examples above, we saw the difference between a serifed font (Garamond) and a sans-serif font (Trebuchet MS).

When choosing a font, keep in mind readability. There are some nice, tried and true fonts that are used often for written documents because they work. Garamond and Trebuchet are two of them. Times New Roman and Palatino are a couple others.

If you work for a company, they may have a corporate font that they've designated for all of their communications. If that's the case, use that one.

You can either change your font before you start typing, or select all of your text afterwards and change it then.

Both the mini formatting menu and Font section of the Home tab have a dropdown menu for font where each font's name is written in that particular font so you can see what type of font it is:

By default, your font list is probably going to look like the list above. Those little clouds with arrows in them mean that if you want to use that particular font you need to download it from Microsoft.

(You can turn this off if you want so that only available fonts are shown. To do so, go to File, then choose Account in the bottom left corner, and click on Manage Settings under Account Privacy. Scroll down to the Connected Experiences section and uncheck the box for Turn On Experiences That Download Online Content. Another option is to uncheck the box that's a little further down that says Turn On All Connected Experiences.)

Back to the font listing.

At the top you'll see any fonts that are used by the theme in your current presentation. Below that you'll see any recently-used fonts. And then after that you'll see an alphabetical listing of all available fonts.

Usually, I'm trying to use a specific font. In that case, click into the field with the current font name and start typing. As you type the font name, Microsoft will autopopulate the name for you. When it lists the font you want, you're good, just click away.

For example, I just clicked into that field and typed "Ti" and it changed the value to Times New Roman for me. All I had to do was click away and my selected text updated to the new font.

If you're not quite sure of the font you want, but know the basic name, you can start with the dropdown menu open and then start typing the font name you want in that field. The dropdown menu will jump to that part of the alphabet and you'll be able to see all choices in that range and click on the one you want from the list.

I will note that PowerPoint was a little weird for me just now when I tried to type in a font name I didn't have. When I clicked away into the presentation, PowerPoint brought up a dialogue box where it tried to name the current font what I had just typed. If that happens to you, click on the No option and it will go away.

You can also use the Font dialogue box to choose a font. Use the Latin Text Font dropdown menu to do so. You won't be able to see the difference between the options there though, and I don't think it gives any additional functionality, so I never use it.

Font Change Case

To change the capitalization of a text selection, you can use the Change Case option available in the Font section of the Home tab. It's the option in the bottom row with an Aa and a dropdown arrow.

Your choices are Sentence Case, Lowercase, Uppercase, Capitalize Each Word, and Toggle Case. You can see in the screenshot below an example of each one applied to the text "this is sample text. and one more sentence. Last one."

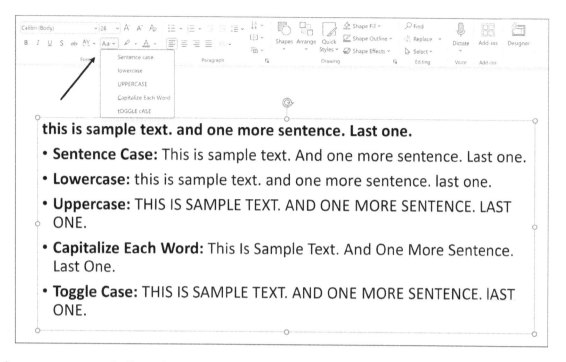

Sentence case capitalizes the first letter in the first word of each sentence. Uppercase puts everything in all caps. Lowercase puts everything into lowercase. Capitalize Each Word changes the first letter of each word to a capital letter. Toggle Case flips the capitalization for every single letter.

For the lowercase and Toggle Case examples, the changes in the above image are subtle. For lowercase, you have to look at the L in the last sentence which is no longer capitalized. And for Toggle Case you have to realize that everything was capitalized except for that last L which was put into lowercase.

In the mini formatting menu, Change Case is not always going to be one of the available choices.

The Font dialogue box only gives you All Caps, which is the equivalent of Uppercase. It does also have Small Caps as an option, though, which I sometimes use in tables of contents or header sections.

Font Color

Both the Font section of the Home tab and the mini formatting menu have an A with a red line (at least initially) under it that allows you to change the color of your text. Click on the arrow next to the A to see sixty possible colors to choose from:

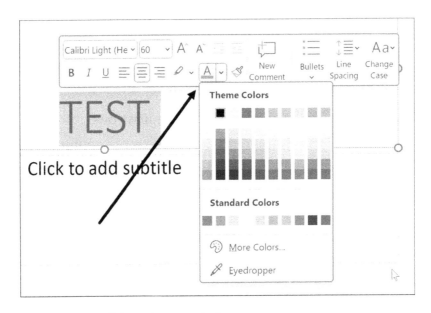

If you see a color you like, click on it to apply it.

In the generic presentation template your color choices are going to be the standard color choices you see in Word or Excel. There are shades of black and gray as well as columns for shades of blue, orange, yellow, and green along with a set of ten Standard Colors that are basically bright rainbow colors.

But here is that same dropdown when I'm in a presentation that has an assigned color scheme:

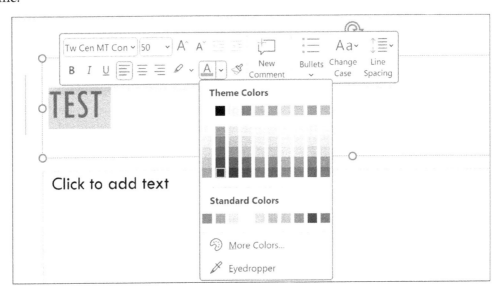

In this case, the Standard Colors and the first three black and gray columns of choices are the same, but then the other seven columns of color choices tie to the colors used in the theme. Which means if you choose one of those colors it's liable to work well with the other colors in the presentation. (Sorry if you're reading in print, you won't see that, but you can try it for yourself in PowerPoint.)

Sometimes, of course, you will need to use a specific color. For example, I have worked for employers who had assigned colors for their brand and all communications had to use very specific shades of each color.

In that instance, click on the More Colors option to bring up the Colors dialogue box. It has a Standard tab and a Custom tab, which look like this:

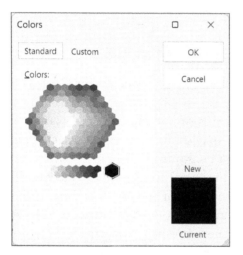 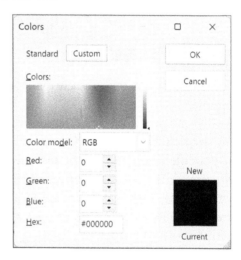

Click over to the Custom tab if you have RGB, HSL, or Hex code values for the color you need to use. Enter the relevant numbers, click on OK, and there you go.

The Font Color dropdown has one more option, the Eyedropper. Click on that option if you have an image or something else in your PowerPoint that uses the color you want. Your cursor will turn into an eyedropper when you do that.

You can either hold the cursor over your selection and it will show you the RGB values for that color, or you can click directly on the color you want to use and it will place that color in the Recent Colors section of the Color dropdown menu. Once you've grabbed the color or the value, it works the same as any other color.

The Font dialogue box also has the same color options but no Eyedropper.

Font Size

To change the font size, I usually go to the Font section of the Home tab, click on the dropdown arrow next to the current size, and select a new value:

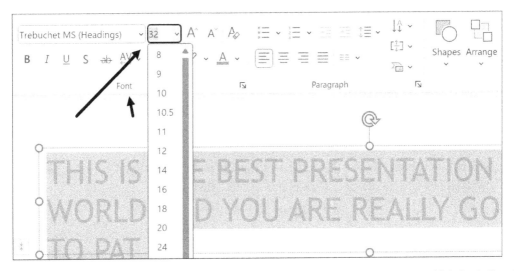

Or I click into that box with the current font size and type the value I want if it isn't listed in the dropdown.

(If you ever select a range of text where the text is of varying sizes, the size you'll see in that font size field will show as X+ where X is the smallest font size in the selected range. So, 12+ for example where the size of the selected text ranges from 12 pt to 20 pt.)

Another option that I never use, but that you may want to use, are the increase font size and decrease font size options that are located to the right of the font size dropdown menu.

There's a bigger capital A with an up arrow and a smaller capital A with a down arrow. Click on either of those to change the font size one step up or down, respectively. The dropdown menu lists the font sizes that are used. So a 12 pt font will go up to 14 pt or down to 11 pt, for example.

These same options are also available in the mini formatting menu.

The Font dialogue box has a Size field. Click into the field and type in a new value or use the up and down arrows to change the font size by .1 pt at a time.

Italicize Text

The easiest way to italicize text is to use Ctrl + I.

In the Font section of the Home tab or the mini formatting menu, you can also click on the slanted I in the bottom row. It's between the options for bold and underline.

In the Font dialogue box, change the Font Style to either Italic or Bold Italic.

To remove italics from text, you do the same thing. Select the text and then use Ctrl + I, click on the slanted I in the menu, or change the Font Style in the Font dialogue box to Regular.

Keep in mind that if your text is mixed italics and regular text and you use an option other than the Font dialogue box, you may need to use the option twice.

Text Direction

By default the text in your presentation is going to be horizontal left-to-right. But there are other options available for text direction, namely rotated 90 degrees, rotated 270 degrees, and stacked. You can find this setting in the top right of the Paragraph section of the Home tab. The dropdown menu there lets you choose which option you want:

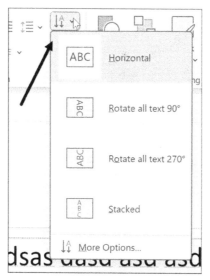

For text boxes, all of the text box has to share the same direction. So if you want different text to use different directions on the same slide, you need to use separate text boxes for each one.

Next to each option you can see a sample. So Rotate All Text 90 degrees turns the text so it runs downward and you'd have to tilt your head to the right to read it. Rotate All Text 270 degrees rotates it in the other direction so you have to tilt your head to the left. Stacked puts one letter per line but doesn't change how the letters are angled.

Clicking on More Options will open the Format Shape task pane on the right-hand side of your workspace, but the Text Direction dropdown menu there has the same four choices.

You may still want to use it though because it does give you a few other choices, including whether or not to Autofit your text to the text box, whether or not to shrink the text if it overflows the text box, and whether to resize the text box to fit the text.

This is also where you can say whether the text should wrap to a new line when it hits the edge of the text box.

Underline Text

For a basic, single-line underline the easiest choice is Ctrl + U. You can also click on the underlined U in the second row of the Font section of the Home tab or the mini formatting menu.

If you want more underline options than that, you need to use the Font dialogue box. As of now (late October 2023), there are sixteen underline options available there in the Underline Style dropdown:

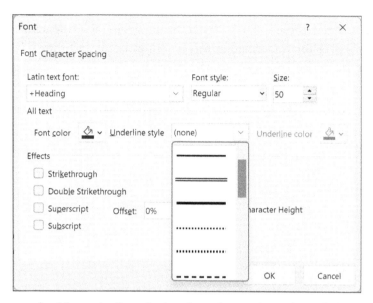

You not only have a double underline choice, but also various dotted, dashed, and wavy line choices. Make your choice and then click OK to close the dialogue box and apply the change.

To remove an underline, you do the same thing again. For Ctrl + U and the U option in the menus, it will either remove a basic underline or transform a non-basic underline to a basic underline. Which means if you used a non-basic underline and try to remove it, you may have to use Ctrl + U or the U in the menus twice to do so.

For the Font dialogue box you just choose the none option from the dropdown menu.

As with italics and bolded text, if the text you select is both underlined and not underlined, you may have to use the Ctrl + U or the U option in the menus two times to get the result you want.

* * *

Clear Formatting

One final note. If you are working in a presentation that uses a theme—so has standardized fonts, colors, etc.—and you change your text away from that, but then later decide you want to go back to the standard look for that presentation, you can use the Clear All Formatting option in the top right corner of the Font section of the Home tab to do that.

* * *

Finally, if you look at the Font section of the Home tab you'll see that there are a few other formatting choices listed there such as strikethrough, character spacing, and text shadow. We're not going to cover them in detail in this beginner book, but they work the same. Select your text, click on the option you want to use, and done.

Format Paragraphs

The last chapter covered the basics of formatting individual letters or words. But sometimes the changes you need to make are at a higher level, the paragraph level or above. So that's what this chapter is for.

As with formatting text, my go-to is the Home tab. There is a Paragraph section there that has all of the options we're going to discuss here and a few more.

Sometimes an option may also be available in the mini formatting menu, but not all of them and not as consistently as with the font options.

You can also right-click in your workspace and choose Paragraph, Bullets, or Numbering from the dropdown menu, as needed. Paragraph brings up a Paragraph dialogue box while Bullets and Numbering both have secondary dropdown menus that let you choose the bullets or numbering to use.

One difference between text formatting and paragraph-level formatting is that you don't have to highlight all of the text to make a change if you're formatting a single paragraph. Just click somewhere in the paragraph and then apply the change you want.

Okay. Let's dive in and walk through some of these options.

Bulleted Lists

Many of the themes in PowerPoint come with bulleted lists already set up. So you bring up a Title and Content slide and you can see immediately that when you add text it will be bulleted. Like here with the Ion Boardroom theme:

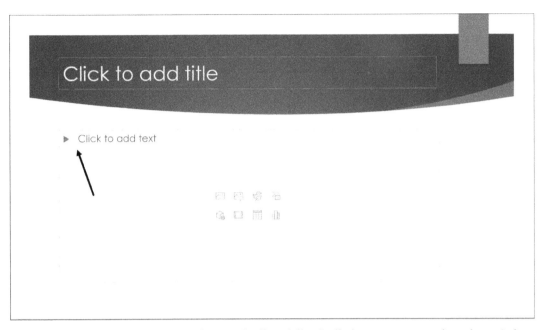

Other themes, like Integral, don't have a bulleted list built in or use one that doesn't have a visible marker. So if you want a visible marker for those themes you have to add it yourself.

To do this, option one is to add the bullet before you start. Click into that text box on your slide, go to the Paragraph section of the Home tab, and click on the dropdown arrow for Bullets:

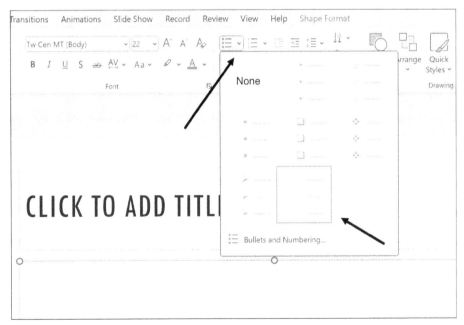

As you can see in the image above, this theme is using a bullet style that doesn't have a shape to it, so to a viewer it's as if there isn't a bullet. To change that, click on one of the six choices you can see there that do use a bullet. If you want there to be no bulleted formatting at all, click on None.

Once you do that, you'll see a grayed-out version of the bullet type you chose and when you start to type it will appear as a fully-colored bullet on the slide.

Here you can see one line of text that I already typed with the bullet fully visible. But since I haven't started typing on the second line that second bullet is grayed out:

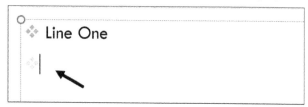

When you choose the type of bullet before you start typing, PowerPoint automatically defaults to creating a bulleted list for you. Each time you hit Enter, it will put a bullet at the start of the next line. If you don't want that, use the Backspace key to get rid of it.

Option two is to wait until you're done. Enter however many lines of text, select them all, and then choose your bullet type. PowerPoint will insert your chosen bullet at the left-hand side of each new line of text you entered.

Above I applied bullets by using the Paragraph section of the Home tab, but as I mentioned earlier, you can also right-click and use the secondary dropdown menu under Bullets:

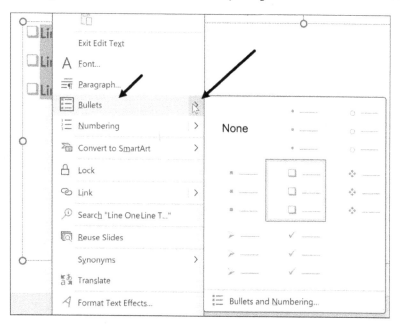

If you click on the Bullets and Numbering option under that dropdown, it will open the Bullets and Numbering dialogue box, which lets you also control the size and color of the bullet:

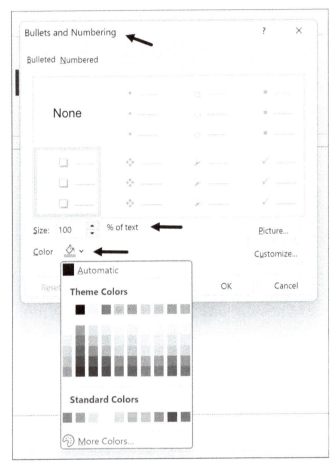

For most bulleted lists, when you hit Enter and then use Tab that will indent the next line of text and use a different bullet either in terms of size or type. You can change from that default, but if you do you may end up having a lot of manual formatting to do each time you want an indented bullet point.

(I'm assuming here that you will not try working with a master slide to make that change.)

This is probably easiest understood if we look at an example:

⬜Default 1

⬜ Default

⬜Default

⬜Default 2

○ Changed Bullet

○ Carried Through Change

○ Carried through change

○ Carried through change

The first three lines here are what the default looks like if I use the shaded box bullet. Each time I indent, the bullet style stays the same, but it gets smaller.

The next four lines I made a change to the first subpoint. I changed the bullet used there to a circle. That then carried through to the next line and also to the subpoint after that next line. Which, all good.

But then…When I tried to create a new main point there at the bottom, it continued to use the circle shape.

So now that final line doesn't match the bullet point used on the other two main points. To fix that, I'd have to manually change it back. And then if I had a subpoint under that, I'd have to change that one to use the circle again.

Honestly, for me, not worth the headache. I'd just stick with the defaults. But there are people I have worked for that tend not to be the ones that do this work who do have strong opinions on what they want to see. So if you work for one of those, you may have to do some manual fixes to get the appearance they want.

If your slide is already using one type of bulleted list and you want to change all of the text on the slide to a different bulleted list, or like mine above to just standardize it to one list, click into the text box, Select All (Ctrl + A), and then make your choice in the Bullets dropdown.

Numbered Lists

Another option you have for points in a slide is to number them. I used to work for an employer who liked to use the Harvard Outline Format, for example. (Complete pain to work with—the format—and more money wasted on something insignificant than you can imagine. Consulting does not believe in the KISS principle.)

Alright. So. To create a numbered list, it works much the same way that a bulleted list does, except you want the Numbering dropdown menu:

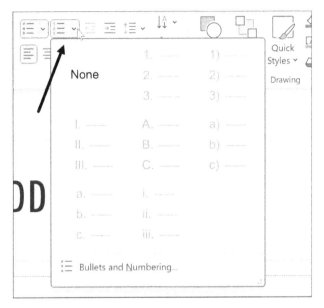

I don't recall this being the case before, but maybe it was. Right now in PowerPoint as I try to create a multi-level numbered list, it just repeats the numbering choice on the next level. Like so:

> I.   **Point 1**
>> I.   **Subpoint 1**
>> II.   **Subpoint 2**
>>> I.   **Subsubpoint 1**
>>> II.   **Subsubpoint 2**
> II.   **Point 2**

See how I'm using a Roman numeral for the first level? And then it uses a Roman numeral for the second level? And the third? If I want to use some sort of standard outline format, that means a lot of manual edits. Because I will want Roman numeral followed by capital letter followed by standard number followed by lower case letter. And that is not what is happening here.

Good news is I can click onto any of the lines for a certain level under a point and change the numbering choice and it changes the associated lines as well. So it took two clicks and two changes to get this:

```
I.    Point 1
      A.   Subpoint 1
      B.   Subpoint 2
           1.    Subsubpoint 1
           2.    Subsubpoint 2
II.   Point 2
```

Now, it's possible you could set up a custom multi-level list in a Master Slide, but that's beyond us. I don't recommend mucking around in Master Slides unless you really know what you're doing because you can really screw things up.

For example, I started working at a new employer a couple months ago and I had to do a presentation, so I grabbed the corporate template we were supposed to use. And someone had borked the thing. You could not get a bulleted list to work at all if it had more than one level. Because someone who didn't know how to work in Master Slides had gone in there and accidentally limited the slide to only one level of bulleted points.

So this is the workaround I'm going to give you instead: If you have to do a multi-level numbered list for a PowerPoint slide, build it in Word. And then copy and paste that list into PowerPoint. It will keep the numbering formats you used in the other program and let you add more lines at each level without an issue.

One final note on numbered lists. Sometimes you will want to start on a number other than 1 or a letter other than A. To make that happen, click into the line you need to change, and then open the Bullets and Numbering dialogue box. (Using either the Numbering secondary dropdown menu when you right-click on the text, or the Numbering dropdown menu in the Paragraph section of the Home tab. Choose Bullets and Numbering from the bottom of either list.)

On the right-hand bottom side of that dialogue box it will say Start At and show a number in a box. Just change the number to what you need it to be. If you're working with letters, then A is equivalent to 1, B is equivalent to 2, etc.

Decrease List Level/Increase List Level

We've already covered one of your options for changing the list level of a point or numbered item. Tab indents or increases the item one level, Shift + Tab decreases it by one level.

But you also have options for this in the Paragraph section of the Home tab. In the top row are options for Decrease List Level and Increase List Level. So if you ever forget Tab and

Shift + Tab, you can always use those instead. They are located directly to the right of the bullets and numbering dropdown choices.

The left-hand one that points to the left is the Decrease List Level option. The right-hand one that points to the right is the Increase List Level option. Just click on your row and use the one you need.

These options are also part of the mini formatting menu.

Specify Amount of Indent

Sometimes you will need to have your text indented by a very specific amount and you won't be able to just use the default formatting in your PowerPoint theme. When that happens, right-click on a line that is at the level you need to fix, and choose Paragraph from the dropdown menu.

This will bring up the Paragraph dialogue box which lets you control Indents and Spacing: You can then change the Before Text value to indent your text the proper amount. Be careful,

Paragraph	? ✕
Indents and Spacing	
General	
Alignment: Left ⌄	
Indentation	
Before text: 0.81" ⬍ Special: Hanging ⌄ By: 0.31" ⬍	
Spacing	
Before: 2 pt ⬍ Line Spacing: Multiple ⌄ At 1.07 ⬍	
After: 0 pt ⬍	
Tabs...	OK Cancel

because your changes will only apply to your selected text. Good news is it will carry through to new lines that you add from that point forward for that level. But if you wait to fix this until the end you may have a lot of fixing to do. (Or a lot of format painting to do, which we're about to cover.)

You can also use this setting with a standard paragraph of text that isn't bulleted or numbered if you want the text to sit away from the left-hand edge of your text box.

Format Painter

Sometimes you can save yourself a lot of effort by getting one line or paragraph formatted correctly and then using the Format Painter which is located in the Clipboard section of the Home tab and looks like a paintbrush.

What the Format Painter does is it takes the text color, font, font size, numbering style, bolding, italics, etc. from the text you select, and then applies that formatting to the text you tell PowerPoint to apply it to.

So in our messy bulleted and numbered list examples above, if I get the formatting on one subpoint the way I want it, I can select that text, click on the Format Painter, and then select the next line of text and it will transfer over all of my formatting for me.

At least for numbered or bulleted lists, right now it looks like I can just click into the line that has my formatting I want, click on the Format Painter, and then click on my other line and all of the formatting transfers. I don't have to select the entire line of text.

But if that doesn't work, then you may need to select the whole line of text or paragraph that's formatted the way you want before you use the Format Painter. Sometimes there's a little trial and error involved.

If you have multiple locations where you want to transfer formatting, you can double-click on the Format Painter when you select it. That will keep it turned on until you either click on it again or use Esc to turn it off.

A few cautions about the format painter.

It is a wonderful tool that can save you a lot of effort, but it will apply the formatting to the next text you click on. So be very careful where you click after you turn it on. If you mess up, use Ctrl + Z to Undo, and try again.

Also, at least in Word and I assume in PowerPoint too, sometimes the way you select the text will impact what formatting is applied. I've had situations in the past where I selected a paragraph starting at the top down and the Format Painter didn't capture the formatting I needed. But if I selected that same paragraph starting at the bottom, it did. So if it doesn't work the way you thought, try selecting the sample text in a different way.

If you need the formatting between paragraphs or bullet points to copy over, be sure to select multiple paragraphs or bullet points in your sample.

Also, know that the Format Painter takes *all* the formatting and transfers it, so be careful there. Sometimes it transfers a little more than you want it to transfer.

The Format Painter tool is also available from the mini formatting menu.

Text Alignment

The next significant formatting change that you may want to make at the paragraph level is the alignment of your text. So far we've been looking primarily at examples that are left-aligned with a ragged right-hand margin.

But you can center text, align it to the right, or justify it. This is best understood with a visual example:

> This is a paragraph of text that has to cover multiple lines so we can discuss the difference between the different alignment options. This one is **left-aligned.**
>
> This is a paragraph of text that has to cover multiple lines so we can discuss the difference between the different alignment options. This one is **centered.**
>
> This is a paragraph of text that has to cover multiple lines so we can discuss the difference between the different alignment options. This one is right-aligned.
>
> This is a paragraph of text that has to cover multiple lines so we can discuss the difference between the different alignment options. This one is **justified.**

The first paragraph there is left-aligned. That means that all of the rows of text along the left-hand side of the page are aligned. You can draw a straight line and connect the start of "this", "we", and "options". But note that the right-hand side is not aligned that same way. That's a ragged right-hand margin.

The second paragraph there is centered. Each line is equally distributed around an invisible center line that runs through that space. You can especially see that in the third line of text where there is a lot of space to the left and right of the text in that line.

The third paragraph is right-aligned. In this case, the words on each line all line up on the right-hand side ("so", "alignment", and "aligned") but the left-hand side is uneven or ragged. See how the second line is longer than the first and definitely longer than the third.

The final paragraph is justified. Both the left and right-hand sides are aligned. To make that happen, PowerPoint adds extra space between the words in the line. Usually the difference is so subtle no one notices, but if you use a lot of big words it can become very obvious. With justified the final line is simply left-aligned.

You can choose your text alignment options in the Paragraph section of the Home tab in the bottom row:

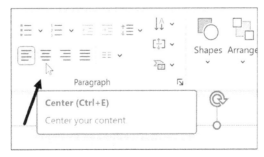

Each option is formatted like the choice. So here we have Align Left, Center, Align Right, and Justify. I have my cursor over the Center option in the screenshot above so that you can also see that each option has a control shortcut.

Ctrl + L will left-align, Ctrl + E will center, Ctrl + R will right-align, and Ctrl + J will justify your selected text. (The only one of those I use often enough to have memorized is Ctrl + E to center.)

The left, center, and right-align options are available in the mini formatting menu on the left side on the bottom. The justify option is on the right-hand side and may not always be available.

You can also choose your paragraph alignment option in the Paragraph dialogue box. It has one final option that isn't available elsewhere, Distributed. That is usually not something you'll want. It takes your text and forces it to cover the entire space in the text box even if that means placing large amounts of space between each letter. (This can be helpful for graphic design projects, but if you're creating book covers or something like that in PowerPoint there are far better tools for that out there.)

The text alignment options we just discussed are related to how the text is arranged left to right within a text box, but there are also options for how text is arranged in a text box top to bottom. Again, this is probably best understood with an image:

This is top-aligned text.		
	This is middle-aligned text.	
		This is bottom-aligned text.

On the left-hand side is the default option you'll normally see, top-alignment. The text starts in the top of the text box and as you add more text it will fill in the text box until it reaches the bottom.

The second example there is an example of middle-aligned text. In that instance, whatever text you add into the text box will be placed so that there is an equal amount of space in the text box above and below the text. As you add more text, your text will expand both upward and downward until you fill the text box.

The final example is bottom-aligned text which starts at the bottom of the text box and then fills the text box from the bottom to the top.

Here I've added another paragraph to each one so you can see the difference in how they handle additional text:

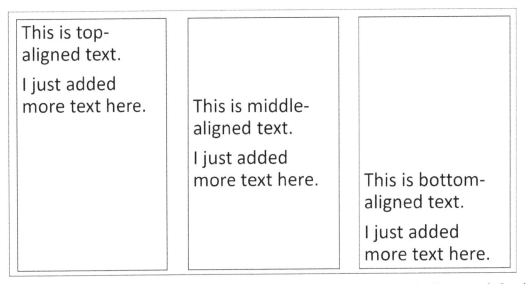

To apply this kind of alignment, click into the text frame, and then go to the Paragraph Section of the Home tab and choose the option you want from the dropdown menu.

The option for this one is a bit buried, at least for me. If you use a bigger screen it might not be as buried for you, but for me it's a tiny little icon on the right-hand side of the Paragraph section of the Home tab. It looks like a box with a line in the middle and arrows pointing up and down. But I can see that it's the one I want because if I hold my cursor over it it says "Align Text". Here it is:

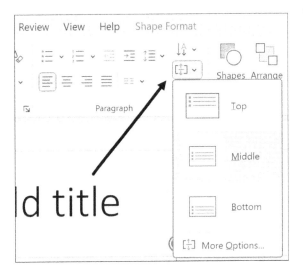

Click on More Options to bring up a Format Shape task pane on the right-hand side of your workspace where you can use the Vertical Alignment dropdown menu to choose Top, Middle, Bottom, Top Centered, Middle Centered, or Bottom Centered. Those last three options combine the Center option with Top, Middle or Bottom.

By default this is not an option available in the mini formatting menu. (That menu is dynamic so if you recently used it then the option may appear for you to select, but since it's not guaranteed to be there, I just skip right past it and go to the Home tab.)

Columns

In the example above I had three separate text boxes to display that text. But if the effect you want is to have your text appear on the page in multiple columns like in a magazine layout, then the best way to do that is to use the columns option with a single text box.

Add your text or click into that text box, and then go to the Paragraph section of the Home tab. The Add or Remove Columns option is in the bottom row and by default shows two sets of lines side-by side:

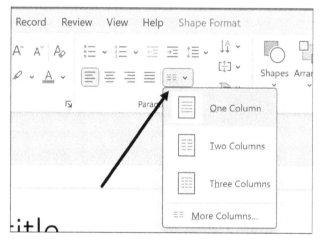

Click on the dropdown arrow and then click on the number of columns you want. If you click on the More Columns option at the bottom, that will open the Columns dialogue box where you can choose any number of columns you want as well as set the spacing between the columns.

Here is an example of the three columns option when I only have enough text for a column and a half:

> This is text that I'm adding to this presentation so that we have enough text to see how multiple columns work in a text box.
>
> Let's go ahead and add yet another paragraph here so that we have
>
> plenty of text to work with.
>
> And maybe one more. Okay, good enough.

It's not very pretty, but it is a good example of how this works. PowerPoint took the text box (the black outline you can see) and divided it up into three sections. It then put text in the first section until that section filled, at which point it started to put text into the second section. Since I didn't have enough text to fill that second section, the bottom of the second section and the third section remain empty.

PowerPoint does not have column breaks like Word, so you can't insert a break to force text into the next column. (At least as of now, their Help specifically states this and says to submit a request if you'd like to see that.) So the only way to balance out your text across columns right now is to use Enter to add enough lines to force your text into place. Not ideal.

The nice thing about using columns is that your text will flow between the columns. But, if your text is pretty static and you want more control over what text appears where, it's probably just as easy to insert three identical text boxes and paste your text into each separate box.

So if you need multiple columns I'd experiment and see which approach works the best for you.

Line Spacing

Another way you can format lines of text is by changing the spacing either between the lines within a paragraph or between different paragraphs of text. For this one, I usually just right-click and choose Paragraph to use the Paragraph dialogue box.

Here are two paragraphs of text. For the first one the spacing between the lines of text within the paragraph is set to .9 which is the default. For the second one it is set to 1.9 which you can see in the dialogue box:

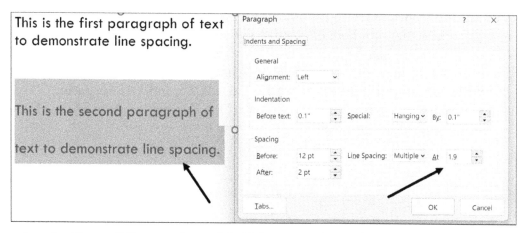

There is a significant difference there, right? That second set of lines don't even look like they belong together they're so far apart.

That Line Spacing dropdown has choices available for single, 1.5, double, exactly, and multiple line spacing. For exactly and multiple line spacing you can then add a value.

Now let's look at the spacing between two paragraphs. I've changed both paragraphs back to .9 spacing between the lines within the paragraph, but now I want to adjust the space between them.

To do that I either need to adjust the After value for the first paragraph or the Before value for the second paragraph.

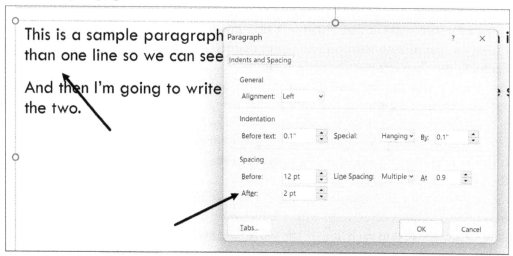

Here I've changed the Before value for the second paragraph to 12. You can see that there's about a line's worth of space between the two paragraphs when I do that.

If two paragraphs have different settings, so maybe one says 2 pt after and the other says 12 pt before and those overlap, PowerPoint combines the two values. So you get a 14 pt space.

Which means that sometimes if you're trying to fix spacing between two paragraphs you will have to look at the settings for both of them to figure out where that value is.

As I mentioned at the start of this section, I tend to right-click and choose Paragraph and go from there. But the mini formatting menu has a line spacing option that can appear on the right-hand side that lets you choose between 1.0, 1.5, 2.0, 2.5, and 3.0 line spacing.

The Line Spacing option is also in the top row of the Paragraph section of the Home tab:

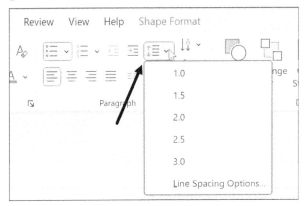

If you click on Line Spacing Options at the bottom of either list it will open the Paragraph dialogue box.

Special Types of Indentation

One final item to discuss in that Paragraph dialogue box. In the Indentation section there is an option for Special with a dropdown menu that lets you choose between none, First Line, and Hanging and then lets you specify a value.

First line will take the first line of a paragraph and indent the text from the left side by a set amount but keep the rest of the lines in that paragraph aligned normally. You can see an example of that in almost all of the paragraphs in most print books. The first paragraph of a section or chapter usually doesn't do this, but every other paragraph usually does.

So if you need that for a paragraph, open the Paragraph dialogue box, choose First Line, and then set the value for indent.

Hanging does the exact opposite. It leaves the first line alone but then indents the rest of the lines of text. This is often used with a bulleted or numbered list where text wraps to the next line so that the text in each line of the paragraph starts at the same point. If you don't set the text to have a hanging indent then the second line of the paragraph will align with the bullet point or number instead.

* * *

Alright, so that's formatting text and paragraphs. A lot of basic beginner presentations just use text so that's where we're going to stop in this book. Because we still need to talk about how to give your presentation and all the fun little bits that go with that. If you want to use tables or charts or SmartArt or any of that, it's covered in the next book in this series.

Animations

If you've ever given a presentation, then you know the annoying feeling when you're trying to talk and your audience is scanning ahead on the current presentation slide rather than listening to you. That's where animations come in handy in PowerPoint. You can design the presentation so that each line of text or element on the slide appears separately.

Animation is added after the slide has been prepared, so enter all the text you want on that slide and then click onto the first line of text and go to the Animations tab:

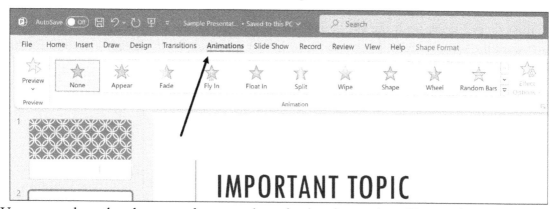

You can see here that there are a large number of animation options. You can have text appear, fade, fly in, float in, split, wipe, shape, etc., etc.

You do you, but I will tell you this from the perspective of someone who has given presentations to thousands of people at a time and also had to sit through hundreds of business presentations, that often the simplest approach (appear) is the best.

Remember, your presentation is there to support what you're trying to say, not to steal the show.

Just my opinion, but maybe ask yourself if this contributes to what you were trying to do or not when you're tempted to go a little overboard in terms of special effects.

Okay, lecture done.

Click on the type of animation you want to use from that Animation section of the Animations tab. PowerPoint will then add that type of animation to *all* of the bullet points in that slide that are at that level:

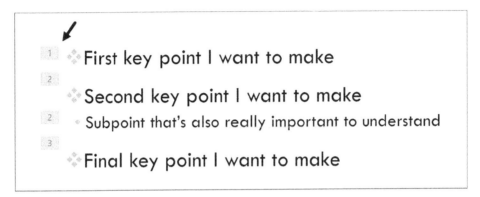

It will also number the items to show you the order in which they will appear.

So if you look at the image above, you can see that my first bullet point is numbered one but then the next two are numbered two. They're going to both appear at the same time unless I change that, because one is a subpoint so initially grouped with the main point. Finally, we have the third main bullet point which will appear third.

Most times I don't want the sub-point to appear at the same time as my main point. So I don't want the second and third line above to appear together. Which means I need to fix that. How do I do that?

First step is to click on the expansion arrow in the bottom of the Animation section of the Animations tab:

This will bring up the Appear dialogue box. Click over to the Text Animation tab:

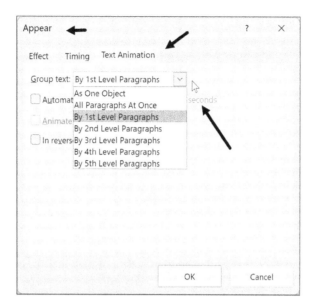

From there you can change the Group Text dropdown option. The default is By 1st Level Paragraphs which is why my subpoint is not set to appear separately.

In my presentation slide I only have two levels of points, so I could choose By 2nd Level Paragraphs and it would work just fine. But if I had a more complex slide then maybe I'd need to use By 5th Level Paragraphs to get each sub-subpoint to appear separately.

I made my choice and now you can see that each line of text will appear separately:

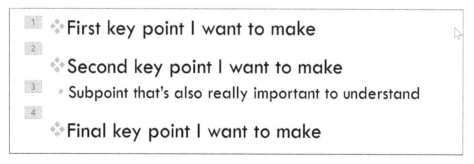

Perfect.

But I still want to see what I've set up. (Often this is crucial when there are photos or videos or other non-text elements on the slide.)

For me, the best way to test a slide like this is to just go to the Slide Show tab and start a presentation from that slide. (We'll cover that momentarily.)

Bring that up and then either left-click, use the down arrow, use the right arrow, or hit Enter when you want the next line to appear. Each of those options will show the next item or advance you to the next slide if there's nothing left. Esc to exit that preview.

There is also a Preview option on the left-hand side of the Animations tab, but it won't work with default settings. That's because it "plays" the slide and the default setting for these animations is to have no delay set up. Which is absolutely fine when you're up there clicking through and giving your presentation. But when you're trying to "play" the presentation, everything hits at once.

If you want to use that option, you need to go to the Timing section of the Animations tab and change the Delay value to something like 00:50. That will give enough of a delay for you to see each element appear by itself.

Keep in mind, too, that if you use the Appear animation it will just have the line show up on the slide. If you really want to see animations at work try one like Fly In or Float In. As you click on each new option the slide should "run" and show you that effect without you needing to Preview.

Another preview option is to click on Animation Pane in the top row of the Advanced Animation section. That will bring up the Animation Pane task pane that will also let you "play" your presentation.

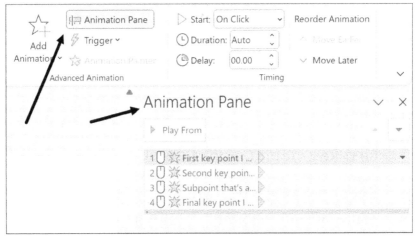

Setting up bullet points like I did above is relatively easy to do. But sometimes I have different elements on my slides or I want the main points visible right away but not the subpoints. The way to create a more complex order is to use this Animation Pane.

As you can see above, it shows each of the animated items for that slide and the order in which they will appear. Each line also has symbols that are supposed to tell you what will make that line appear (a click by default which is represented by that white image of a computer mouse) and what type of animation will be used. Next to that you can see the text that starts that specific line.

It's better though to hold your cursor over each item to see a text description of what will happen. Because when I was just now experimenting with different animation styles on the same slide that little green star didn't change all that much:

And yet each of those first three lines there uses a different animation. You can see in the image above that I've held my mouse over that third line and it uses the Split animation style.

To do what I was just doing and apply different types of animation to different lines of text in your presentation (something that's probably not a good idea due to the distraction factor), just select each line individually and then click on the animation you want.

Okay, back to the Animation Pane.

When you click on a specific item in the Animation Pane, there's a dropdown arrow that appears at the very end of that line. Left-click on that arrow to choose a different way to start the line. Your options are click, with previous item, or after previous item by a set period of time.

Usually click is the option you want. But if you're going to have the slide run on its own for an audience, then the after previous item option would let that happen. Finally, with previous item will group two of your elements together so they appear at the same time.

For example, let's say you have two subpoints and you want both of those to appear together, but you don't want the third subpoint to appear just yet. You can't use the level setting we discussed before because it would apply the same rule to all three. But what you can do is go to the second of the two subpoints (assuming it's already set to appear after the first subpoint), and change the timing option for that second subpoint to Start With Previous. That should make both of those items appear at the same time.

To change the order in which an item appears, click on that line in the Animation Pane, and then use the up and down arrows at the top of the pane to move the item around in the numbered list. That will change the item number on the slide as well:

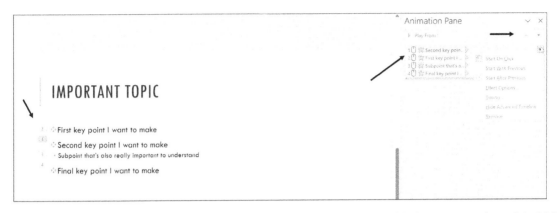

Here I moved that first line to the second appearance position and it is now numbered 2. If I run this slide, you will see "Second key point…" appear before "First key point…"

In the image above, the horizontal black arrow on the right-hand side is pointing to the up and down arrows you can use to shift an item up or down in the order.

You can also see the dropdown menu for that first row, which has the start options as well as timing and effect options. Those are also available in the Advanced Animation and Timing sections of the Animations tab.

If you expand your list of animation choices in the Animation section of the Animations tab, you'll see that there are also animation options for placing emphasis on an item in your presentation or for having an item exit your presentation. They work the exact same way.

As I said before, using animation is very handy sometimes. Just don't overdo.

Other Tips and Tricks

Before we move on to how to actually give a presentation, I wanted to touch on a few other tips or tricks that might be helpful.

Add Notes to a Slide

When I advised you to keep the text on your slides to the bare minimum, I can imagine that some of you thought to yourselves, "But then how do I remember that detail? Or what if I forget what the bullet point is about?"

Well, good news is that you can add notes to your presentation that are either, (a) visible when you print the presentation for yourself, or (b) visible on your computer as you present but not on the screen that participants see.

To add notes to your presentation slide, go to the right-hand side of the gray bar below your main workspace and click on Notes:

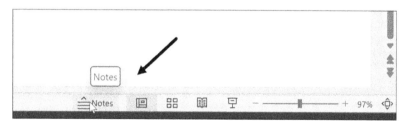

That will open a task bar at the very bottom of the screen that says "Click To Add Notes".

You can also go to the Show section of the View tab and click on the Notes option there to get the same task bar. However you manage to open it, simply click on that space and type in whatever note you want to add like I did here:

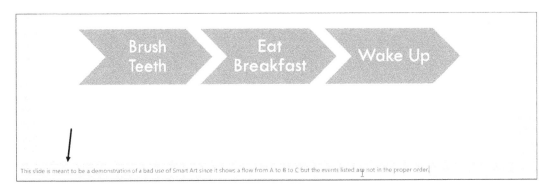

If you have a lot of text to add in the Notes section, you can make that section bigger by holding your mouse/cursor over the border between that notes pane and your slide until you see a white arrow pointing up and down. Left-click and drag upward. That will increase the size of the Notes section while decreasing the size of the slide.

We'll talk about printing later, but if you want to see how those notes look on a Notes Page printout, you can go to the Presentation Views section of the View tab and click on Notes Page. You'll see something like this:

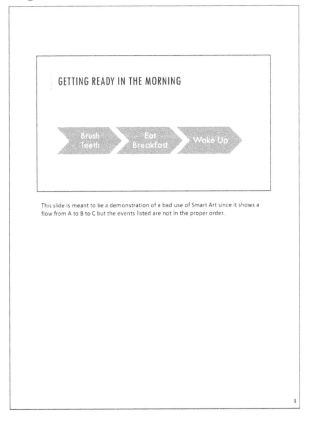

It has the slide at the top and then any added notes in the section below that. You can, if you want, print this for your participants, but remember that they will just read the notes instead of listen to you. So notes pages are best used for the presenter alone or as handouts after the fact.

To return to the standard view click on Normal in that Presentation Views section of the View tab.

Spellcheck

To run spellcheck on your presentation, go to the Proofing Section of the Review tab and click on Spelling. It should be the first option.

It works pretty much the same as in Word.

If there are no spelling errors, PowerPoint will just tell you that.

If there are spelling errors, PowerPoint will open a Spelling task pane on the right-hand side of the screen. That pane will identify the misspelled word at the top. Below that you can choose to Ignore Once, Ignore All, or Add (to the dictionary) if it's not a misspelling. If it is a misspelling, there will be a list of suggested words it could have been where you can click on one of the choices and then tell PowerPoint to Change this one instance or Change All to change all misspellings in the entire document.

If you're not sure which spelling is correct, below the suggestions box will be a definition for the currently selected option. (This can come in handy when trying to figure out whether you wanted discrete or discreet, for example.)

Do be careful with using Change All and Ignore All because they apply to all instances of that word and you don't get to evaluate each instance separately.

Also, just a reminder that spellcheck is not a substitute for a final readthrough. I will sometimes end up with a cuss word that I didn't mean to include because it's one letter off of the word I did mean to use. Spellcheck doesn't catch that.

It also doesn't work with similar words. Just now as I was proofing this document I had used "lest" instead of "lets". Spellcheck misses things like that. So you should read through one last time no matter what.

Find and Replace

Ctrl + F is the easiest way to find a word in your document. Using that will bring up the Find dialogue box where you can type the word you want. There are checkboxes below the field where you type what you're looking for where you can choose to match case and/or find whole words only.

So if I want to find all uses of "Tom", I'd check both of those boxes so I don't end up finding words like tomorrow as well.

Note that it does seem to also look in placeholder text that was used in a presentation. So, for example, I just searched for "to" in a presentation where I only had three slides and it brought up some slide masters that used phrases like "Click Icon To Add Picture."

If that ever happens to you and you need to get back to your presentation, go to the Slide Master tab and click on the Close Master View option.

Ctrl + H will bring up the Replace dialogue box which has fields for both what to find and what to replace it with. You also have options there for match case and find whole words only. Use them.

It can be especially important with replace to use those boxes because you don't want to accidentally turn "tomorrow" into "Steveorrow" when what you really meant to do was replace "Tom" with "Steve".

You can bring up both the Find and Replace options via the Editing section of the Home tab as well if you ever forget the control shortcuts.

Replace Font

The Editing section of the Home tab is the only place I know of where you can replace a font. Click on the dropdown arrow for Replace and you'll see an option there for Replace Fonts.

This will open the Replace Font dialogue box, which has a dropdown for which font you want to replace and which font you want to use instead. Make your choice and then click on Replace.

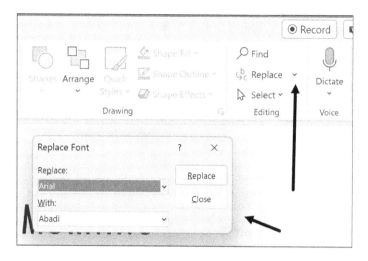

The dialogue box *does not* default to your current font so you need to know what fonts you're already using before you try this.

Also, it did not work on SmartArt for me just now, so you'll need to scan through your presentation and see if there was any text you thought should've changed but didn't.

And, finally, be careful with this if you have a lot of fancy formatting or lots of text in your presentation already, because sometimes fonts that are the same point size take up different amounts of space on the page. That means formatting that worked for your original font may not work for the replacement font and you'll need to fix that.

One more thing, it may not be perfect. I used this on a work presentation template someone had set up using a font that wasn't available. And it did replace that font in everything I can see on the slides, including the master slides. But, every single time I open that presentation it also tells me that the font I replaced is missing. So clearly somewhere it didn't get replaced, but I wasn't able to find it and neither was this replace font option.

Undo/Redo

We discussed this in the basic terminology section, but I wanted to circle back to the Undo option and also discuss Redo.

Undo will back out of what you just did. If I apply a font to text and don't like it, the easiest way to change that back is Ctrl + Z.

If you ever undo something and then change your mind and want it back, the easiest way to do that is Ctrl + Y.

But sometimes you may take multiple steps before you realize you want to undo something. For example, maybe I add a table to a presentation and I do a lot of fiddly little formatting to it where I change column widths, add text, and change colors and then at the end of the day I realize that, no, I just need to back out those last five or six steps.

In that case, the best option is the Undo arrow at the very top of the workspace. It's the arrow pointing to the left and will always be available as long as you've done something in the presentation. (If you've yet to do anything it will be grayed out.)

Click on the dropdown arrow on the right side of that Undo option, and you'll see a listing of the last X number of steps you took. Here we have sixteen steps that can be undone but the list can be longer than that:

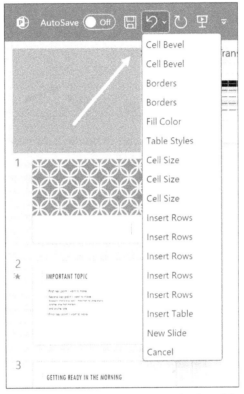

The top item is the last thing you did. The bottom item is the oldest step that you can undo.

Each item listed gives you some idea what it was about but not a great idea, so you kind of have to know what you just did or how far back you want to go.

In this case, if we look from the bottom up, I inserted a new slide, added a table, expanded that table from two rows to seven, and then started changing the column widths and messing around with formatting of the table.

If I want in one step to go back to that original inserted table without all that additional formatting, then I could click on the last of the listed "Insert Rows" entries in that list.

That undoes everything that happened after that point. I am now back to a new slide with a two-row table in it.

Now, maybe I messed that up. I undid all of that and now I have a table with only two rows and all of the columns are all the same width. But I actually wanted those five rows I'd added.

To Redo part of what I just undid, I can use Ctrl + Y or click on the arrow at the top that points to the right. Sadly, as I write this, I can only do so one step at a time. But it is pretty easy to use Ctrl + Y multiple times and I honestly rarely need to redo something I undid.

Zoom

You can zoom in or out on your presentation slides by using the slider in the bottom right corner of your workspace.

The bar perpendicular to the line shows where you currently are in terms of zoom level. The actual percentage is listed at the far right of the bar.

By default mine is zoomed to 97% for a new presentation, but that changes as additional task panes appear. When the Designer tab opens, it drops to 80%, for example.

To change the zoom level on your slide, either click on the bar to the left or right of the current marked spot or left-click on that marker and drag until the main workspace is the size you need.

You can also go to the Zoom section of the View tab and click on Zoom to bring up the Zoom dialogue box, which lets you choose from 400%, 200%, 100%, 66%, 50%, and 30%. You can also change the Zoom to Fit value to any percentage you want.

I often use this to get back to 100% when needed.

Note that with Zoom, the size of the slide changes but not the size of the workspace where the slide displays. So if you go for a high zoom percentage you will not see the full slide.

This is different from how the slide workspace will resize when you change the size of a taskpane that surrounds that workspace. So sometimes it may work better to click and drag along the edge of one of the visible task panes to make more space for the main slide area in your workspace.

Headers and Footers

If you want to print your presentation slides, chances are you may want to include headers or footers. To do so, go to the Insert tab and click on the Header & Footer option in the Text section. That will open the Header and Footer dialogue box:

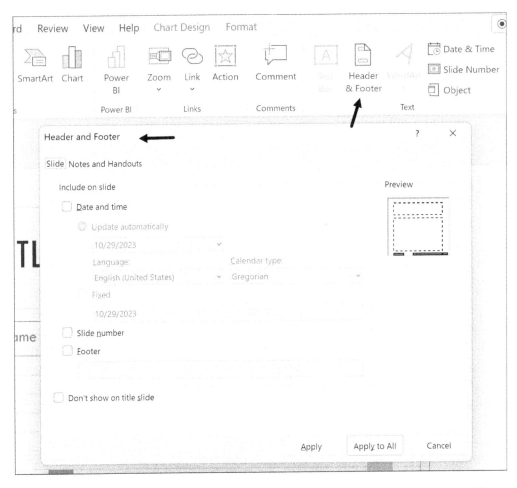

Your options for what to insert are limited. On a slide you can insert Date and Time, Slide Number, or a custom Footer.

You can also choose to not include that information on the title slide but just include it on every other slide in the presentation.

For Notes and Handouts, you can choose between Date and Time, Page Number, a Header, and a Footer.

As you click on each choice, the little thumbnail image on the right-hand side will put a black box where that element will appear. You can't change the location that element will appear in unless you go and change your master slides, which we are not going to do. So you're stuck with wherever that element is set up to appear for your chosen presentation theme.

Present Your Slides

Okay. You've created a presentation. Congrats. Now it's time to present it. How do you do that?

Go to the Start Slide Show section of the Slide Show tab, and click on From Beginning or From Current Slide on the left-hand side:

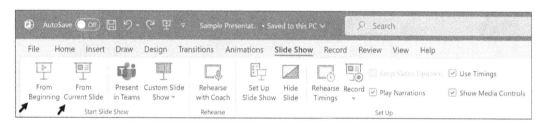

Usually you want to do From Beginning unless you're testing a presentation slide, in which case the option that lets you just start at the current slide is very handy.

If you're on a laptop or desktop computer and not connected to another monitor or anything like that, your entire screen should now be the presentation. You'll either start with the first slide or the last one you'd had selected, depending on the choice you made.

To navigate to your next slide or bring up any text on your current slide that was set to appear, you can left-click, use Enter, or try the right or down arrows.

If you ever go a little too far and want to go back a slide or a bullet point, use the up or left arrows.

You can also right-click and choose Next or Previous, but I never use that.

To exit your presentation before you're done, use Esc. Otherwise when you reach the end of the presentation the screen will be black and you'll see a message that says "End of Slide Show, Click to Exit." You can left-click or Esc will work there too.

There are some fancier options to choose from if you right-click on a presentation, like what your pointer looks like under Pointer Options, but if you're going to use them get those set up before you start presenting.

You can also see the Presenter View by right-clicking. So if you want to know what that view will look like while just working with your own screen, that's how to do that.

The Presenter View looks like this:

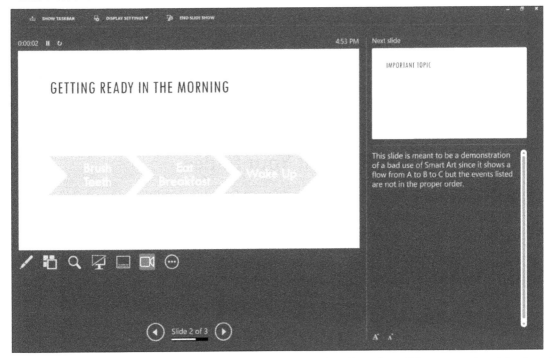

Your current slide is on the left-hand side. The notes related to that slide are on the right-hand side bottom section. Above the notes on the right-hand side, you can see which slide is up next and what it will look like when it appears.

So, for example, that next slide actually has four bullet points on it but in this preview we don't see them because when that slide comes up it will not show those automatically since I have them set to appear one at a time.

If you have your computer connected to an external monitor or a projector, Presenter View should launch automatically. The current slide will show on the external monitor or projector and your screen will show the next slide and notes.

There are some additional options below the current slide that you may want to play around with as well, but we won't cover here.

You can turn Presenter View off by right-clicking and choosing Hide Presenter View.

Print

Often it's a good idea in smaller group settings to also print your presentation slides so people can take notes as they listen to you.

You can find your print options by going to the File tab and then clicking on Print. Or use Ctrl + P. Both will bring up the Print screen:

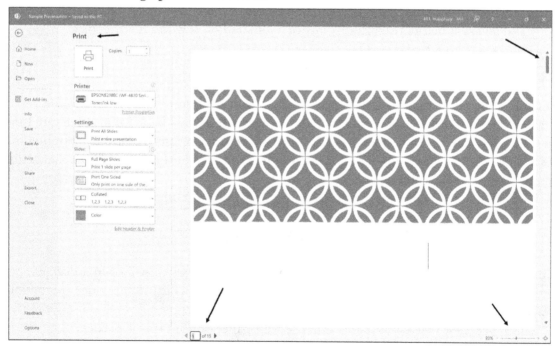

On the left-hand side in the second panel under the heading Print are your print options.

To the right of that is the preview section that takes up most of the space on the screen. That section will show you how the presentation will look when printed.

Below the preview are navigation arrows that let you move from page 1 to 2 to 3, etc. or back. There are also scrollbars on the right-hand side of the current visible slide that will let you see the other pages that are going to print. And in the bottom right corner is a slide where you can adjust the zoom level.

Now let's talk about all those settings under Print.

* * *

Print

At the very top of the print options is the button you click on to actually print. It's currently a square with a black and white icon of a printer that says Print below the icon.

Copies

Next to that is where you specify the number of copies to print. Click into the box and type the number you want or use the up and down arrows to change the value.

If you have never printed this presentation before, it might be a good idea to start with one copy and review it before you print twenty or a hundred or however many copies.

Printer

Directly below those options is a dropdown where you can select which printer to use.

Mine defaults to Microsoft Print to PDF because a few years back I noticed that if I had an Office program open and that program listed my personal printer as the default printer that it sometimes took a very long time for the program to open. So I always have to change this setting to my actual printer when I need to print.

I think the default setting is for Office to list your most recently used printer.

Printer Properties

Under the printer dropdown is a link for Printer Properties which will open a dialogue box with choices. You need to have your printer selected before you use this since the options available will be impacted by the printer you're using.

This is generally where you'd go to choose your paper or print tray if needed.

Settings

Under Settings you have a few choices to make. Make sure your printer is selected before you use this section.

Print All Slides / Print Selection / Print Current Slide / Custom Range

The first choice is which slides to print. The default is Print All Slides. That will print all of your slides.

Print Selection requires that you already selected a subset of slides before you clicked on print. Print Current Slide will print the slide that was showing in the workspace when you chose to print.

Custom Range will take you to the Slides field directly below that dropdown. You can then enter which slide numbers to include. Commas between numbers means to print each one you list. So, 3,6,9 will print slides 3, 6, and 9. But a dash between numbers means to print the range. So, 3-9 will print slides 3, 4, 5, 6, 7, 8, and 9. You can combine commas and dashes so something like 3,4,5-7 will print slides 3, 4, 5, 6, and 7.

Click away from that box and the preview section will update to show the slides that will print.

If you have sections in your document, which we did not learn in this book, the section names will also be options for you to choose at the bottom of the dropdown menu. PowerPoint will print all of the slides in that one section if you choose one of the options listed there.

Slides

If you're trying to print a custom range, you can just skip using the dropdown altogether and go straight to the Slides field and put in the slides you want. PowerPoint will change the dropdown to Custom Range for you.

Print Layout and Handouts Dropdown

The next dropdown menu defaults to Full Page Slides so that's the title you'll see, but there are a lot more options under that if you click on the dropdown arrow.

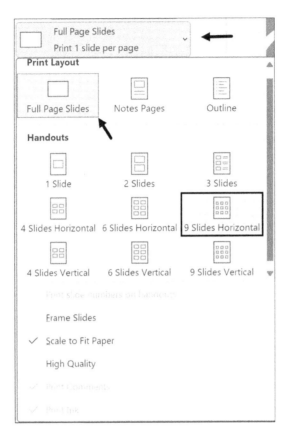

With Full Page Slides each printed page will have one slide per page and it will fill the page.

The Notes Pages option will print with your slide on the top third of the page and any notes displayed under that. So this is a good one for you as the presenter, but maybe not for your audience because you want them to listen to you not read the slides.

The Outline option just prints the freestanding text on each of the slides in a long list. It will not print the contents of tables or any images or anything else.

The 1 Slide Handout option puts the slide in the middle third of the page with open space above and below it.

The other slide handout options with 2 to 9 slides per page do exactly what they say. They fit 2, 3, 4, 6, or 9 slides onto the page arranged either vertically or horizontally. You can see what each option will look like in the preview section.

Below all those choices there are also some options that you can check or uncheck by clicking on them.

They are: Print Slide Number On Handouts, Frame Slides, Scale to Fit Paper, High Quality, Print Comments, and Print Ink. Experiment with selecting or unselecting each one until you get the preview appearance that you want.

For example, my sample presentation had comments still in it. When I went to print, PowerPoint wanted to print an entire page for one of my slides that was just the comments for that slide. It also wanted to mark that slide as having a comment on it. I didn't want that, so I had to click on the Print Comments option to uncheck it.

Print One Sided /Print on Both Sides (Long) / Print on Both Sides (Short)

The next option lets you choose whether to print on one side of the page or on both sides of the page. This will only be visible if the printer you have connected to allows that. For slides or other landscape layouts (where the top is longer than the sides) you generally want to print on both sides and flip on the short edge. For notes pages or other layouts that are longer along the side than across the top you generally will want to flip on the long edge.

Collated / Uncollated

Here you choose whether to print one presentation at a time (collated) or each page of the presentation X number of times before printing the next page (uncollated). Which choice you want will depend on whether you want people to have the full presentation up-front or whether you intend to hand out each page of the presentation as you reach it.

Color / Grayscale / Pure Black and White

This option lets you choose whether to print in color, grayscale, or pure black and white. The black and white option strips out colored sections and makes them white not black, so it's the option that will use the least amount of ink. The grayscale option keeps those colored sections but transforms them to shades of gray. It's easy enough to see what each one will look like by making your choice in the dropdown menu and then looking in the preview section.

Edit Header & Footer

At the very bottom there is a link you can click on to edit the header and footer sections of your presentation. Click on that to bring up the Header and Footer dialogue box which we discussed earlier. Note that it has two tabs, one for Slides and one for Notes and Handouts, so you need to make your choices on the correct tab.

Page numbers are always good to have. I often like to also include the name of the presentation and author even if that's already on the title slide since slides can become separated.

Conclusion

Alright, that's pretty much it for a beginner-level introduction to PowerPoint. It's probably not everything you're going to need because we didn't cover inserting tables or images into your presentations. Nor did we cover SmartArt or WordArt. But I like to keep these books to a certain length that isn't too overwhelming and I think we've hit that point. So I'll cover the rest of that in the next book in the series.

If you don't want to continue on with me, you can, now that you have the basics, use PowerPoint's help options to get the rest of the way there.

In PowerPoint 365 as it exists in October 2023, Help can be found as a separate tab on the far right set of the tab choices. Click there and you'll see five options: Help, Contact Support, Feedback, Show Training, and What's New.

For users of 365, it's probably especially important to occasionally check in on that What's New option because 365 is constantly evolving, and sometimes the changes may be big ones or ones that would make your life easier if you knew about them. They certainly have been with Excel over the last couple years where some really great new functions have been added.

If you click on the What's New option it should open a task pane on the right-hand side of the workspace that has links to what they've added recently.

(Of course, nothing is ever perfect so when I was writing the first draft of this book that wasn't working for me at the time. The problem with all these connected options is that sometimes that connection fails and then you have nothing there.)

Anyway.

Help works the same way. You click on the Help option in the Help section of the Help tab and it opens a Help task pane where you can look up a topic that you want to learn more about:

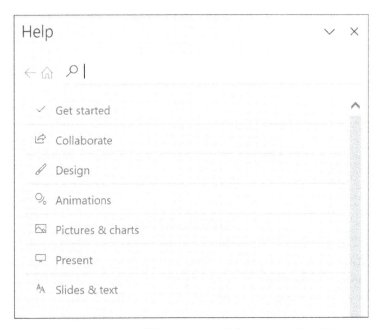

Either use the search bar at the top or click on one of the topics listed there to see more about that topic. There's text descriptions as well as videos.

You can also usually just hold your mouse or cursor over each of the options under a tab and PowerPoint will give you a description for that particular task. Like here where I held my mouse over the Shapes option:

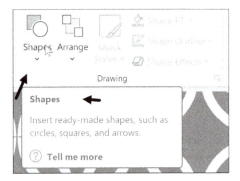

Often those descriptions have a Tell Me More choice that you can click on to bring up Help specific to that option. That will once again open the Help task pane, but this time to that particular topic.

Now, what do you do when Office has put all of their help topics online and your version of PowerPoint seems to not be willing to connect to them like, oh, I don't know, me when I was writing the first draft of this section?

You can always do an internet search. I usually type "microsoft powerpoint 365" and then whatever topic I'm trying to learn about like "shapes".

Often the top result or one of the top results is from the Microsoft website. I look for links that say support.microsoft.com first or in this case the top link was microsoft.com. Those are the best place to start. Microsoft has really good help available, it's usually going to be up-to-date, and you don't risk clicking on something you shouldn't.

Google these days also has little answers to questions they pull onto their search results. Sometimes those work, too. They also tend to offer video links, which often are also good resources.

Personally, I tend to avoid watching random Office videos online because I once found a great helpful video on a topic that answered my question wonderfully only to realize that it was a complete rip-off of a video someone else had done a year before that.

Since I try not to reward assholes for being assholes that copy the hard work of others, that made me avoid random dude on the internet publishing tech help videos. But you do you. If you need the answer, you need the answer. I just always try to start with the official resource first.

Okay, so that's about it. Reach out if you have a question and can't find the answer. I don't check email every day these days, but I do check in and will try to help. And if you want to learn more from me then check out the next book in this series, *Intermediate PowerPoint 365* which covers tables, images, videos, SmartArt, and more.

Index

About the Author

M.L. Humphrey is a former stockbroker with a degree in Economics from Stanford and an MBA from Wharton who has spent close to twenty years as a regulator and consultant in the financial services industry.

You can reach M.L. at mlhumphreywriter@gmail.com or at mlhumphrey.com.